Pyramids of Túcume

Pyramids of Túcume

THE QUEST FOR PERU'S FORGOTTEN CITY

*Thor Heyerdahl, Daniel H. Sandweiss,
and Alfredo Narváez*

with 177 illustrations, 43 in color

THAMES AND HUDSON

Dedicated to the people of Túcume, past and present

Title-page: The pyramids of Túcume.

First published in the United States of America in 1995 by Thames and
Hudson Inc., 500 Fifth Avenue, New York, New York 10110

Library of Congress Catalog Card Number 95-60012
ISBN 0-500-05076-7

Printed and bound in Great Britain

Contents

Preface

RISING OUT of the flat coastal plains of northern Peru, the vast, barren ruins of the pyramids of Túcume, though eroded over the centuries, still bear witness to their original grandeur. Covering over 220 ha (540 acres) and including 26 major pyramids as well as myriad smaller structures, the ancient city is truly impressive. First built around AD 1100 by people of the Lambayeque culture, it survived and even grew under successive waves of conquest by Chimú and later Inca armies, only to fall into ruins within a few years of the Spanish conquest.

Excavations at Túcume have gone on more or less continuously since 1988, when Thor Heyerdahl first visited the site. Although in many ways we can never do more than scratch the surface of such an immense site, we have come to understand its history much better than when we first started excavations. This book summarizes what we have learned so far and relates it to the broader prehistory of the Lambayeque Valley, the north coast of Peru, and the Andes. (The technical details of our work will be published later, as *Occasional Papers of the Kon-Tiki Museum*.) Although each of us has written about the work for which he is directly responsible, the results are the product of a coherent plan of research and of constant interaction among all involved.

Thor Heyerdahl sets the stage by discussing prehispanic seafaring in Peru (Chapter 1) and then provides a personal narrative of his experiences at Túcume and how he came to start the project (Chapter 2). Dan Sandweiss then reviews the archaeological and ethnohistoric background necessary to place Túcume in its local and regional context, and briefly discusses previous investigations at the site and the research program of the Túcume Project (Chapter 3). The following chapters present the results of our excavations: Dan Sandweiss translated the text of chapters 4, 5 and 7. Alfredo Narváez describes his work in the Monumental Sector (Chapter 4); at the Huaca Las Balsas (Chapter 5), where he discovered modeled mud friezes including a scene showing reed boats; and in two cemeteries on the south side of the site (Chapter 7). Dan Sandweiss discusses his work outside the monumental precinct of Túcume, in Sector V on the west side (Chapter 6) and on the central La Raya mountain itself (Chapter 8). Dan and Alfredo end this section with a summary of their conclusions (Chapter 9), and Thor closes the book with a discussion of the continuities in culture and technology from ancient to modern Túcume (Chapter 10). Since 1988, Thor has lived among the modern descendants of ancient Túcume, and he provides an informed perspective on their lives and customs.

THOR HEYERDAHL
DANIEL H. SANDWEISS
ALFREDO NARVÁEZ

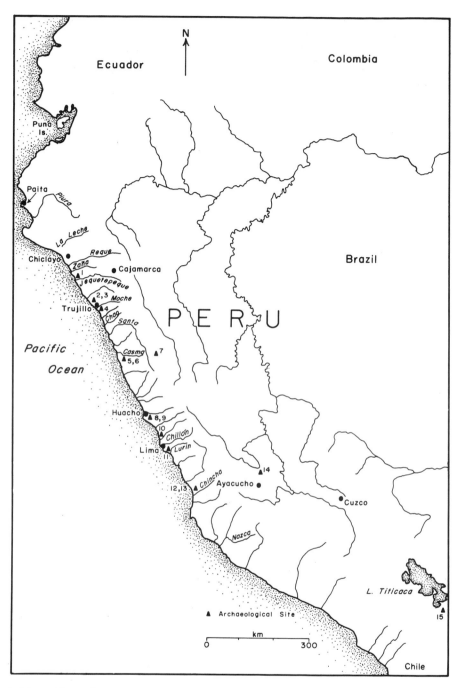

1 *Map of Peru, showing major sites mentioned in the text. Key: 1 Pacatnamú,
San José de Moro; 2 Chan Chan; 3 Huaca Dragón; 4 Moche pyramids;
5 Sechín Alto; 6 Pampa de las Llamas-Moxeke; 7 Chavín de Huánatar;
8 Huaca Carquín; 9 Huaca Bacín de Oro; 10 El Paraíso; 11 Pachacamac;
12 La Centinela; 13 Lo Demás; 14 Huari; 15 Tiahuanaco.*

Thor Heyerdahl

Túcume

and the Maritime Heritage of Peru's North Coast

The coastal desert

THERE ARE few territories with a past so well preserved and yet so little known as the coastal plains of Peru. Deprived of rain by the lofty cordilleras of the Andes that tap the west-bound trade-wind clouds on their eternal drift from the Atlantic side of South America, the Pacific coast of Peru is a desert, but one which preserves a boundless wealth of antiquities. Throughout its length, the 2000-km (1200-mile) long coastline of Peru is a narrow belt of sand, open beaches, and rocky cliffs, sheltered by the Andes (*ill. 1*).

All along this arid coastline there is ample evidence of intensive former habitation by a diversity of culturally advanced civilizations. Ruins of adobe walls, burial fields pitted by tomb-robbers, colossal stepped pyramids and other monumental structures can be found, eroded and deformed by the infrequent but torrential El-Niño rains and drifting sand.

Today, as in the early 16th century when the Spanish conquistadors arrived, a road runs southward from Tumbes, where Pizarro landed, past towns and villages and into the very heart of Peru. In the northern coastal plains, only 6° south of the equator, it passes near the tiny village of Túcume, closer to the borders of modern Ecuador than to the Peruvian capital of Lima. One branch of the modern Panamerican highway runs through Túcume, which is rarely marked on any map although the modest houses lie at the foot of South America's largest accumulation of pyramids (*ill. 2*).

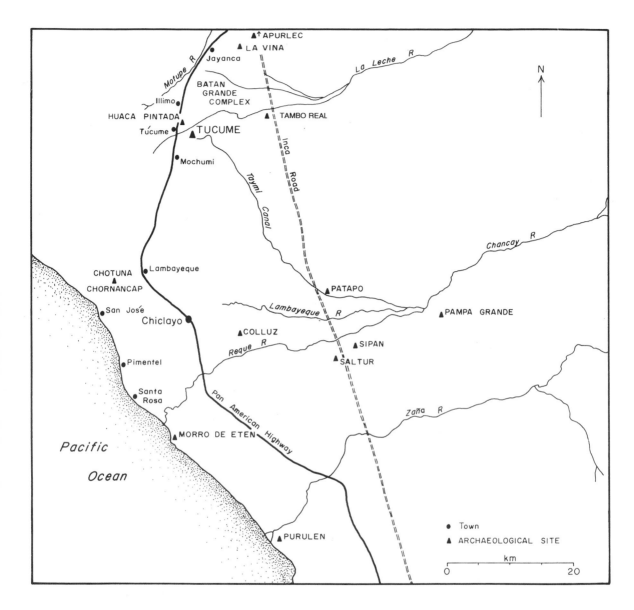

2 Map of the
Lambayeque Valley area,
showing Túcume in its
regional archaeological
context. The area labelled
'Batán Grande Complex'
includes a number of
pyramids and sites such as
Huaca Las Ventanas and
Huaca Lucía. North of
Lambayeque, only the old
Panamerican Highway is
shown. (After Shimada,
1990: fig. 2.)

When the invading Spaniards rode past the Túcume pyramids on
the Inca road they were amazed at the sight of such enormous monuments from a forgotten past. But modern tourists have rushed by on
the new highway in their thousands, ignoring what they missed in their
hurry. For the Túcume pyramids are successfully camouflaged both by
erosion and even more by their very dimensions. In the tropical sun-
light they show up in the distance like bright sandstone mountains
with the blue Andes as shadows behind. Until emerging into the lime-
light in recent years, the colossal buildings at Túcume have towered
unnoticed over the plains, as if left there by the Creator (ills 3–6).

To the people in Túcume, this naked wilderness of eroded pyramids in their backyard is known as *El Purgatorio*, The Purgatory. For more than four centuries they have regarded the ruins as shameful remains of their pagan ancestors, a place where past and present medicine-men communed with devils. Only the Director of the Brüning Archaeological Museum in the nearest town of Lambayeque fully understood the importance of the ruins for science and for tourism. But his enthusiasm did not reach the authorities in Lima, nor the tourists who rushed by. Until tomb-robbers hit upon unbelievable treasures in a similar pyramid at nearby Sipán, the Túcume pyramids continued to slumber, neglected, under carpets of sand.

This would have been strange indeed in any other country, but perhaps not quite as strange in Peru. The Túcume plains are part of the wide Lambayeque Valley which is dotted with impressive pyramids. Short distances apart the traveler can find such important sites as Sipán, Batán Grande, Chotuna, Pampa Grande, Zaña, and Ucupe. The valley must have been extremely rich and densely populated in early pre-Inca times, although little more than ruins of its former grandeur remained when the Spaniards arrived some five centuries ago.

The conquistadors from Europe found the Lambayeque Valley still intensively cultivated through artificial irrigation. The original pyramid-builders had watered vast areas of the surrounding desert plains for untold centuries when the highland Incas preceded the Spaniards as conquerors of the coast. Today, Túcume, with the adjacent algarrobo forest of Batán Grande, seems like an oasis in the arid desert that is Peru's coastal plain, crisscrossed by pre-Inca irrigation channels. These impressive canals were built by skilled hydraulic engineers during Moche times, in the first millennium AD. The largest, the Taymi Canal, more than 70 km (45 miles) long, runs close alongside the Túcume pyramid complex. From Túcume it was navigable for medium-size rafts of balsa wood or reeds down to the sea in one direction, and way inland in the other, until regulated by modern sluices.

An ancient road runs the 20 km (12 miles) down to the sea, past the fishermen's town of Mórrope and the legendary site of the two large pyramids, Chotuna and Chornancap, barely inland from the shore, where oral tradition records that Naymlap, the founder of the first Lambayeque dynasty, had landed. Now, as when the Spaniards arrived, both fresh and dried fish brought from the sea are an important part of the diet of the people of Túcume.

The same roads that hastened the Spanish advance had also helped the Inca Tupac Yupanqui to conquer the Lambayeque Valley, and the

3 (overleaf) A view of the Túcume archaeological complex, looking east from Huaca del Pueblo. This immense site, covering 220 ha (544 acres), had been virtually forgotten and was almost untouched by archaeologists until Thor Heyerdahl organized a massive program of excavations.

rest of the Inca empire, three generations earlier. With the already existing network of roads, these well-organized warriors from the high Andes divided the Pacific lowland into provinces and communities, as well controlled from Cuzco and Tomebamba as was the Roman empire from Rome. The Incas have with good reason been considered the Romans of medieval South America – they were great conquerors and statesmen who absorbed their culture from other, earlier civilizations. The Incas are generally regarded as the peak of Peruvian civilization, but archaeological excavations along the entire coast are now disclosing details of the little-known but impressive earlier civilizations, all different from each other and yet clearly related.

The history of these forgotten cultures has never been written because they were partly destroyed and partly absorbed by each other and finally swallowed up by the Inca invaders a few generations before the Spanish chroniclers came. If we are ever to understand the intricate network of interrelated and yet seemingly independent Peruvian cultures, we first have to appreciate the ability of the aboriginal Peruvians to communicate over long distances.

The Inca emperors dominated a nation so vast that it had two capitals, Cuzco in Peru and Tomebamba (now Cuenca) in modern Ecuador, both as high up in the Andes as average peaks in the Swiss Alps and further apart than Paris and Rome. Inca caravans and administrators, as well as armies, benefited from roads built by others before them who had also had need of long-distance communication. Modern archaeology has demonstrated that many of what had been called Inca roads are actually of pre-Inca origin. The possibility should therefore not be overlooked that some of the pre-Inca civilizations, like those of Tiahuanaco, Chavín, or coastal valleys such as Lambayeque or Chicama, were pan-Peruvian, or at least temporarily linked together by religious ties or organized commerce.

Indeed, mounting evidence from the whole of Peru suggests that the early communities in the coastal valleys were not as isolated from each other nor from those in the Andean highlands as was hitherto presumed. At least a millennium before the Incas descended to conquer the Pacific coast, merchants in the Lambayeque valley obtained great quantities of sea shells from Ecuador and perhaps Panama, and lapis lazuli from the central coast of Chile. Thus, the cultural elite of well-organized societies such as those of Sipán, Batán Grande, and Túcume were able to absorb cultural impulses from a coastline at least as long as that of the subsequent Inca empire.

From history we know that the Incas, who traveled on foot, controlled and influenced peoples throughout the deserts, highlands and jungles from the borders of Colombia to Ecuador, Peru, Bolivia, and well into Chile and Argentina. Although an inland and land-locked people, they thus came to rule over coastal settlements in their vast empire. Not only were people in Túcume eating produce from the sea when the Spaniards arrived, but, as recounted by the chroniclers, the Incas in the distant highlands had fish brought from the Pacific by relay runners. The chronicler Guaman Poma[1] recorded that clams from Tumbes on the north coast were brought live to the Inca in Cuzco.

It has for too long been assumed that all Peruvians in pre-Columbian times had neither the vessels nor daring to take them further than inshore fishing in the crudest of craft. This misconception stemmed from the dearth of information concerning daily life along the coast prior to the Inca period. Only in the last 30 years have archaeologists turned their attention to a great number of coastal sites where they have found that communities in the pre-Inca period based their economy to a great extent on fishing and maritime trade.

From the moment the Spanish conquistadors ascended to the Inca cities in the mountains and were confronted with their gold and splendor, they were so impressed that they credited the Incas with all the achievements of Peruvian culture. The conquered coastal peoples, from whom the wealthy Incas had forcibly acquired most of their wealth, left only a slight impression on the newcomers from Europe and their chroniclers. The little information the chroniclers did record of their first meeting with Peruvians along the coast is therefore of great importance. Certainly, the people the Spaniards met on the coast were already strongly influenced by their involuntary contact with Inca customs and culture. But the invaders from the highlands had surely not taught them how to build improved watercraft nor turned them into better mariners. Indeed, whatever the arriving Spaniards observed of maritime activity on their first contact with Peru will bring us the closest we will ever get to a correct image of what life had been like for centuries along these coasts. Only by combining historic and archaeological evidence will we be able to interpret and understand what excavations reveal to us in Túcume.

Coastal navigation in the Inca period

Before Francisco Pizarro and his companions set sail on their first explorations down the Pacific coast of South America, they had already heard of the Inca empire from their own countrymen.

Bartolomé de Las Casas, who had come to America at the time of Columbus' last voyage, wrote in his *Historia de las Indias* that the Cuna Indians in Panama had given the Spaniards information about Peru as early as 1512, seven years before Cortés reached Mexico and a year before Balboa could confirm the Cuna Indian claim that there were two oceans, one on either side of their isthmus. The son of a Cuna chief said of the ocean the Spaniards had not yet seen that 'other peoples navigated there with ships or vessels a little smaller than ours, using sails and paddles. . . . and he gave much news concerning the peoples and riches of Peru, and the balsa rafts in which they navigated with paddles and with sails.'[2]

In 1527, Bartolomeo Ruiz, Pizarro's pilot, was the first to confirm this, as his own little vessel met one of these Peruvian rafts tacking northward against the Niño current. The raft was already north of the equator when it was intercepted by the Spaniards who were following the current southward into waters unknown to Europeans. This historic event, subsequently much publicized, was first reported in a letter from Juan de Samanos to King Carlos V of Spain, written before Pizarro had yet reached Peru. Samanos reported:

They captured a vessel which carried twenty persons on board, of whom they threw eleven overboard. Of the others who were captured, the pilot retained

three. He set the others ashore . . . The three who were kept as interpreters were well treated and were brought back with them. This vessel which I say he captured appeared to have a capacity of up to thirty *toneles* [36 gross tons]. The flat underbody and keel were constructed of logs as thick as posts, lashed together with ropes of what they call *hennequen*, which is a kind of hemp. The upper part was of more slender canes, tied together with the same lashings, and there the crew and cargo went dry while the bottom was awash. It carried masts and yards of very fine wood, and cotton sails in the same shape and manner as on our own ships. It had very good rigging of the said *hennequen*, . . . and some mooring stones for anchors formed like grindstones.[3]

Among the cargo, the first Inca property to fall into European hands, Samanos lists ornaments of gold and silver, colorful costumes of both wool and cotton, jars, silver-framed stone mirrors, and delicate balance-scales for weighing gold, besides a heavy load of sea shells.

This first European encounter with sea-faring Peruvian merchant mariners was also recorded by Francisco Xeréz[4] and other chroniclers, and we learn that three women from the sailing raft were captured by the Spaniards and trained to speak Spanish. They later accompanied Pizarro on his final push southward to Peru, and helped him to open friendly negotiations with an aristocratic *orejón* (literally 'long-ear') visiting the north coast port of Tumbes on a mission from Cuzco, 1500 km (over 900 miles) away.

Off Santa Clara island in Ecuador, Pizarro overtook five sailing balsas, and with the help of his interpreters he traded peacefully with the crew. Pizarro's companion, Miguel de Estete, returned to Spain immediately after the Conquest, and in a report of 1535 to the Council for the Indies, he described this first advance towards Peru. In his journey down the coast Pizarro arrived at a large gulf with an island in it called Puná. Rafts came from the island, sent by its ruler with an offer to Pizarro to ferry him, his men and his horses across to the island on the rafts.

These rafts are made from very thick and long logs; they are as soft and light on the water as cork, and they tie them together solidly with some kind of cables they use, and over them they install a high framework so the merchandise does not get wet. And in this manner, by placing a mast on the largest log in the middle, they fasten a sail and navigate the entire length of these coasts. And these are very secure embarkations, for they can neither founder nor capsize because the sea lifts them on all sides.[5]

A good summary of the chroniclers' reports on subsequent events is given by W.H. Prescott in his *History of the Conquest of Peru*:

When at some distance from shore, Pizarro saw standing towards him several larger balsas, which were found to be filled with warriors going in an expedition against the island of Puná. Running alongside of the Indian flotilla, he invited some of the chiefs to come on board his vessel. . . . It was not long before several balsas were steering for the vessel laden with bananas, plantains, yuca, Indian corn, sweet potatoes, pineapples, coco-nuts, and other rich products of the bountiful vale of Tumbes.[6]

Francisco Pizarro lost no time in returning to Spain for some 150 armed soldiers. His cousin Pedro Pizarro accompanied him when he came back and anchored off the island of Puná in 1531 to prepare an attack on Tumbes. It is from Pedro that we learn how the Peruvians outsmarted the Spaniards with the help of their balsa rafts. Some of the Spaniards embarked in their own caravels, whereas 'the rest of the men embarked on some balsas which were then with us, and which belonged to the people of Tumbes, who offered to carry some Spaniards and baggage upon them.'[7] The Spaniards were carried to some small islands where they went ashore. When they fell asleep the Peruvians sailed away on their balsas, returning with more companions to kill the stranded Europeans.

Pedro Pizarro adds that the same tragedy would have befallen himself and his companion Alonso de Mesa if it had not been for the fact that the latter was ill and did not want to get off the balsa. Believing him to be asleep, the Peruvians set sail, but de Mesa was in fact awake and his shouts alerted Pizarro and Francisco Martin who were still ashore. They tied up the Peruvians watching them and in the morning set sail for Tumbes. On nearing the coast, however, the Peruvians dragged their captors into the sea, nearly drowning them, and regained control of the balsa raft. 'At last they left us with only what we wore upon our backs, and so they robbed many who had put their belongings upon the balsas believing that the Indians would carry them safely; among [those who did so] were captain de Soto and others.'[8]

What the Spaniards did not know until they had conquered the highlands was the marked difference between the Incas and the seafaring peoples the Incas had defeated on the coast. Later they were to learn what was recorded by the chroniclers Inca Garcilaso and Cieza de León: the aboriginal inhabitants of Tumbes had only practiced on the Spanish newcomers the same tricks they had played on their Inca enemies earlier. Just before Pizarro's party came down the coast, the old Inca ruler Huayna Capac, then on his death bed in Quito, ordered a fleet of balsa rafts to take some of his own messengers from the highlands out to Puná Island. They sailed from Tumbes with the order to demand complete submission from the rebellious island chief, Tumbala. Tumbala complied, and Inca troops with leaders of royal blood were transported from the mainland to the island, together with Inca officials who were to organize the island district. The Inca chiefs later returned to Tumbes, ordering a large part of the island garrison to return to the mainland later. But Tumbala devised a cunning plan. When the Inca convoy was out in the open sea, the islanders cut the ropes which held the logs of the rafts together, and pushed the Inca soldiers into the sea. Cieza commented:

6 Huaca Las Estacas, one of the many pyramids of Túcume's Monumental Sector.

With great cruelty they killed them with the arms they secretly carried. And thus killing some and drowning others, all the longears [Inca nobles] were killed and nothing was left on the rafts but some cloaks with other jewels of theirs.[9]

Inca Garcilaso, himself a highland Inca of royal blood, shared his people's dismay at the humiliation the coastal mariners brought on his own kin. He recounted the same story and added:

The Indians generally know how to swim, but this did not avail them; for those of the coast, being so used to the sea, had the same advantage over the

inland Indians as marine animals have over those which live on land. Thus the islanders remained with victory, and they enjoyed the spoils, which were rich and numerous. They joyfully saluted each other from balsa to balsa, and wished each other joy of their deed, thinking, like a rude and barbarous race as they were, that not only were they free from the power of the Inca, but they were strong enough to deprive him of his empire. Full of this presumptuous vanity, they returned, with all possible dissimulation, for the other captains and soldiers who had remained on the island, took them on board, and killed them in the same place and in the same way as they killed their companions.[10]

It is important to note the references to the contrast between the ruling Inca landlubbers and the coastal mariners recorded before the Spaniards had yet reached the highlands. Subsequently the chroniclers paid very little attention to the subdued coastal dwellers and their watercraft. Evidently the navigable balsas were still in use and even of importance during the Inca rule of the coast, as the Incas themselves had no alternative type of vessel. The Spaniards, however, brought the European tradition of plankbuilt boats, and as they took charge of all trade and communications in the country, large sea-going balsa rafts became of secondary importance and gradually disappeared. Yet, for coastal traffic and as landing barges bringing crew and cargo ashore on the shallow Peruvian beaches, the flat-bottomed, unsinkable balsa rafts proved so superior to the European vessels with keel and open hull, that some large balsas survived until modern ports with wharves were built in all coastal towns.

We learn from Xeréz, who took part in the advance into Peru in 1530, that the conqueror Pizarro himself made use of 'balsas of wood which the Indians make, on which the horses were carried over.'[11] Gonzalo Fernández de Oviedo Valdés, who was already in Panama when Pizarro fitted out his expedition, also recorded that Pizarro's horses were disembarked from balsa rafts, and he adds some important details: 'Their cooking places are in the center, and they have lateen sails [*velas latinas*] and oarsmen at the sides with their paddles.'[12]

Pascual de Andagoya had been the pioneer who first sailed along the mangrove swamps of Panama as far as the Biru tribes near the northern borders of Colombia. It was his reports that led to the expeditions of Pizarro and Ruiz. He wrote from this northern extremity of South America: 'I received accounts both from the chiefs and from merchants and interpreters, concerning all the coast, and everything that has since been discovered, as far as Cuzco; especially with regard to the inhabitants of each province, for in their trading these people extended their wanderings over many lands.'[13] Referring specifically to the aboriginal peoples along the coast from northern Ecuador to south of Tumbes in Peru, he reported:

They go to the sea to fish, and navigate along the coast in balsas made of light logs, which are so strong that the sea has much ado to break them. They carry horses and many people, and are navigated with sails, like ships . . . The inhabitants have a manufactory where they make cordage of a sort of *nequen*, which is like carded flax; the cord is beautiful, and stronger than that of Spain, and their cotton canvas is excellent.[14]

A most detailed description of how the balsa rafts were lashed together of an odd number of logs, the longest in the middle, was recorded by Augustín de Zárate. He also described how the rafts had a platform on top and could carry 50 men and three horses.[15] From the Italian chronicler Girolamo Benzoni,[16] who came to Peru immediately after the Conquest, we get the first primitive drawing of Peruvian fishing vessels. He states that all along the coast the Indians were great fishermen, and illustrates the kind of watercraft they used for setting their nets. One drawing shows a larger vessel of seven logs (curved up in the bow) carrying a crew of eight men and navigated with sail and paddles. Two small three-log rafts are each straddled by a single fisherman dragging a fishnet between them (*ill. 7*). Even today old fishermen remember this custom in use off the coast of the Lambayeque valley, referring to the big raft as the 'mother-balsa', on which the fishermen on the little 'caballitos' jointly assemble their catches. Today one-man fishing craft of from three to seven balsa logs are still in use in coastal villages north of Lambayeque. One-man 'caballitos', made from three bundles of *totora* reeds, are used by fishermen in the Lambayeque valley as well as in Huanchaco further south. When they can afford it, the owners of these 'caballitos' have a modern trawler serving as a joint mother vessel.

Benzoni states that there were also balsas made of up to nine or eleven logs and adds: 'They are made of various lengths and thus they carry sails according to their size; and a proportionate number of rowers.'[17]

7 *Girolamo Benzoni published this first primitive illustration of Peruvian fishermen in 1565. The fish are caught in nets strung between one-man 'caballitos' of three balsa logs, and collected on the larger balsa with a sail and eight-man crew.*

The Peruvian sailing technique

Although Benzoni's attempt to illustrate the way Peruvian mariners hoisted sail is crude and obviously inaccurate, he has clearly tried to depict a mast of the type more precisely shown in drawings by such naval artists as G. Juan and A. de Ulloa (*ill. 8*).[18] This is important, for it documents that two different types of sails were in use in ancient Peru: the lateen or triangular sail, as reported by Fernández de Oviedo in describing the rafts transporting Pizarro's horses; and the square sail on a double-mast drawn by Benzoni. Both types have survived until modern times. The square sail on a bipod mast was found on reed balsas on Lake Titicaca, and on a single mast on the huge rafts of balsa logs used on the coast of Lambayeque, until the end of the last century. The lateen or triangular sail on a single mast is the form used on the numerous little balsas of from three to seven logs still seen in fishing villages all along the Peruvian coast northward from Lambayeque towards Tumbes. A single mast raised on the largest central log is clearly described by Estete in his report on the very first balsas the Spaniards saw.

Another variety of the triangular sail is shown in an illustration drawn in 1582 by Richard Madox, reproduced in a recent study of indigenous Peruvian watercraft by W. Espinoza Soriano.[19] In this drawing the apex of the triangular sail is pointed down to the very bow of the raft and the sail is supported on two slender rods converging down to deck without any mast. This peculiar form of rigging conforms precisely with that typical for the sailing rafts of southeastern Polynesia, as shown in great detail by Beechey[20] in his report on the discovery of Mangareva Island. Similar sails, also triangular with the tip down to the deck but closer to the center of the raft, can be seen on the *jangadas* or balsa rafts of Brazil.

The next time a Peruvian balsa was depicted by a European it was shown with a triangular sail, the tip of the triangle at the mast head. This rough but informative drawing appears in the book of an experienced navigator, the Dutch Admiral Spilbergen, reporting on his voyage around the world in 1614–17 (*ill. 9*). Reaching Peru he speaks of 'the savage vessels, called *Balsem*' which sailed swiftly in the wind. When his fleet entered Paita harbor, Spilbergen recorded how Indian fishermen, who had been out fishing for two months in their well-made craft, brought them their catch.[21]

Spilbergen does not comment on how these indigenous fishermen could have navigated their balsa raft for two months in the open ocean outside Paita bay, where the Humboldt Current runs like a giant river. The raft is shown sailing under full sail towards the Dutch fleet, with neither paddles nor steering oar. The lateen sails, hoisted on two independent single masts, are attended by two standing mariners; three

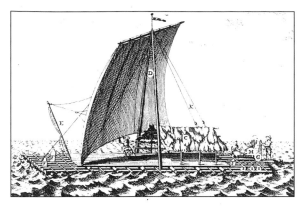

others are squatting and handling broad boards inserted vertically in the cracks between the logs. Stone anchors resembling millstones are shown on deck as noted on the first balsa encountered north of the equator by the Spaniards. Unwittingly, and with no comment, Spilbergen here gives us the first illustration of a balsa raft being navigated merely by lowering and raising boards called *guaras*, an ingenious system of deep-sea navigation not understood by the European visitors until the middle of the subsequent century.

But before the century ended, in the 1680s, English buccaneers began to harass shipping in the waters off northern Peru. Among them was William Dampier, who paid particular attention to the large balsa rafts and their cargo. Like Spilbergen, he entered Paita bay with its main village of Colán, where he found that all the Indians were fishermen and went to sea in balsa rafts. These varied in size and type according to the taste and needs of their owners, wrote Dampier, and he went into great detail describing a huge type used for conveying merchandise, weighing up to 60 to 70 tons, in the open ocean. Some of them had large cabins on two floors, leaving barely space outside for one helmsman astern and another in the bow. The cabin consisted of a solid framework of light balsa logs lashed together with one lower and one upper deck of planks. The lower deck, only just above water, was for the crew and their necessities, and on the deck over their heads was the main cargo, fenced in by planks. With these top-heavy cabins, around 3 m (10 ft) high, such rafts were in need of ballast in the form of huge stones placed on the main logs below the lower deck and awash together with such cargo as would resist water.[22]

These monstrous cargo balsas, wrote Dampier, were so clumsy to navigate with their huge sail hoisted on a mast coming up through the cargo space, that they could only sail before the prevailing winds from

8 *(above left) Drawing of a balsa raft by Juan and Ulloa (1748). A bow; B stern; C thatched hut; D poles serving as masts; E kind of bowsprit; F center-boards; G center-board serving as rudder (guara); H cooking-place; I water-bottles; K main-stays; L flooring or deck.*

9 *(above right) The Dutch admiral Spilbergen was the first to illustrate, in 1619, the method of navigating a balsa raft with the aid of* guaras. *Three men are shown raising and lowering these vertical boards to steer the raft, while two others attend to the sails. Note the water jars and anchor stones.*

south to north. In a north wind the sail was lowered and the vessel drifted. With inadequate deck space for free *guara* navigation, these clumsy cargo freighters could not maneuver like normal balsas. Therefore 'they take particular care to have free deck space when they undertake long voyages, as for example from Lima to Trujillo, Guayaquil or Panama.'[23]

Not until 1736 did two inquisitive Spanish naval officers, G. Juan and A. de Ulloa, study the sailing technique of balsa rafts, intent to discover how seemingly primitive vessels with neither keel, rudder, nor steering oar could sail like ships in the open ocean. They found large numbers of deep-sea-going balsa rafts in the Ecuadorian port of Guayaquil, which regularly frequented ports in Peru all the way down to Paita and Sechura. From there Peruvian merchant mariners with balsa rafts sailed on down to Callao and even the Chincha islands.

The balsa rafts measured by Juan and Ulloa were between 25 and 30 m (80 and 100 ft) long and 6 to 8 m (20 to 26 ft) wide, with bipod masts and one or more cabins on the bamboo deck covering the logs (see *ill. 8*). Merchant balsas generally carried 20 to 25 tons. Indians and mulattos in the Guayaquil area moved on to their balsa rafts with their entire families in the rainy season when they were cut off from their small farms. They lived on board in thatched huts with the same conveniences as on shore, moving continuously along, fishing and also subsisting on the preserved meat and plant food carried aboard to last throughout the rainy season. The sails were square, hoisted on a boom that could be swung around at the mast-head where the two poles met. Some balsas had an extra foresail hoisted on an additional bipod mast. Then the authors add:

Hitherto we have only mentioned the construction and the uses they are applied to; but the greatest singularity of this floating vehicle is that it sails, tacks, and works as well in contrary wind as ships with keel, and makes very little leeway. This advantage it derives from another method of steering than by a rudder; namely, by some boards, three or four yards in length, and half a yard in breadth, called *guaras*, which are placed vertically, both at the head and stern between the main beams, and by thrusting some of them deep in the water, and raising others, they bear away, luff up, tack, lay to, and perform all the other motions of a regular ship. An invention hitherto unknown to the most intelligent nations of Europe . . .[24]

Not even today, more than two and a half centuries after Juan and Ulloa's written documentation, have modern mariners and anthropologists fully grasped that flat-bottomed rafts can be steered into the

10 A balsa raft as seen by Alexander Humboldt in Guayaquil bay in 1810 when such ocean-going vessels still carried cargo from Ecuador far down the Peruvian coast. Note the bipod mast and a raised guara astern, where a meal is being prepared on an open fire.

wind. Their explanation of how *guaras* function left no deeper impression on readers than did Spilbergen's unwitting drawing of *guaras* in use, or the records of the conquistadors who met balsa rafts sailing against the elements. Yet the two observant naval officers explained at length that the combined surfaces of inserted *guara* boards served like a keel, but in addition the ratio between submerged boards fore and aft would determine which end of the craft would best resist the leeway and which would turn over with the wind, thus permitting the crew to set a predetermined course and change it at their will. In their own words: 'The method of steering by these *guaras*, is so easy and simple, that when once the balsa is put on her proper course, one only is made use of, raising, or lowering it as occasions require, and thus the balsa is always kept in her intended direction.'[25]

Alexander Humboldt, after whom the powerful coastal current off Peru is named, illustrated in color in 1810 a balsa raft in Guayaquil bay, around 25 m (80 ft) long and with a multi-room bamboo cabin and open kitchen-fire on deck (*ill. 10*). In the early 19th century W.B. Stevenson found sailing balsas with 25 to 30 tons cargo still sailing from Guayaquil past the coast of Lambayeque down to Pacasmayo and Huanchaco, 'having on board five or six hundred quintals of goods as cargo, besides a crew of Indians and their provisions.'[26] In the early 1840s F.E. Paris published the first exact technical draft of all the details of the balsa rafts in the Guayaquil area (*ill. 11*), which he found so 'well suited to the localities to be still preferred to all other craft.'[27]

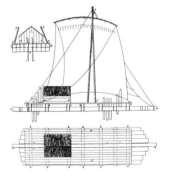

11 The building principles of the aboriginal balsa raft of northwestern South America: a plan made in Guayaquil by Paris (1841–1845). The vertical boards are the center-boards or guaras.

Finally, H.H. Brüning, founder of the museum that still bears his name, photographed balsa rafts carrying goods between ships anchored at sea and the vast but shallow beach of the Lambayeque valley. One of these is of a size that dwarfs the *Kon-Tiki* raft which later sailed from the same coast to Polynesia. It carries a sail of enormous dimensions, made of locally hand-woven Peruvian cotton such as was praised by the conquistadors. The flags of an anchored steamship as well as the wake of the raft and the bulging of its sail clearly show that the huge balsa is heading into the wind (*ill. 12*).[28]

Unlike the Spaniards, the Incas, who had no boats of their own, were interested in keeping alive the balsa raft traffic along the coast. One important reason was that the red *Spondylus* (spiny oyster) shells from Panama and Ecuador had been valued more highly than gold and silver in Peru since the late Preceramic period, even in the highlands. In her study of coastal life in the Inca period, the Peruvian historian María Rostworowski discusses the significance of the trade in *Spondylus* shells. She quotes a document of 1549 from Atico on the coast, showing the existence there of experts in inlaying mosaics of *Spondylus* shell into woodcarvings. According to the local chief, these shells were imported from the coast of Ecuador, and Inca Huayna Capac was so impressed by the work of the artists that he ordered 50 of them to be transferred to Cuzco to practice their skill in the capital. Chincha, in southern Peru, with the offshore islands, was the major center for maritime trade in Inca times, probably because of its vicinity to Cuzco.[29] Rostworowski points out that the chief of Chincha received special privileges from Inca Atahuallpa. 'When one day Francisco Pizarro asked the Inca cautiously the reason for this privilege, Atahuallpa answered him that he was a friend, the most important chief in the Plains who commanded over a hundred thousand balsas in the ocean.'[30]

Apart from the benefits to be gained from coastal traffic, the Incas showed little interest in the watercraft used by their merchants. In his own *Royal Commentaries*, Inca Garcilaso limits himself to some sparse comments on the vessels used by the subjugated coastal tribes. He describes the one-man 'caballitos' of totora reeds, and mentions that the fishermen travel from four to six leagues into the ocean on them and more if necessary, which would take them into the middle of the Humboldt Current. He did not believe that they put up sails on the reed-boats because of the lack of support (although he knew they hoisted sails on the reed-boats on Lake Titicaca), but he adds: '. . . they hoist sails on their wooden rafts when they navigate the sea.'[31]

12 A large balsa trading raft photographed on 6 November 1899 by Hans Heinrich Brüning off the north coast of Peru. The wake of the raft and the orientation of its bulging sail and the steamship's flags show that the raft is sailing into the wind. The crew on deck are dwarfed by the enormous cotton sail. (Courtesy of Brüning-Archiv, Hamburgisches Museum für Völkerkunde, Hamburg, Germany.)

When Francisco Pizarro reached Lake Titicaca on his advance through the highlands, he witnessed the vast number of reed-boats with sails in use on the lake. What is less well known is that he embarked here with his horses on balsa log rafts. From a manuscript by Vicente Valverde on the unrest that followed the Conquest between 1535 and 1539, we learn how Francisco Pizarro encountered a problem on the shore of the mountain lake:

After he had arrived at the outlet of the lake, he had rafts constructed, since he found there a light kind of timber which is suitable for that kind of purpose, and which Huayna Capac, the father of the two ruling Incas, had made the Indians carry on their shoulders a distance of 300 leguas to that place, to build balsa rafts which he went on board for recreation on this lake during the festivals.

The Spaniards embarked on a little flotilla of balsa rafts, but the current took them and Pizarro lost eight horses with their heavily armed riders. Pizarro ordered more logs of the same type of wood to be brought there and built two rafts. Hernando Pizarro sailed on one with 40 Spanish soldiers, and Gonzalo Pizarro and Alonso de Toro went on the other with their horses.[32]

Balsa rafts in Inca oral history

Inca memories about their ruling predecessors in Tiahuanaco begin and end with balsa navigation. The Inca festivals at Lake Titicaca were in honor of the seafaring man-god Con-Ticci-Viracocha, the representative of the sun on earth, who had first appeared to the mountain Indians when he and his white and bearded followers sailed on a fleet of balsas from an island in Lake Titicaca to found Tiahuanaco, in modern Bolivia. It was a pan-Peruvian belief that the last of the Viracocha people finally embarked at Manta, on the coast of present-day Ecuador, and sailed into the open Pacific, leaving a memory which caused confusion throughout the Inca empire when Pizarro arrived from the sea.

Inca Huayna Capac, who had ordered the balsa logs which Pizarro found at Lake Titicaca to be taken there, had special reasons to appreciate balsa rafts. His own father, Inca Tupac Yupanqui, had first used balsa rafts on his victorious expedition to Brazil, taking 10,000 soldiers and their provisions down the tributaries of the Amazon, with between 30 and 50 men on each raft. Later he embarked on his famous expedition into the open Pacific, following literally in the footsteps and wake of his ancestor-god Virococha, first from Cuzco to the coast at Manta in Ecuador, and then into the open ocean. The famous chronicler and navigator Sarmiento de Gamboa writes in his *History of the Incas*:

Marching and conquering on the coast of Manta, and the island of Puná, and Tumbes, there arrived in Tumbes some merchants who had come by sea from the west, navigating the balsas with sails. They gave information of the land whence they came, which consisted of some islands called Avachumbi and Ninachumbi, where there were many people and much gold.

The Inca did not believe the merchants and consulted his necromancer, who in fact confirmed their claim. Tupac Yupanqui then determined to voyage to the islands himself and had an immense number of balsas constructed, and sailed with over 20,000 men. The fleet successfully reached the islands of Avachumbi and Ninachumbi, and returned, bringing back 'black people, gold, a chair of brass, and a skin and jaw-bone.' Tupac's expedition was said to have taken 'nine months, others say a year, and, as he was so long absent, everyone believed he was dead.'[33]

Father Miguel Cabello Valboa, who worked among the indigenous Peruvians for 36 years, refers to Inca Tupac's ocean voyage in two of his books. A copy of the manuscript of his first work, *Miscelánea antártica* is preserved in the New York Public Library and was published in Lima in 1951. The text includes a reference to Inca Tupac's first encounter with the Pacific on the jungle coast of Ecuador and of his voyage on a large number of balsa rafts to the islands in the South Seas.[34]

In his *History of Peru*, Cabello also cites the impressive travels of Inca Tupac, and includes a chapter on 'His voyage by sea'. He concludes:

I dare not confirm this deed, however, nor determine the islands in question, but the Indians report that the Inga brought back from this expedition a great number of prisoners whose skin was black, much gold and silver, a throne of copper, and skins of animals similar to horses. One is quite ignorant of where in Peru or the ocean washing its coast he could have found such things.[35]

When Cabello and Sarmiento recorded these relatively recent events in Inca oral history, the Europeans had not yet discovered any inhabited island in the open Pacific, only the uninhabited Galapagos group. These islands were so close to Ecuador that they were regularly visited by fishermen on balsa rafts from early pre-Inca times[36] into the 17th century[37] and even later.[38] Whereas Father Cabello admitted his ignorance as to where there could be inhabited islands off the coast of Peru, the navigator Sarmiento decided to find them. He persuaded the new Viceroy of Peru to organize an expedition, led by Commander Mendaña, in which Sarmiento participated as navigator. He had obtained exact sailing directions from the learned Inca *amautas* and the expedition left Callao in 1567, setting a course west–southwest, directly for Easter Island. But after 26 days, quarrels with Sarmiento made Mendaña change course to northwest, just before they would have discovered the island, and they continued at sea until they landed among 'black' people in Melanesia. To return against the trade-winds and contrary currents, the Mendaña expedition had to sail first far north and then to Peru by way of the north Pacific and Panama. Tupac's balsa fleet must have done the same, and thus could have returned with black islanders and trophies of gold and copper from Central America.

Since 1947, when the balsa raft *Kon-Tiki* (ill. 13) sailed from Callao to Polynesia, 14 manned rafts of balsa logs or totora reeds have sailed from Peru and Ecuador. Two reached the Galapagos and 12 reached islands in Polynesia, of which five continued to Melanesia, and four successfully traveled on to Australia. There are strong reasons to suspect that Inca Tupac Yupanqui's *Nina-chumbi*, or 'Fire-island', was Easter Island; not only because it fits Sarmiento's information both in direction and distance,[39] but also because Easter Island's discoverer (Jacob Roggeveen from Chile in 1722) and rediscoverer (Felipe González from Peru in 1770) both expressly state that they found the island because the islanders sent up smoke signals all along the coast to attract attention when they approached. There can be no doubt also that the *Ava-chumbi* of Inca Tupac is the Kava islet in the Gambier group of Mangareva, the next inhabited island nearest to Peru after

13 The balsa raft Kon-Tiki, *reaching Polynesia upon a voyage from Peru in 1947. Thor Heyerdahl undertook this hazardous voyage after a year of research in the Marquesas Islands to challenge the generally accepted dogma that no aboriginal Peruvians could have reached Polynesia for lack of seaworthy craft. This was the beginning of Thor Heyerdahl's enduring interest in the two types of ancient Peruvian watercraft and East Pacific archaeology that brought him back to Peru when he organized excavations at Túcume.*

Easter Island. The noted Polynesian anthropologist Sir Peter Buck, ignorant of Inca history but the leading authority on Polynesian traditions, quotes an old Polynesian manuscript in his work *Ethnology of Mangareva*. This states that a visitor to Mangareva called Tupa sailed to the island through a passage subsequently named *Te-Ava-nui-o-Tupa* (great-channel-of-Tupa). The manuscript also tells how, before Tupa returned to his own country, 'he told the Mangarevans about a vast land . . . which contained a large population ruled by powerful kings.'[40]

Clearer proof of the seafaring exploits of the Peruvians in pre-Conquest times could hardly be asked for. And although both Melanesia and subsequently also Polynesia were discovered by Spaniards sailing from Peru, respectively in 1568 (Solomon Islands) and 1595 (Marquesas Islands), the anonymous merchant mariners who set Inca Tupac on his right course, or the still earlier Peruvians who brought their sweet potato, yuca, gourd, and totora to Polynesia, merit respect for their real discovery of land in the open Pacific.

Inca Tupac's voyage of exploration in the Pacific took place so few years before the European arrival that it may almost be considered to have occurred in historic times. But of importance in interpreting the archaeological material at Túcume is also the fact that the oral history of the tradition-minded Peruvians goes further back, to pre-Inca periods. Whereas the Incas started their history with their first progenitor Manco Capac emerging mysteriously from a cave as a child of the Sun, the lowland people on the coast around Lima had another version of his appearance – as a fraudulent immigrant mariner who came up from the coast to hide in a cave, inventing his miraculous solar origin. This accusation was first recorded by the Jesuit Anello Oliva, one of the few 16th-century writers who lived with the lowland population. He was told that the first royal Incas were descended from mariners who sailed down from Ecuador:

Many made voyages along the coast and some were shipwrecked. At last one branch took up its abode on an island called Guayau, near the shores of Ecuador. On that island Manco Capac was born, and after the death of his father Atau he resolved to leave his native place for a more favorable clime. So he set out, in such craft as he had, with two hundred of his people, dividing them into three bands. Two of these were never heard of again, but he and his followers landed near Ica, on the Peruvian coast, and thence they struggled up the mountains, reaching at last the shore of Lake Titicaca.[41]

Balsa rafts in coastal traditions

Along the whole Peruvian coast there are traditions and legends of arrivals and departures by mythical heroes and ordinary voyagers. Father Joseph de Acosta recorded that the Indians at Ica, and also those of Arica, hundreds of miles further south, told the Spaniards that in ancient times they used to sail into the South Seas where they visited some islands very far away towards the west.[42]

Captain de Cadres recorded the sailing directions to the nearest of these islands from an aged informant named Chepo, who said it took two months to sail from Ica to reach an uninhabited island called Coatu with three mountains and many birds. Keeping this island to the left, the next landmark was an inhabited island called Quen with a chief called Quentique, and ten days further west lay an even larger populated island, Acabana. Amherst and Thompson, publishing the old record, comment justly in a footnote that this is an exact sailing direction to Easter Island, with the uninhabited bird islet of Sala-y-Gómez followed by Mangareva ten days further west.[43] Sala-y-Gómez is the nesting place for the sooty-terns of Easter Island and the three naked hills ashore are so distinctly seen from a distance that later European discoverers marked it erroneously as three islands, and this modest rock islet is still commonly shown thus on maps.

Historic traditions on the Peruvian coast maintain that not only the first highland Incas, but also the founders of their own pre-Inca cultures on the coast came as navigators. The first king of the Chimú dynasty and founder of Chan Chan on the coast near Trujillo, is the legendary Takaynamo (Taykanamo in the oldest manuscript). Texts recorded in the Province of Trujillo in 1604 state that his original homeland was forgotten, but a great lord had sent him to govern the land. He arrived on balsa log rafts, but followed the local custom of using yellow powder and a loincloth of cotton, 'and the balsa of logs is used on the coast of Payta and Tumbez, from which it is presumed that this Indian did not come from a very distant region.'[44]

The memories of this cultural hero of the Chimú are so similar to those of the legendary founder of the pre-Chimú hero Naymlap of the Lambayeque Valley further north, that the two have sometimes been thought to be the same person, with two different names. However, this cannot be so, for in the Lambayeque royal genealogy 12 generations of the Naymlap dynasty were followed by a period of regional kings before finally the Chimú arrived from the south and conquered the valley, only a few generations prior to the Inca conquest of the entire Chimú kingdom.

The story of King Naymlap landing on the coast is still part of oral history in the Lambayeque valley. Again it was the learned Jesuit Father Cabello Valboa who first put it on record during his long sojourn on this coast. Since his text has a direct bearing on the foundation of the pyramid complex of Túcume, we will cite it in some detail:

The people of Lambayeque say – and all the folk living in the vicinity of this valley agree with them – that in times so very ancient that they do not know how to express them, there came from the upper part of this Piru, with a great fleet of Balsas, a father of families, a man of much valor and quality named Naymlap . . .

This Lord Naymlap with all his followers came to land and go ashore at the mouth of the river (now called Faquislianga), and leaving their balsas there, they went inland intent to settle. And after walking half a legua [less than two kilometers], they built some palaces in their own style, which they called Chot, and in this house and palace they convoked with barbarous devotion an idol which they brought with them, made in the image of their own Lord, and this was carved in green stone. This they named Yampallec (which means figure and statue of Naymlap). Having lived many years in peace and calm with his people, the Lord had many sons, when the time came for his death, and as he did not want his vassals to know that death also had power over him, they buried him secretly in the same royal habitation where he had lived, and announced for the entire land that he (for his own virtue) had taken wings and disappeared. His absence was felt so strongly by his followers, even though they had already a great number of children and grandchildren and were very devoted to the new and very fertile land, that they abandoned everything and left blindly without guidance to search for him in all parts. And thus nobody remained in the land except those who were born there, who were not few . . .

Naymlap's oldest son Cium then ruled until he in turn was placed in an underground vault where he died.[45] After King Cium, Cabello lists the names of ten more generations of kings, ending with Fempellec who 'was the last and most unfortunate king of this dynasty, because he decided to remove to another place that relic or idol which we have said Naymlap had placed on the throne of Chot.'[46]

Fempellec's attempt to remove this image was unsuccessful, and when furthermore he slept with a demon in the guise of a beautiful woman, disaster ensued. Torrential rains, unheard of in the area, were followed by drought and hunger. The priests understood that the cause of these troubles was Fempellec's crimes and so they caught him, tied him up and threw him into the ocean. 'And with him finished the line and dynasty of the Lords of the Lambayeque valley.'[47]

After recording the complete history of the Naymlap dynasty from the first to the last of the 12 kings, Father Cabello returns to the earliest period with a brief but important assertion:

During the life of Cium, hereditary son of Naymlap (and the second Lord in these valleys), it is said that his sons parted to start new families and settlements bringing with them much people. One named Nor went to the valley of Cinto, and Cala went to Túcume, and others to other places.[48]

Since both Naymlap and his oldest son Cium were secretly buried inside their own temple-residence of Chot, Túcume was founded as a second settlement after Chot by Naymlap's own grandson Cala. Thus Túcume had been under the rule of ten generations of the Naymlap hierarchy when the unfortunate king Fempellec made his futile attempt to remove the imported green stone statue and had to pay for his conduct with his life.

From then on Túcume and the rest of the Lambayeque Valley seem to have experienced periods of less glory and repeated conquest. The memories preserved from these generations are fragmentary but tell how the kingdom of Lambayeque broke up into separate states after

Fempellec's execution until 'a certain powerful tyrant named Chimo Capac came with an invincible army and took over all these valleys'. After his death he was succeeded by his son Oxa, 'and this was at the time and occasion when the Incas marched victoriously in the provinces of Cajamarca . . .'[49]

Oxa, says Cabello, lived in dread that the Cuzco Incas would descend from the highlands and conquer the lands the Chimú intruders had occupied on the coast. His fears proved well founded, and, according to Cabello's informants in Lambayeque, the Incas made the descendants of Oxa their vassal rulers for five generations until the last, Secfunpisan, was overthrown when Pizarro and his conquistadors landed on the coast of Peru and put an end to all the indigenous cultures.

From the above it appears that the Lambayeque people divided their own history into four periods, all of which began with immigrants: the Naymlap period, which brought the Lambayeque culture; the Chimú period; the Inca period; and the Spanish Colonial period. According to the legend, prior to the landing of Naymlap's fleet there was seemingly no important organized society in the valley. But there are nevertheless hints of an earlier population: Naymlap was recalled to have come with some customs of the local people (the use of yellow powder and cotton loincloths), and 'those who were born there' remained in the land when those who had come with Naymlap left to search for him after he had disappeared.

The local genealogies give us no hint of when Naymlap arrived and built the temple of Chot, nor when his grandson Cala founded the temple-city of Túcume. There is also a gap of an unknown number of generations when the original kingdom was broken up into independent republics, until the conquest of the entire area by the Chimú invaders, who ruled first as lords on their own account for three generations, and next as vassal kings for the Incas for five further generations, until the Spanish Conquest.

The importance of the oral history of the culturally advanced societies in pre-Columbian Peru should not be underestimated, as has been verified by modern archaeology. If we were to translate the memories of the Lambayeque people, whose descendants still dominate the villages of the valley today, into archaeological terms, we should expect to find the following stratification from the bottom up: a formative and in part Preceramic period; a Lambayeque period; a Chimú period; and finally a Chimú–Inca period preceding the Colonial Spanish. Although the archaeological record for the entire region is far more complex, it does indeed include all these periods.

Conclusion

This introduction to the account of our archaeological investigations at Túcume is intended to show the importance of the sea to the aboriginal population along the Pacific coast of South America, with emphasis on the north coast of Peru. By combining the oral history of a culturally advanced nation with the eyewitness records of those who came with Pizarro, we find that the local population had seaworthy craft and the knowledge how to sail them in pre-Colonial times. Scholars have all too long underestimated and even ignored the maritime aspect of life along the Peruvian littoral prior to the arrival of European norms for watercraft. In spite of modern experimental ocean voyages on manned rafts made from logs of balsa wood or bundles of reeds, the erroneous impression has prevailed that the ancient Peruvians were a land-locked people with the most primitive forms of watercraft. Canoes were in use on the jungle rivers of the Inca empire, but the lack of boats with hulls on the open sea coast has invariably been pointed to as evidence of a lack of development, in surprising contrast to the extremely high level of Peruvian technology in all other fields. What had not been understood was that the very special coast of Peru, with endless stretches of Pacific surf breaking directly ashore upon unsheltered beaches and cliffs, called for vessels without an open, vulnerable hull. The Europeans, as heirs to the medieval custom of building boats as air-filled shells with keel and rudder, could not perceive that a non-European principle of building vessels with neither hull, keel nor rudder could make secure and controlled ocean navigation possible.

Yet the Spaniards met the Peruvians navigating north of the equator bound for Panama, with over 30 tons of merchandise on board. They had cabins and cooking places on deck, and carried food and water for weeks at sea. We also have a record of balsa rafts returning to Peru after fishing in the open ocean for two months, and distributing their catch, presumably dried, to an entire Dutch fleet. Pizarro personally met a whole fleet of balsas carrying Inca troops from Peru to an island off Ecuador, and he and his men preferred the balsa rafts over their European longboats for conveying their troops and horses through the surf on the Peruvian coast. Indeed, the Spaniards were greatly impressed by the seamanship they met with in Peru, and praised the rigging of the balsa rafts. We do the coastal population of pre-Spanish Peru great injustice if we confound them with the highland Incas who had conquered them, and label them as landlubbers.

Thor Heyerdahl

Túcume

A Temple City Called Purgatory

THE FIRST EUROPEAN to visit Túcume and record his impressions was the Spanish chronicler Pedro Cieza de León. After landing with some of the conquistadors on the coast further north, he rode through the coastal deserts into the fertile Lambayeque Valley, and left for posterity brief descriptions of the settlements he found along the Inca road:

Túcume . . . sublime and beautiful, green with luxuriant growth and plantations, and furthermore with great edifices which, although destroyed and in ruins, testify to its greatness in the past.[1]

His words also convey the impression the site had on our group of modern travelers, four and a half centuries later, when we took a short walk off the busy Panamerican highway to see what is the greatest complex of prehistoric pyramids in South America. 'There are 26 pyramids here and all are untouched,' explained our companion. He was Walter Alva, the Peruvian archaeologist who first told us about the site. It had lain in oblivion since seen by the conquistadors; untouched except for the gnawing teeth of time.

I could hardly believe my own eyes. The Spanish conquistadors were used to completely unexpected sights when they arrived to explore what at that time was a New World for Europeans. We, who looked at the same sight in 1987, were neither accustomed nor prepared for something unfamiliar in advance from tourist guides or textbooks. Except for our locally born guide, my companions were visibly as dumbfounded and amazed as I. I literally felt like a visitor to another planet – there was nothing like these strange and colossal ruins on our own familiar Earth. 'You try to get the government interested,' said Walter Alva. He had tried in vain.

The birth of a project

Next day, with the impression of the gigantic prehistoric monuments clear in my mind, the Norwegian Consul General in Lima helped me to get an audience with the Foreign Minister of Peru. We could not find Túcume on his large wall map. His staff had never heard the name. But if I had seen something worth excavating there, I would be welcome to do so in accord with the Archaeological Commission of the National Institute of Culture, provided funds were obtained abroad.

A few months later a contract was signed in Lima between the Institute and the Kon-Tiki Museum in Oslo, Norway. I was to organize a Peruvian project with funds from the Norwegian museum that housed the *Kon-Tiki* raft. Thus the balsa raft which in 1947 sailed from Peru to Polynesia to prove the ancient Peruvian craft seaworthy, would now bring funds from the museum's ticket sales back to Peru, to look for evidence of prehistoric seafaring in the pre-Inca temple-city of Túcume.

It was not without reason that I expected to find evidence of balsa raft navigation among the pyramids of Túcume. I had just seen what Walter Alva had rescued from the hands of the tomb robbers in Sipán.

Sipán and Walter Alva were unknown names to me until the very day Walter took me to Túcume. Their names were then also unknown to our Peruvian companion Guillermo Ganoza, who was a noted amateur archaeologist and collector of pre-Inca coastal art. It was he who had brought the impressive ruins of Chan Chan, the former Chimú capital near Trujillo, to the attention of the outside world by inviting the entire board of the *National Geographic Magazine* in Washington to come and see them. On the day we both ended up in Túcume, Guillermo was driving me and some friends northward from Chan Chan in search of a lonely pyramid I had once seen and never could find again; we were simply sidetracked on the way. We seemed lost in the midst of endless stretches of desert dunes with no sign of life, when an old friend suddenly popped up from nowhere. He was Dr Christopher Donnan, archaeologist and museum director from the University of California, who was digging among these dunes because they covered the walls and mounds of the pre-Inca city of Pacatnamú. But we had an even greater surprise: he told us how, a little further

14 Walter Alva, the excavator of Sipán.

north on the coast, at a place called Sipán, tomb robbers (*huaqueros*) had recently broken into a pyramid and discovered the largest gold hoard of the century. Thus we heard for the first time of Walter Alva (*ill. 14*) and his confrontation with the looters in Sipán.

A few hours later we reached Sipán and found Alva deep down at the bottom of the looters' shaft, at the foot of a spliced bamboo ladder, so long and shaky that a descent seemed as risky as an ambush by the thieves. Walter Alva carried a loaded gun as he was under constant threat from people in the nearby village of Sipán who had sworn revenge for a relative killed in a raid by the police.

Alva's greatest prizes among the treasures he had confiscated were two splendid masks of gold. One represented a human face with blue eyes, the other a grinning feline with pink teeth, as if stained in blood. The blue irises of the human face were achieved by skillful inlays of blue lapis lazuli in eyeballs of silver, in turn inserted in the mask of gold (*ill. 15*). The bloody feline teeth were made of natural reddish *Spondylus* shell (*ill. 16*).

Here immediately was irrefutable proof of long-distance maritime activity. Lapis lazuli was not easily obtained. It could have come from nowhere else but the only quarries in America, on the central coast of Chile. Nobody could have walked thousands of miles down the coast through deserts and foreign tribes. And coastal navigation southward would have been exceedingly difficult against the full force of the Humboldt Current which runs northward along the coast until it turns west off northern Peru and flows directly to Polynesia. To travel from the Lambayeque beach to central Chile would entail sailing some 80 km (50 miles) out to sea and then turning south outside the coastal current. A homeward voyage would be much faster and close to land. Not even the *Spondylus* shell for the pink teeth could be obtained in Peru. It required navigation in the opposite direction, into the tropical waters of Ecuador and Panama, where Pizarro's advance party captured a balsa raft loaded with *Spondylus* shell.

These pre-Inca art objects were dated by Walter Alva to the Moche period, about AD 300. Thus, more than a thousand years before the voyages of Columbus, skilled craftsmen in the Lambayeque valley were familiar with materials from the entire Pacific coast of South America, and they knew both how to work and where to find the substances they needed.

When I held the strange blue-eyed human-head mask from Sipán in my hands I immediately remembered the pan-Peruvian traditions of the white men they said had come by sea and brought their ancestors'

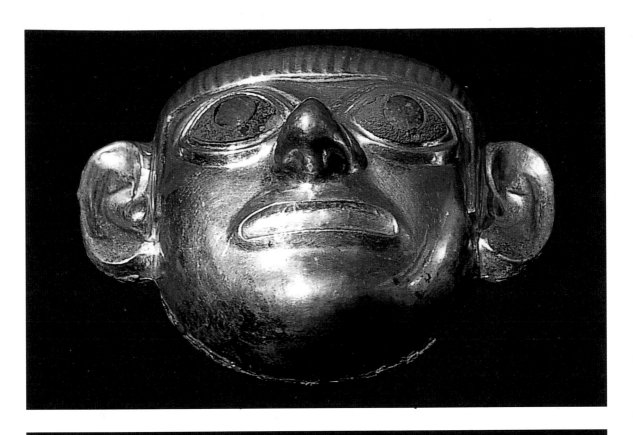

culture. The immigrant King Naymlap, who had built his first pyramid in the Lambayeque valley, had landed on the nearest beach. Only archaeology could tell us who he was and where he originated. He certainly came from somewhere where non-European civilization was already well advanced, and lapis lazuli known.

Walter saw my enthusiasm and looked at his watch. The sun would set in two hours. We had a long drive back to Trujillo. Sipán was a small site with only two pyramids, he said, but if we hurried up we had time to drive a bit further north to Túcume, a place where he knew there were 26 pyramids all in a cluster (*ill. 17*).

Thus I and my companions heard of Túcume for the first time, and arrived there just a few minutes before the sun set. Walter had cleared some steps up to a terrace on a rocky volcanic cone that rose like a natural cathedral amidst the ruins of majestic man-made structures. We got barely a glimpse of a lifeless prehistoric city of pyramids glowing like red hills in the last rays of the sun (*ill. 18*), before the unreal vision was swallowed up in the tropical night.

I knew that what I had seen would change my life. How could I free myself from this sight? Unknown people like ourselves had lived here. What would these walls enclose and these pyramids contain?

'You should organize excavations here,' I heard Walter Alva suggest. Was he joking? Guillermo was not joking: 'This is more impressive than Chan Chan,' he exclaimed. And back among the treasures from Sipán in Walter's museum, he placed a paper in front of everybody present. Walter and I had to sign a pledge: I was to organize excavations at Túcume and Walter was to be the responsible field director.

Settling in Túcume

Our unofficial pledge grew into an authorized project later when I signed the long agreement with the National Institute of Culture in Lima, before flying to Chiclayo near the north coast to check in at the Hotel Turistas. Some 30 km (18 miles) south of Túcume, this was the nearest place to sleep. But I had come to work. Peru was in great crisis, with both its currency and the terrorist group the 'Shining Path' equally out of control. Communications were badly affected. The old Panamerican highway to Túcume resembled fossilized waves after rains and floods five years before, and there was no money for repair. Shaken to bits together with the taxi on arrival at Túcume, I discovered that it was impossible to call another taxi to get back. Thieves had stolen the entire telephone line connecting Túcume to the outside

world. And it was a waste of time to put up a new one, for either thieves or terrorists would pull it down again and sell it for copper at the market in Chiclayo.

To solve my communications problems, Guillermo presented me with an old trailer so I could sleep on the spot. I parked it hidden from the village, between algarrobo trees and behind a small isolated pyramid. All I could see from my hideout were the other, huge pyramids. They formed a separate world and resembled the shadow of a dragon's crest against the night sky until the sun rose behind them and turned them first yellow and then red when it sank behind the tiny pyramid that was part of my own world. The highway was no further away than earshot, as I realized when a lorry rumbled past in the otherwise silent night.

I bought the land I was living on from an old couple in the village who wanted to move into town. On it was the small pyramid, a piece of algarrobo forest, and some long abandoned fields. I had to fence it all in, for I had learned that the village of Túcume was the home of three noted highway robbers, among them the respected *El Zorro*, 'the Fox', who came out of prison as fast as he went in, for he shared part of his fortunes with the villagers and part with the police. Theft was considered bad in Túcume, but not too bad. The first fence I put up

17 Aerial photo of the archaeological complex at Túcume, with La Raya Mountain rising over the site.

18 (opposite above) The pyramids of Túcume at sunset: a general view of Huaca Larga, looking north-northeast.

19 (opposite below) Thor Heyerdahl on horseback, riding through the west side enclosure of Huaca Larga, Túcume.

20 (above) The magnificent burial of 'the Lord of Sipán' (Tomb 1), identified as a Warrior Priest as depicted in Moche fineline drawings of sacrificial ceremonies.

21 (right) Gold human-head bead from the necklace of the 'Old Lord' (Tomb 3) at Sipán.

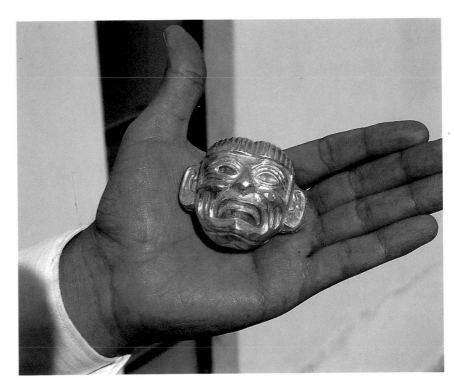

was made from wooden posts and thorny twigs. This was openly harvested by friendly old women who carried it off for their kitchen fires. Then I started to build a solid house and fence of large hand-made adobe blocks, such as used by the builders of both the ancient pyramids and the present village houses. Mud was pressed into shape in wooden molds and sun-dried to become as hard as tuff.

I bought a bed, ready to move in as soon as the first room was completed, but there was no door and so the mattress was stolen the very same night. I paid a watchman to sit in the door, but next night the bed, too, was stolen, through the window. I dug a well next to the house, with a hand-pump and a tube to a tap, and hid the pump at night. But somebody came with a hacksaw and stole the tube with the tap. I decided to add a second floor to the house, which would jut out on all sides to prevent thieves climbing up. This required a supply of cement for columns and beams so the upper floor would not crumble in the event of a Niño flood or an earthquake. The sacks of cement were piled high inside a little storage hut built for security, and a watchman volunteered to sleep on top. Day by day it seemed as if the watchman was sleeping closer to the floor. Then one day he quarreled with his wife who came running to confide that her husband had a friend who helped him drive away sacks of cement every night.

Superstition was another interesting aspect of local life. I was told that to get along with the people of Túcume, I had to be on friendly terms with more than twenty *brujos* – witch-doctors or medicine-men – in the area around the pyramids, as well as the village priest and the mayor. The priest was highly civilized and amiable, and both he and the soft-spoken mayor, a certain descendant of the pyramid-builders, became my close friends. It took time to know more than half a dozen of the most important *brujos*, the most famous of whom was Santos Vera, whose name was renowned all over Peru. He later became my best collaborator in clearing thieves away, while two of the other *brujos* became foremen on our digs, useful for their ability to pacify the spirits.

Before I really understood the importance of the *brujos* I had made it a habit to run around inside my fence for exercise every day. One morning I found a hole in the fence next to the small pyramid, and a dead rooster was hanging head down from a branch in a tree. Some kids, I thought, and kept on running. Next day a dead dog lay on the ground under the rooster. Perhaps the rooster was poisoned to kill foxes and the dog has eaten from it, I thought, and decided to have them both buried. But before I had time, a local couple from Chiclayo came on a visit, and the wife screamed when she saw the rooster and the dog. This is witchcraft, she shouted, we have to find a *brujo* who knows how to stop the evil it is meant to cause! I took it as a joke, but the couple ran away to the village and came back soon after with a bag of red chilli-peppers. They had found a *brujo* who told them what to do, and they strewed the chillis in a ring around the dead dog in the sand. This helped. Next day both animals were gone, and also the chilli-peppers. But witch-doctors kept on finding openings in my fence, and around the foot of the pyramid they left behind innocent twigs placed in a cross, empty medicine bottles, or bits of red ribbon tied to a piece of bark.

When I gained the confidence of the village people, they told me that a duck and 12 ducklings of pure gold lived inside my pyramid. Many people had seen the golden duck a few years before when it came waddling through the village with all the ducklings in a row behind. The villagers had tried to catch them, but they escaped and finally disappeared back into the pyramid. Much later, when I had about a hundred workmen employed in the excavations, all hired in the village, I was to learn that new rumors were circulating in the village: I had personally dug and found the golden duck with its ducklings. I had sold them, and with the money I had provided many village families with the employment they so badly needed. An intrepid woman opened a little one-room bar in the village and called it The Golden Duck.

One of the largest pyramids lay apart from the others and rose like a mountain with eroded vertical cliffs right next to the main school-yard in Túcume. It was literally part of the village itself and was therefore called Huaca del Pueblo, the Village Pyramid (*ill. 22*). Twice we all woke in the morning to discover that members of the Shining Path had been in Túcume during the night and planted their red flag on top of the Village Pyramid. Armed with stenguns they had knocked at some doors and shouted threats against the mayor who belonged to the government party, but apart from daubing slogans on some walls they left without doing any harm. The terrorists were most active in the big cities and in the highlands where they originated. The people on the north coast were laughter-loving, friendly, and peaceful. They were blessed by the cool coastal current from the distant Antarctic which blended so well with the rays of the tropical sun. Little was demanded from them by the outside world, and little was given to them except the water from the mountains flowing in their ancestral irrigation canals, which caused green fields and gardens to emerge like islands in a sea of desert sand.

22 Huaca del Pueblo, a huge eroded pyramid in the middle of the modern village of Túcume.

But inside the Village Pyramid lived a beautiful white lady the older generation still feared. She was said to be so light that when she emerged from the pyramid she danced weightless along the tops of the fence-posts, and so beautiful that men had great difficulty avoiding looking at her. But if they did, they would die. Worse still was the ugly sea monster that lived in the main pyramid area – formerly in a lake that had since disappeared, now inside the mountain-pyramid in the midst of all the ruins. There were still old people who had spoken to those who had seen it when it lived in the lake. It was a rayfish, *raya*, and so the mountain was named La Raya.

Never before had I heard of a mountain named after a fish, but the belief was so firm that people passed through the ruins around La Raya only in daytime. Even then they rode as if through canyons along two main donkey trails which connected farms on the other side of the mountain to the main village of Túcume. But at night only the *brujos* ventured into these ruins. The young women serving me with my daily soup and goat-with-rice meal at the Túcume market had never been inside the pyramid area, although it was virtually on their doorstep, for their grandfather had seen the devil there and the ray would come out and take them. Initially we found it difficult to get workmen for the dig. Even the bravest who did agree to spend the night as watchmen in a little plywood hut returned next morning and refused to continue the job, for spirits came at night and tried to strangle them. Not even the *brujos* could convince them. We had to resort to Padre Pedro, the village priest, who came with holy water which he sprinkled on the walls (*ill. 23*). The spirits disappeared until we forgot them and moved the shelter to another place; they then reappeared and we had to get Padre Pedro back.

Everyone talked about these ghosts and supernatural beings that they had heard of and most of them had seen, but never about a real murder that actually took place among the pyramids just after my first visit. Walter Alva and a draftsman who had come to map the site discovered blood in the sand. They thought someone had killed a fox, but there was too much blood. Following the tracks they found a dead man at the foot of one of the pyramids, completely naked, with a bullethole in his head. There was no way to identify him; no one knew him; nobody was reported missing. The police removed him. Who was he? Who had killed him? There seemed to be no answers, so the episode was never mentioned again.

When my house was ready I employed a marvelous cook from the village. Chona was the happiest being I had ever seen: if she was not smiling or laughing she was singing. But one day she was serious, her old father was ill, could I help take him to the doctor? With the aid of my faithful driver Pizarro, also a pure Tucumano, we got the old man into our pickup and turned right outside the gate, heading for the Panamerican highway. The old man protested violently, he had tried the doctors in Chiclayo with no result. Now he wanted to go to a

23 *Thor Heyerdahl had to bring Padre Pedro into the Túcume pyramid site to bless the guards' hut again in 1991. This ceremony was needed to remove the fear of the local watchmen, who insisted that spirits from the tombs tried to strangle them at night.*

Túcume doctor. He was so set on his intentions that we had to turn left instead, set on the four-wheel drive, and bump along a mule track into the algarrobo forest. After a couple of kilometers the tracks ended, and with Chona as path-finder Pizarro and I helped the old man out of the car and struggled to support him between us on a walk through the forest trees. We found an adobe hut where an incredibly fat man sat outside his door, too heavy to get up when he saluted us. This was the doctor, a *brujo* of the friendly class called *curandero*. His diagnosis was was obtained by killing a guinea-pig and studying the intestines. His cure was a brew for the patient to drink while he rubbed him with the skin of the little local rodent. But this required the whole night and we were to come back and fetch the patient early next morning.

When we returned the next morning the old man was gone. He had left on foot. We caught up with him as he came out of a shortcut through the forest, walking briskly. The pain was gone, the old man cured. Chona triumphed. A week later the man died.

Not all *brujos* were *curanderos*. Some were evil and even killed through witchcraft, but nobody dared to denounce them for fear of their revenge. My local anthropologist friend Victor Fiestas spoke about them from personal experience. Fiestas was the son of a fisherman from the coast near Túcume, his features bore clear evidence of previous generations with no foreign blood. He himself was a man of the ocean who had paid his way through the Anthropology Department at the University in Trujillo by fishing with his family off the local coast. He specialized in the maritime aspects of past and present local culture, and from the moment I arrived he showed me ancient documents concerning balsa rafts, some with two masts. To my great surprise he also took me to several beaches and secluded coves north of Túcume where the fishermen still sailed their small balsa rafts every day into the open Pacific long before sunrise. Navigating only with sails and *guara* boards, they returned loaded with fish in the afternoon to their tiny ports, such as Yasila, La Islilla, Nonura, Matacaballo, and Chulluyache Viejo. But suddenly Fiestas disappeared; I learned later that he was in hospital with an incurable illness. Some time still later someone told me he was totally paralyzed and that there was no hope for him. Months passed, and we were all sure Fiestas was dead.

Then one day Fiestas, broad, tanned, and smiling, stood in my door. I confessed I thought he was dead. Almost, he said, for he could only move his eyes, and the hospital had given him up, when his family brought a *brujo* to see him. When the *brujo* came for the third time he carried an old soiled shirt which Fiestas recognized as his. The *brujo* had dug it up at a cemetery, where some other *brujo* must have buried it to please a client by killing Fiestas through sorcery. After rubbing Fiestas all over with his old shirt, the *brujo* commanded him to sit up. Slowly the paralyzed patient, after a half a year motionless in bed, sat up. Then the *brujo* ordered him to stand up with no support, and to think of the last movements he made before he had lost his ability to move his legs. Fiestas obeyed automatically. He took some fumbling steps, then he walked, and was cured. And completely, for a few months later he persuaded the Peruvian Navy in Sechura to organize a regatta for balsa raft fishermen on the north coast. The rafts sailed into the open Pacific to a flagship on the horizon and back again, as easily as any sailing ship.

The people of Túcume never made me feel like a foreigner. Traditionally, ever since the time of Naymlap, anyone who came to settle among them became one of them. To judge from their pitch-black hair, tanned skin, and typical Peruvian features, a minimum of foreign blood had mingled with theirs, in spite of conquests by both the Incas and the Spaniards. Proud, friendly, and generally very attractive, they often resembled the Polynesians more than any other people. Whether tilling the ground in Túcume or pulling in their nets in the open ocean, the great majority of the village people of the plains and coasts of north Peru are as pure representatives of the people Pizarro met when he landed as it is possible to find today. Strangely, the word *gringo*, for fair-haired foreigners, uttered with contempt in other parts of Latin America, is a respectful compliment among the people whose past I had come to study.

The start of excavations

Professional archaeologists began to arrive from universities in Peru and abroad and we were able to find strong men willing to work in Túcume, where most families lived only off their own scattered farmlands. The first problem was to decide where to start to dig. The site was huge. With all its sand-covered mounds and walls the pyramid complex of Túcume covers about 220 ha (540 acres). At Sipán professional tomb-robbers had shown the way and the work left for archaeologists was salvage. In the vast area at Túcume only the outskirts showed any evidence that looters had ventured into the neighborhood, digging like farmers with pick and shovel. However, our tools

24 (right) Excavations in the North Plaza of Huaca 1, 1989.

25 (below) Over the last 500 years the sporadic but catastrophic El Niño rains have eroded the pyramids of Túcume. The material washed off Huaca 1 has formed stratified sediments, around 5 m (16 ft) deep, as seen here in a view of excavations in the North Plaza.

would be the mason's trowel and the painter's brush, for our task would be to dig not for royal treasures, but for evidence telling us how the builders of the pyramids had lived, the common people as well as the elite.

We were to discover that a few professional archaeologists had visited the pyramids, but without leaving any traces behind (see Chapter 3). These visits gave us no guidance but full freedom in our choice of where to begin excavations in an area containing 26 pyramids and numerous other buried remains in the sand between them.

The Túcume Archaeological Project got under way in 1988, initially co-directed by Walter Alva and Arne Skjölsvold of the Kon-Tiki Museum. On 28 August of that year, Walter laid out a 1-m square with string at the foot of a Túcume pyramid, and began scraping the crusty surface with a trowel. This was the official opening of the first excavations inside the pyramid area, and the pyramid was arbitrarily named Huaca 1, Pyramid One (ill. 24). Little did we know that Walter would have time to do no more, for his helpers called him back to the looters' pit in Sipán. There was evidence that the tomb-robbers had not had time to remove everything. And thus Walter returned to Sipán and discovered the splendid tomb of the 1500-year-old nobleman who became known as the 'Lord of Sipán' (ill. 20).[2]

Work had to continue in Túcume once we had started, and Walter sent us a younger Peruvian colleague to replace him for the few days he thought he would be delayed in Sipán. But no sooner had the Lord of Sipán been brushed clean in his tomb and transported with all his buried treasures to the Brüning Museum, when his team found

26 The start of excavations in the South Plaza of Huaca 1 in 1988. The low walls of numerous enigmatic ash-filled chambers are visible.

another tomb; and still another.[3] The little pyramid of Sipán seemed to contain an inexhaustible supply of royal burials (*ill. 21*).

In the meantime Hugo Navarro, Walter's replacement, decided to cut bigger slices of cake in proportion to the dimensions around us. Instead of 1-m squares, he lined up 100-m squares at a time, where digging started with trowel and brush. Millimeters became centimeters and by the time we had reached a meter's depth, wheelbarrow loads by the hundreds of pure sand had been rolled away. Nothing was found in the sieves – no trace of human activity, only sterile silt which had descended as mud from the terraced wall of the pyramid above over the centuries. We could see the stratification of mud from Niño years – the periodic episodes of torrential rain – like superimposed pages of a book in the vertical profiles of the dig (*ill. 25*).

Disappointed at finding nothing, Hugo changed tactics and we dug a test trench down and along the wall of the pyramid. This descended some 5 m (16 ft) before we reached the foot of the pyramid which already rose about 40 m (130 ft) above the ground, yet still we found nothing but silt from the wall above.

We then moved from the north to the south side of the pyramid, where the remains of a buried wall outlined what had been a huge plaza. Here even the surface was covered with broken, white sea shells and ancient potsherds. Immediately below the surface the trowels uncovered a haphazard complex of low adobe walls enclosing tiny rooms too small to be for habitation (*ill. 26*). A mixture of sherds from large urns, some displaced human bones, and a thick coat of black ashes was a common feature of nearly all these shallow-walled enclosures. Scattered among them were numerous complete, extended baby burials, all girls of about a year old. Did they represent offerings? They seemed to be secondary and not ancient. But the ever-present carpet of black ashes was surprising. Was this the first discovery of cremation burials in Peru, such as we were familiar with from Easter Island and Ecuador? If not, it had to be the remains of burnt offerings. And all the ashes must have been brought here from elsewhere in urns, for the adobe enclosures would have turned red from fire if the burning had taken place in them.

Wherever we dug, in all directions, the enclosures with ashes appeared, and, as Hugo hesitated to destroy them by digging underneath them, the excavated area expanded outside the level plaza and up into the undulating higher level east of the same pyramid. Here another pattern of low adobe walls took over and continued seemingly endlessly eastward and northward. Rows of well-preserved niches emerged, all the size of a comfortable and roomy easy chair or throne, and sometimes actually placed in tiers like seats in an amphitheater. Sadly, they were all empty and clean, with no marks from use. Had they once contained mummy bundles, images, or other treasures robbed by the Inca intruders? We found to our surprise that the sand covering all these niches was neither windblown nor silt from the pyramid wall, but fill mixed with pre-Colonial potsherds, rags, shells, bone, and carbon, all carried in by the ton, intentionally to hide what was beneath.

Walter's temporary replacement was hoping to make some important discovery while he was in charge of field operations and he decided to widen the area of investigation. Since I have always made it a policy to let the responsible archaeologist follow his own plan and draw his own conclusions, he soon had his little army of workmen and students inching their way up and down the nearest mounds, without going deeper than the upper level of occupation floors with the tiny, walled niches. With a hundred years at our disposal we might have uncovered the upper layer of all the Túcume ruins, and yet learned nothing about anything earlier than the very last moment when the site was abandoned and the empty structures hidden by the fill. Hidden from whom, though? From the advancing Spaniards?

The more we dug the more questions we asked ourselves without finding any answers. When it became obvious that Walter would not complete his obligations in Sipán within any foreseeable time, good luck brought two very experienced archaeologists to share the responsibility as co-directors of the Túcume Archaeological Project:

27 *Some of the exhibits in the temporary site museum established in the laboratory and warehouse buildings set up with Kon-Tiki Museum funds in 1991. This has since been replaced by a larger permanent site museum set up by the Peruvian government.*

Alfredo Narváez from the National University in Trujillo, and Daniel H. Sandweiss, then a Research Associate of the Carnegie Museum of Natural History and now an assistant professor at the University of Maine in the United States. Both had many years of archaeological field experience in northern Peru. As the official representative of the National Institute of Culture in Peru, Alfredo was to be the Resident Archaeologist, and with his Ph.D. in archaeology from Cornell, Dan represented the Kon-Tiki Museum and was chief editor of project reports. He held the responsibility for co-direction on behalf of Dr Arne Skjölsvold, who could only free himself from his obligations as Research Director of the museum in Norway on annual inspection tours. The team was also joined by María del Carmen, a Peruvian archaeologist and Dan's wife, and besides her we engaged a number of Peruvian and foreign archaeologists, as well as 20 students of archaeology from the universities in Lima and Trujillo. An old house in Túcume village was restored and extended to house the students, and contracts for mutual scholarly collaboration were signed with the University in Trujillo and the National Museum of Anthropology and Archaeology in Lima.

We were in full operation. Project headquarters were set up by the Kon-Tiki Museum at the entrance to the Túcume Pyramid area. These buildings included a temporary museum (*ill. 27*) to house and exhibit the objects that kept coming out of the ground as long as excavation lasted. This has now been replaced by a permanent site museum by the Peruvian Ministry of Tourism. Laboratory work continued through 1994 and there is much work for future teams at Túcume.

Daniel H. Sandweiss

Cultural Background

and Regional Prehistory

Peru's written history began in 1532 with the Spanish Conquest, but its prehistory stretches back at least 12,000 years. Over the last century, archaeologists have worked to uncover and write the prehistory of Peru from the fragments left behind by the prehistoric inhabitants. In this task, they routinely draw on the research of *ethnohistorians*, who study the peoples of Peru through early post-Conquest documents, and *ethnographers*, who study the living descendants of these peoples. These other sources are particularly important when dealing with the sites and cultures closest in time to the European invasion. Túcume is such a case, and we draw on both ethnohistory and ethnography in our interpretation of the site and its inhabitants.

Lambayeque and Túcume

The coast of Peru is an arid desert broken only by the rivers which descend from the Andes mountains to the east. It is along the river valleys that irrigation can be practiced and large populations supported. Although in southern Peru the foothills of the Andes reach right into the sea, with the river valleys forming narrow canyons all the way to the shore, the situation is different in the north, where Lambayeque and Túcume are located. North of the Santa Valley at about latitude 9° south, the coastal plain grows ever wider and the valleys become bigger and bigger (see *ill. 1*). The northernmost and largest of these valleys is Lambayeque, formed of the coalesced flood-plains of three rivers – from north to south the Motupe, the Leche, and the Lambayeque. The Lambayeque River actually consists of the Chancay River (not to be confused with the Chancay River just north of Lima), which splits into the Lambayeque and Reque rivers and the Taymi Canal where the river emerges on to the coastal plain (see *ill. 2*). In places, over 30 km (18 miles) of coastal floodplain separate the Andean foothills from the shoreline in the Lambayeque Valley. North of Lambayeque is the immense Sechura desert.

In ancient times, the three valleys of the Lambayeque area were joined by irrigation systems to the Saña and Jequetepeque valleys to the south. This five-valley complex 'probably accounted for almost *one-third of the total cultivated area* and almost *one-third of the population of the entire Coast!*' (italics in original) according to geographer Paul Kosok.[1] Kosok calls this five-valley system the 'Lambayeque Complex'; here, we will use the term 'Lambayeque Valley Complex' to refer to the three most closely united river drainages: the Motupe, the Leche, and the Chancay/Lambayeque/Reque.

As the condor flies, the site of ancient Túcume lies some 28 km (17 miles) to the north of Chiclayo, the modern center of the Lambayeque Valley. The pyramids and other remains are spread in a circle around the base of a natural hill which rises over 140 m (460 ft) above the surrounding landscape and cover about 220 ha (540 acres). This hill is known today as 'Cerro La Raya' – the Mountain of the Ray – and it sticks out of the flat coastal plain like a beacon.

The modern village of Túcume is located about 2 km (1¼ miles) to the west of the site, next to a large pyramid (the Huaca del Pueblo or Village Pyramid) which is part of the Túcume complex. Because the coast of Peru is an arid desert, the modern villagers depend on irrigation agriculture just as their ancestors did. When rains do come, as part of the sporadic El Niño phenomenon, they are a terrible disaster: fields and farms are flooded and plagues of insects, rodents, and tropical diseases ravage the crops and the people. The most recent strong El Niño was in 1983, and the descriptions of local residents sound little different from those of their ancestors in 1578, the first major event after the Spanish Conquest of the Andes.[2]

In a normal year, irrigation water for Túcume comes from two sources: the Taymi Canal, which draws on the Reque River to the south, and from the Leche River to the north. Principal market crops today are rice, maize, cotton, and sorghum, while a variety of fruits and vegetables are grown mainly for local consumption.

Lambayeque and coastal Peruvian prehistory

People first arrived in the Andean region at least 12,000 years ago. Archaeologists refer to the initial occupation of the Andes as the Preceramic Epoch, divided into the Early (10,000+ to 6000 BC), Middle (6000 to 2500 BC), and Late (2500 to 1850 BC) Preceramic Periods.[3] Although the first hunters and gatherers probably traveled south along the spine of the Andes mountain chain, they had descended westward to the Pacific coast no later than 11,500 years ago.[4] Once in the coastal environment, marine resources became an important part of their diet, and ocean-oriented activities must always have played a significant role in daily life and/or seasonal rounds. Indeed, the sea has remained important in Peruvian coastal lifeways throughout prehistory and up to today: as recently as the 1960s, Peru was one of the world's leading fishing nations. Some archaeologists have convincingly argued that the rich bounty of the Pacific Ocean supported the first steps towards civilization on the Andean coast.[5]

Based on the food remains found at different early coastal sites, the Early and Middle Preceramic hunters and gatherers of the Peruvian coast spent part of their year hunting sea mammals and sea birds, fishing, and gathering mollusks, seaweed, and other foods along the shore; they would have passed the rest of the year inland, gathering plants and hunting small game. Later coastal cultures continued to exploit both seafood and landfood (albeit in different economies), and the combination of terrestrial and marine resources is one of the defining characteristics of the Peruvian coastal cultures throughout prehistory.[6]

In the Late Preceramic Period, from around 4500 years ago, ancient Peruvians began to construct monumental architecture. Large temples were built at this time in the highlands, but the majority of Late Preceramic monuments are found on the coast between the Chillón Valley near Lima and the Chao Valley, to the south of Trujillo (see *ill. 1*). Though small by comparison with many later structures, the Late Preceramic temples represent a big jump in size and complexity from buildings of preceding periods. The largest of the Late Preceramic sites is El Paraíso, in the Chillón Valley, which covers 58 ha (140 acres) and has nine major buildings built from more than 100,000 tons of stone.[7]

Agriculture, which had begun earlier, became more significant, and many of the important Andean crops were domesticated by the Late Preceramic Period. In addition to numerous food crops, these included 'industrial' plants such as cotton, used to make textiles and nets, and gourds, used as containers and as floats for fishing nets. On the coast the bulk of the animal protein in the diet still came from the sea.[8]

Some scholars argue that the monumental structures of the Late Preceramic Period indicate coastal society had become significantly more complex, with power accruing to a small elite, probably chiefs and their close relatives. Others feel that the Late Preceramic temples could have been built by egalitarian groups without the need for hereditary chiefs or rulers.[9]

Although Preceramic sites are known on the Peruvian coast both north and south of Lambayeque, only one such site has been reported in the Lambayeque Valley Complex itself. Walter Alva briefly mentions a midden with stone tools, animal bones, and sea shells on the Pampa de Eten, near the shore between the Reque and Zaña rivers. Alva concludes that the site's inhabitants must have been maritime hunter-gatherers. Unfortunately, no dates or details are available for this site.[10] It is highly unlikely that Preceramic people would have ignored an area as well-watered and rich in resources as Lambayeque. The absence of Preceramic sites in this area surely reflects the lack of a systematic search for early sites as well as problems of preservation – the valley floor has been irrigated and farmed for thousands of years, while later sites are built over many of the uncultivated hillsides.

The Initial Period (c. 1850 to 600 BC) is so named because it marks the time when pottery first came into use in Peru. Pottery had been made for over a thousand years in Ecuador and Colombia before being adopted in Peru; no one is sure why the delay occurred. In any event, along with the introduction of this new technology, buildings on the coast became even larger, and irrigation agriculture apparently began. Initial Period monuments are more widely spread than those of the Late Preceramic Period, reaching as far north along the coast as the Lambayeque Valley Complex. Although marine foods continued to be important in coastal Initial Period diets, a shift inland of major centers reflects the increasing importance of cultivated plant foods that accompanied the advent of irrigation agriculture.

The debate over the level of socioeconomic complexity of Peruvian coastal societies continues for the Initial Period. The greatest concentration of Initial Period monumental architecture occurs in the north-central coast Casma Valley, where the site of Sechín Alto has the largest structure known from the Americas for its time. Shelia and Tom Pozorski argue that Initial Period Casma had a state-level society, probably the first in the New World. They point to the large size and complex nature of the architecture at sites such as Pampa de las Llamas-Moxeke, where they found evidence for planned construction, extensive centralized storage, and separate residential areas for elite and commoner inhabitants. Working at Initial Period sites in the Lurín Valley near Lima, Richard Burger notes that the monumental structures were built in successive increments over several hundred years. Pointing also to the lack of significant differences in wealth found in Initial Period burials, he argues that the monumental constructions of the Initial Period could have been built by egalitarian groups without rulers wielding coercive power.[11]

Following the Initial Period is a time referred to as the Early Horizon (c. 600 to 200 BC). A 'horizon' occurs when a single style or set of styles spread rapidly through a large region of former stylistic diversity. The Early Horizon in Peru was originally defined as the period when a single art style was thought to have expanded rapidly from the site of Chavín de Huántar in the north central highlands of Peru to most of the Central Andes. More recent work has shown that much 'Chavinoid' art actually dates to the Initial Period or perhaps even the Late Preceramic Period. Chavín de Huántar became the center for the religion expressed in 'Chavín' iconography only later, in the Early Horizon. Certainly by the end of the Early Horizon, most Peruvians – including those on the north coast – lived in highly complex, stratified societies.[12]

In the Lambayeque region, the late Initial Period and Early Horizon societies are generally referred to as part of the Cupisnique culture.[13] Important sites of this time include Purulén, Huaca Lucía, and Morro de Eten (see *ill. 2*). Purulén is a late Initial Period monumental site located near the coast in the Zaña Valley, the next valley south of the Lambayeque Complex. The site covers about 3 sq. km (2 sq. miles) and consists of 15 mounds, composed of fill faced and retained by stone walls, and surrounded by living areas, refuse, roads, and quarries. Walter Alva excavated one of the mounds and found it to be a stepped platform with a central staircase, sunken rooms, and rows of cylindrical columns. The mound had two architectural phases, one superimposed on the other; at the end of the occupation, the buildings on top of the mound were burnt.[14]

Located some 7 to 10 km (4 to 6 miles) to the northeast of Túcume, the Batán Grande area contains one of the region's most important concentrations of prehispanic monuments. Research over many years by Izumi Shimada and his colleagues has shed much light on the prehistory of this zone. Although its apogee came later, important structures were already present in Batán Grande by the Initial Period. Huaca Lucía, or the Temple of the Columns, is an Initial Period, two-tiered platform with a central staircase and 24 cylindrical columns made of conical adobes (sun-dried mud bricks) and mud mortar. On abandonment, the columns were dismantled and placed carefully on the clay floor and the whole structure was buried in clean sand. During later periods, the filled temple was used as a cemetery.[15]

Morro de Eten is a large hill overlooking the ocean on the southern flank of the Lambayeque Complex. Work at this site by Carlos Elera uncovered a number of Early Horizon burials, including that of a shaman. This individual was buried with two bone spatulas, an anthracite mirror, and a carved bone rattle which may have been inserted repeatedly into the leg while the shaman was alive, eventually forming a socket in which the rattle could be carried. Structures on Morro de Eten include a road leading to a cliff above the ocean, facing the setting sun, and a small, two-tiered, stone-faced and rubble-filled mound. On the upper tier of the mound, Elera found a large stone interpreted as an altar and surrounded by burned and broken shells of *Spondylus*, the sacred mollusk brought from Ecuador.[16]

The Early Intermediate Period (c. 200 BC to AD 600) was a time of cultural florescence in Peru. Many societies had reached a state level of sociopolitical organization, particularly on the coast. Art, probably in the service of religion and state, was highly developed and technologically sophisticated; media included pottery, textiles, gold, silver, copper, and alloy metalwork, and carved wood, bone, and shell. On the coast, the best-known cultures of this time are the Nasca in the south and the Moche in the north. A variety of smaller polities characterized the northern and central Peruvian highlands, while the Tiahuanaco empire arose in the highlands of Bolivia and southernmost Peru.

During the Early Intermediate Period, the Lambayeque area fell under Moche influence. The capital of the Moche state was at the site of the same name in the Moche Valley (see *ill. 1*). Here, two huge pyramids known as the Huaca del Sol (Temple of the Sun) (*ill. 28*) and the Huaca de la Luna (Temple of the Moon) dominate a sand-covered landscape at the base of a large hill. Although a large part of the Huaca del Sol was eroded when Spanish treasure seekers diverted the course of the local river, archaeologists estimate that as many as 143 million adobes had been used to make this massive, solid mound. Between the two pyramids, sand now covers a vast area of houses, administrative buildings, and cemeteries. Catastrophic natural processes buried these

28 *Huaca del Sol (the Pyramid of the Sun), in the Moche Valley, once the seat of Moche power.*

structures at the close of the Early Intermediate Period, causing the site to be abandoned between AD 500 and 600.[17]

Although Moche sites have been excavated, the Moche culture was until recently best known from its naturalistic, red and white pottery. Modeled and fine-line painted scenes often show recognizable objects, animals, plants, and human activities. Lengthy study of Moche iconography by Christopher Donnan and his colleagues has shown that all these representations are part of a limited number of 'themes', probably myths.[18] Recently, excavations of high-status burials at Sipán in the Lambayeque Valley and San José de Moro in the Jequetepeque Valley have added significantly to our knowledge of Moche culture.[19]

Although other Early Intermediate Period sites are known in Lambayeque, Sipán is the only one for which we have extensive information. The site of Sipán lies well inland of Túcume, up the Reque River towards the point where the mountains begin to close in on the Lambayeque Valley (see *ill. 2*). At the foot of the large, adobe pyramid known as the Huaca Rajada (Split Mound) because it is divided into two sections, a low, unimpressive platform was found to contain the richest burials ever excavated by archaeologists in Peru. In 1987, police showed archaeologist Walter Alva a collection of beautiful gold, silver, copper, and alloy objects just captured from looters (see also Chapter 2). Alva located the looted tomb in the low platform at Sipán, cleaned it, and began excavations near by. Since that time, he has discovered three royal tombs: the Warrior Priest; the Bird Priest; and the Old Lord of Sipán (*ills. 20–21*), who may have been an earlier Warrior Priest. Each of these important personages had been buried

in a deep tomb cut through the pre-existing adobe platform, and each was accompanied by sacrificed retainers and impressive quantities of finely worked precious-metal objects, shell-bead pectorals, and other offerings. Comparison of the nature and arrangement of the grave goods in the tombs at Sipán, as well as those more recently discovered at San José de Moro, and the personages depicted on the pottery have shown that the mythical figures were represented in life by real people. This discovery has revolutionized our understanding of the rituals and organization of Moche society.[20]

29 Huaca Fortaleza at Pampa Grande.

During the Middle Horizon (*c.* AD 600 to 1000), environmental and cultural change went hand in hand in the Central Andes. For the first time cultures of the south highlands began to exert a notable influence over peoples of the north. The Tiahuanaco Empire continued to dominate southernmost Peru and Bolivia, while the Huari Empire expanded north and west from its capital at Ayacucho in southern Peru (see *ill. 1*). Archaeologists debate the nature of Huari, particularly whether it grew imperially by military conquest or its influence was exerted through commercial relations or religious authority. By the end of the Middle Horizon, the southern empires had declined and fallen, and the northern region returned to local traditions.[21]

At the close of the Early Intermediate Period, during the late 500s AD, a prolonged and severe drought plagued Peru. On the north coast, occasional El Niño events punctuated the dry spell with catastrophic rains and flooding. These disasters seem to have caused the abandonment of the old capital in the Moche Valley and led to the establishment of new centers during the final phase (V) of the Moche culture (*c.* AD

600 to 750). Of all the new sites, Pampa Grande in the Lambayeque Valley was the largest (*ill. 29*), and was probably the capital of the reorganized Moche state in the early Middle Horizon. This site is strategically placed at the valley neck just above the point where the Chancay River splits into the Taymi Canal and the Reque and Lambayeque rivers – the major sources for irrigation water for much of the coastal plain. Spread out over an alluvial fan on the side of the valley, Pampa Grande consisted of rooms, workshops, and storehouses of masonry and several adobe pyramids. The largest is Huaca Fortaleza, a huge stepped platform reached by a long inclined ramp running perpendicular to the front of the mound before zigzagging up the different levels of the platform. This marks the beginning of a long Lambayeque tradition of building stepped pyramids reached by ramps.[22]

Around AD 750, Pampa Grande was burned and abandoned, bringing an end to Moche V and giving rise to the regional Lambayeque culture. It seems clear that the Lambayeque area was never conquered by highlanders from Huari, although their influence had certainly been felt since Moche V. Shimada has argued that the Lambayeque culture at Batán Grande, which he calls Sicán, arose as an independent synthesis of Moche and Huari elements. Little is known about the Early Sicán Period (AD 750 to 900). During the Middle Sicán Period (AD 900 to 1100), the Religious-Funerary Precinct at Batán Grande may have been the center of a religious polity which controlled much of the Lambayeque region. Many of the adobe pyramids with ramps at Batán Grande date to this time, and most of the Peruvian gold objects in museums throughout the world were probably looted from Middle Sicán cemeteries.[23] Shimada recently excavated the tomb of an important Middle Sicán person at Huaca Loro in Batán Grande, the first such tomb ever excavated scientifically. Over 1.2 tons of grave goods were uncovered, around 75% of them metal – much of it gold.[24] Previous work by Shimada and his colleagues found metallurgical workshops in the Batán Grande area which date back to at least AD 800 and continued in use through Inca times. The presence of these workshops and the iconographic designs in the local, Sicán style on many of the metal objects show that the Sicán people themselves produced much of the metalwork found in their graves and sites.[25]

Shimada identifies a figure represented frequently on pottery and in other media as the principal diagnostic feature of Middle Sicán iconography. He calls this figure the Sicán Lord, and suggests that representations of the motif virtually cease at the end of the Middle Sicán Period.[26]

Other post-Moche V Middle Horizon sites are known from the Lambayeque area, including Huaca Pintada near Túcume and the Early Phase at Chotuna near the town of Lambayeque.[27]

Around AD 1050 to 1100, near the start of the Late Intermediate Period (*c.* AD 1000 to 1470), the Lambayeque area saw radical changes. Like Pampa Grande before it, the major Middle Sicán pyramids at Batán Grande were burned and abandoned, and the focus of power in the region seems to have shifted to Túcume.[28] At the same time, the Lambayeque Valley Complex was dotted with important sites. It may be that a number of small polities shared Lambayeque culture, with Túcume as *primus inter pares*, exerting influence over the region as the principal religious center. In the Motupe drainage, the huge site of Apurlec covers more area than Túcume, but lacks the concentration of massive pyramids that makes Túcume the primary center. In the Leche drainage, Batán Grande continued to be occupied, though the major pyramids were abandoned; other sites include La Viña, which might have been the capital of the Jayanca polity known from the ethnohistoric documents. In the Lambayeque Valley proper, major sites include Chotuna (*ill. 30*) and Chornancap near the shore and Colluz moving inland, all with adobe pyramids. Where the valley begins to narrow still further inland, Pátapo on the north side and Saltur on the south are large sites consisting of adobe compounds at the base of hills and stone structures on the hillsides.[29]

For the first part of the Late Intermediate Period, the Lambayeque Valley Complex was politically independent from the rest of Peru, whether or not it was politically united under Túcume leadership. At

30 Huaca Mayor at Chotuna.

Batán Grande, Shimada calls this period Late Sicán A/B, dating it to AD 1100 to 1350. He finds major changes in pottery, in particular the near absence of the Sicán Lord representation, as well as in settlement pattern. However, there are sufficient continuities to argue for only local change, not foreign conquest. Late Sicán A/B is roughly contemporaneous with the Middle Phase at Chotuna and Chornancap.[30]

Around AD 1350, or perhaps a little later, the Chimú Empire of the Moche Valley conquered the Lambayeque region. Many of the existing sites continued to be occupied, although the Chimú oversaw continued growth and modifications to them.[31] An analysis of the Chimú or Inca period pottery from Batán Grande is not yet published, but that area probably experienced the same trend as at Túcume, where Chimú and Chimú-inspired pottery types were added to the local ceramic assemblage, but the traditional Lambayeque types continued to be produced without modification.[32] This pattern makes sense: like the later Inca, the Chimú ruled largely through local lords, so the bulk of the population and the elite remained ethnic Lambayeque people.

The Inca Empire began expanding out of Cuzco, in the south highlands of Peru, in the early to mid-1400s. At its greatest extent, the Incas controlled the Andean chain and adjacent Pacific lowlands from central Chile and Argentina to the north of Ecuador. Over 30,000 km (18,600 miles) of roads connected the huge empire, and a complex system of way-stations, known as *tambos*, fortresses, and administrative centers facilitated imperial rule. Though a mighty military power, the Inca also used statecraft to conquer and control the multitude of diverse ethnic groups and factions whom they incorporated into their empire.[33]

The Inca conquered Lambayeque about AD 1470 and controlled it until the Spanish Conquest in 1532. This period of Inca imperial expansion is known as the Late Horizon. Like the Chimú before them, the Inca ruled largely through local lords; new, Inca-inspired pottery types were added to the ceramic inventory without eliminating local types that dated as far back as AD 1000. Most of the same sites continued to be occupied, although a few Inca installations were established and new construction was carried out at a number of sites. The Inca coastal road ran along the Andean foothills, crossing the Reque River near Saltur, the Lambayeque River, the Taymi Canal near Pátapo, and the Leche River just east of Batán Grande. At its closest point, the road lay some 14 km (9 miles) due east of Túcume; a short distance before crossing the Leche River, it runs by Tambo Real, an Inca state installation which included pottery workshops (*ill. 2*).[34]

One of the intriguing questions about Inca archaeology on the north coast of Peru is why Inca sites are so scarce. The ethnohistoric record leaves no doubt that the entire north coast was under Inca dominion for over 60 years, yet recognizably Inca sites are few compared to many other parts of the empire. Lambayeque was one of the most productive regions of all Peru, and it is surprising that only one small *tambo* has been found. Fortunately, our work at Túcume has shed some light on this question.

In 1532, the Spanish conquistadors under Francisco Pizarro entered Peru at Tumbes, the northern extreme. On their march to the highland city of Cajamarca to meet the Inca ruler Atahuallpa, they passed close to Túcume. As best we can tell, the site was still occupied at that time and was probably the major center for the region. Yet a mere 15 years later, Túcume lay abandoned and in ruins.

Túcume ethnohistory

What can we learn about Túcume from the early historic record? We must start with the nature of that record. First, the early historic documents about Lambayeque in general and about Túcume in particular were all written by Spaniards – there is no known early native chronicler for the region. Second, the available sources fall into two major categories: oral history of prehispanic events and rulers, and documents generated by Spanish colonial officials trying to administer the region. Each category has its strengths and weaknesses.

The principal source of oral history is the Naymlap legend, recorded independently by Cabello in 1586 and Rubiños y Andrade in 1781. Written when some people born before the Spanish Conquest were still alive, the Cabello version is closer in time to the supposed events described and more complete than the Rubiños y Andrade rendering. However, the two accounts are very similar, providing independent confirmation of the details of the Naymlap story.[35]

In Chapter 1, Thor has detailed Cabello's version, and I will summarize it here. The great lord Naymlap arrived in Lambayeque on balsa rafts with his subjects and retainers and built a palace at Chot. On his death, he was succeeded by eleven consecutive rulers in his line, beginning with his oldest son Cium. Cium's 12 sons spread throughout the valley to found their own settlements; among them, Cala went to Túcume. Naymlap's old retainer Llapchillulli also founded a settlement, at Jayanca. Because Cabello first lists the rulers of the whole valley, presumably Cium's sons' settlements remained subordinate to the named head of the dynasty. The last of Naymlap's line was Fempellec, who committed a great sin that brought on thirty days of rain and caused his subjects to throw him in the ocean. After Fempellec's death, an interregnum of unspecified length followed before the Chimú Empire conquered the area and placed a native Chimú lord named Pongmassa over the valley. Pongmassa was succeeded by his son Pallesmassa and grandson Oxa, during whose reign the Inca passed through Cajamarca in the neighboring highlands. After Oxa came six more rulers of the same family; the Spanish Conquest occurred during the sixth lord's reign. Cabello says that after word of the Inca in Cajamarca reached Lambayeque in Oxa's reign, the lords of the valley lived in constant fear of being deposed by the highlanders; however, he does not specify when the Inca conquest of Lambayeque actually took place.[36]

Archaeologists and ethnohistorians are divided on whether the Naymlap story has some element of historical truth, or whether it is purely mythical. Did Naymlap and each of his descendants exist and rule as the legend states? Does the Naymlap story conflate a long process or repetitive events into a simplified and coherent narrative? Is the more recent part of the story history and the early part legend? Or is the whole thing simply a water myth?[37]

Among those who believe that Naymlap may have existed, there is debate over when he arrived, from what direction, and which archaeological site is the location of Naymlap's palace. Cabello says that Naymlap's fleet came from 'la parte suprema', the upper or supreme part. Does that mean the north or the south? Most scholars now agree with Kosok that the use of balsa log rafts and other evidence indicate a northern origin in present-day Ecuador.[38]

According to the Naymlap legend, the great leader built his palace at a place called 'Chot'. Most archaeologists have equated this with the site known as Huaca Chotuna;[39] however, Shimada argues that the nearby site of Chornancap would better fit the description in the legend.[40] Much depends on the date assigned to Naymlap's arrival.

Many scholars have tried to determine when Naymlap stepped on to the shores of Lambayeque. Following Means, Kosok estimated 25 years as the average length of reign of the named rulers and calculated a date of c. AD 1025.[41] More recently, Shimada has suggested that different lines of evidence could be used to argue for an arrival at the start of Moche V, or of Early, Middle, or Late Sicán.[42] Donnan offers arguments for a date of either c. AD 750 (the start of his Early Period at Chotuna, equivalent to the start of Early Sicán) or AD 1150 (the start of his Middle Period at Chotuna, equivalent to Late Sicán); he favors the Early Period arrival.[43] From a purely Túcume-centric point of view, if the story is history and a grandson of Naymlap founded (not merely took control of) Túcume, then we would have to support an arrival date very similar to Kosok's, sometime in the 11th century AD.

In addition to the Naymlap story, Cabello provides one other piece of information concerning Túcume. He writes that when the Spanish conquistadors first passed through the region in 1532, they were received by the lord of Jayanca, who 'had just concluded certain wars with the Túcumes, a people who had given themselves over to devotion of the Chimús, the capital enemies [of the lord of Jayanca]'.[44] That two neighboring polities could have been warring while under overall Inca jurisdiction has been taken by some to indicate the loose nature of Inca control over the region.[45] The Naymlap legend offers another perspective on the conflict between Túcume and Jayanca: all of the known polities in the Lambayeque Valley Complex were said to have been settled by Cium's sons (Naymlap's grandsons) – except Jayanca, which was settled by Llapchillulli, a member of Naymlap's court who was a master in making feather garments. If Lambayeque was a loose federation based on kinship, fictive or real (see Chapter 9), this detail could explain why Jayanca was alienated from Túcume and perhaps the rest of the Lambayeque Valley Complex.[46]

Beyond Cabello's brief notice of the war with Jayanca, there are only glimpses of prehispanic Túcume in other, administrative documents dealing with the region. Ramirez has found and collated evidence for 15 different kinds of specialists in the Túcume polity recorded within 45 years of the Conquest: carpenters, cooks, *chicha* (corn beer) makers, spindlemakers, merchants, potters, fishermen, cloak painters, silversmiths, saltmakers, shoemakers, chairmakers, weavers, dyers, and deer hunters. The bulk of the population, however, were farmers.[47] Túcume was thus a typical coastal polity, composed of groups of specialists, some full-time and exclusive (such as fishermen), some part-time; some living under their own specialist lords, though subject through him to the paramount lord of Túcume (fishermen are again an example), some attached to the paramount or subordinate lords (such as cooks). Through their different specialists and by controlling a variety of resource zones, the lords of coastal polities such as Túcume had access to almost any coastal product they might need.[48] For instance, the abundance of marine shells and the presence of fish bones at Túcume are archaeological evidence for supply from the shoreline. The ethnohistoric record names the lords of various early

Colonial fishing groups subordinate to Túcume, such as Don Diego Mocchumi.[49]

Whether the coastal lords also controlled lands in the highlands before the Inca conquest is not clear, but such was the case under the Inca. For instance, in 1540, Túcume still had lands in Guambos in the highlands of modern Cajamarca, which at that time were worked by Indians from Jayanca.[50] In 1561–82, Túcume *mitmaq* (groups of Indians which the Inca state resettled in areas distant from their home) were in Cajamarca.[51] Indians from Túcume were sent to Simbal in the upper Moche Valley to build walls around coca fields which the Inca state had taken over from the local lords; after the walls were built, the Túcume men returned home.[52] Netherly suggests that sending these people so far to carry out a simple task which local folk could easily have done 'may have been an exemplary punishment' for a 'regional polity which was loyal to the Chimú and hostile to the Inca.'[53]

Although the lords and subjects of Túcume are often mentioned in the administrative documents of the 16th century, we have only one eyewitness account of the site of Túcume from the early Colonial Period. Pedro Cieza de León was a Spaniard who traveled through the former Inca empire some 15 years after the Conquest. Although often engaged in military campaigns as a foot soldier, Cieza was a careful observer who kept notes and later wrote long accounts of what he had seen and heard. In 1547, he rode from Jayanca through the valley of Túcume (the lands watered by the Taymi Canal), and described how, although ruined, the remains of Túcume still bore witness to its former grandeur.[54] If Túcume was abandoned so quickly, where did the people go? Local tradition and the presence of an early church point to Túcume Viejo, just north of the archaeological site,[55] though the population of this hamlet could never have rivaled that of Túcume at its height under the Inca. Rapid depopulation of the coast may account for some of the difference, but there must be other explanations as well (see Chapter 9).

During the early years of the Colony, Spanish conquistadors were granted *encomiendas*: 'the right to enjoy the tributes of Indians within a certain boundary, with the duty of protecting them and seeing to their religious welfare. An *encomienda* was not a grant of land.'[56] *Encomiendas* were often roughly equivalent to the prehispanic polities, but sometimes a polity was divided among two or more *encomenderos*. Such was the case at Túcume: in 1536, Francisco Pizarro gave the Indians of Túcume to Juan Roldán and Juan de Osorno.[57] The subsequent history of Túcume's *encomenderos* and of the various subdivisions of the original Túcume territory is quite complex, but does not concern us here.[58]

In the 1570s, Viceroy Francisco de Toledo carried out a policy of resettlement of the native communities into a smaller number of more easily administered *reducciones*, a process which on the north coast had been started a decade earlier by Cuenca. By the end of the 1570s, the pattern of settlement in Peru was no longer a reliable indicator of pre-hispanic life. Among the many things lost in the *reducciones* was the knowledge, built up over millennia, of where to position settlements to best avoid natural disasters. One such disaster is El Niño. Major El Niño events occur only once or twice a century. In 1578, the first serious El Niño of the Colonial Period ravaged the north coast of Peru with flood, insects, diseases, and other plagues. While ancient Túcume lay on the slopes of La Raya Mountain above the floodwaters, many of the new settlements in Lambayeque were situated on the floodplain and were washed away. In an inquest carried out two years later, witnesses for the native lord of Túcume spoke of the terrible destruction. In the words of one, the river left its bed and 'passed through the middle of this village and carried away the houses of the Indians and that of the caçique [lord] and the hospital and the community houses, and . . . the church.' Some people left the region altogether, heading north or south; the remaining inhabitants of Túcume were forced to seek refuge 'on the hills and the high huacas [pyramids]' – in other words, ancient Túcume.[59] They did not, however, move back permanently, and even the modern village of Túcume (different again from Túcume Viejo), was seriously damaged by the 1982–3 El Niño. Since then, a small population has moved on to the northeast side of the site but most are still exposed to the devastation of the next flood.

History of research at Túcume

As we have seen, Túcume was mentioned in early Spanish accounts, but it was not until the beginning of this century that scientific observers began commenting on the site. The first was the German agricultural engineer Hans Heinrich Brüning (1848–1928), who spent many years in northern Peru in the late 19th and early 20th centuries. Brüning was intensely interested in the present and past native peoples of the region, and he made numerous contributions to the ethnography, ethnohistory, and archaeology of northern Peru. In addition to his publications about the people and their dying language, he gathered a large collection of antiquities which he sold to the Peruvian

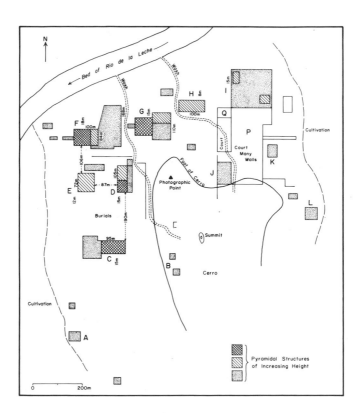

31 A sketch map of Túcume by Alfred L. Kroeber, 1926 (redrawn from Kroeber 1930: Plate XXXI).

government before leaving Peru in 1925. Brüning's collections became the core of the museum in Lambayeque which still bears his name.[60]

Brüning considered Túcume 'the most interesting ruins' in Lambayeque.[61] He was a skilled photographer, and among the hundreds of plates he made in the Lambayeque region and elsewhere along the coast, many are of archaeological sites including several dozen views of the pyramids at Túcume.[62] Ancient irrigation systems also figured among Brüning's many interests, and he briefly mentions Túcume in his discussion of the Taymi Canal;[63] this canal runs close to the site and was probably first built between AD 1000 and 1100 when the site was founded.

Next to visit and publish on Túcume was American anthropologist Alfred L. Kroeber (1876–1960), who spent a day there in 1926. Kroeber writes that Túcume 'was not mentioned to me in Chiclayo or Lambayeque . . . Brüning . . . recognized the importance of the Purgatorio; and it was on the basis of his statement that its ruins are [the most conspicuous and grandiose of this province of Lambayeque] that I looked it up.'[64] Like many other writers, Kroeber refers to the site by one of its local names, El Purgatorio (Purgatory), distinguishing the site from the nearby, modern village of Túcume.[65] Though he did

not excavate, he did make a sketch map of Túcume (*ill. 31*), described the pyramids, took a panoramic photograph of the monumental sector (*ill. 32*), and purchased a number of pots from local looters who said that they came from the site. Kroeber assigned these pieces to his Late Chimú Style, which he dated to 'late times' immediately before and during the Inca Period (Late Horizon). Several of the vessels illustrated in Kroeber's report show clear Inca influence, and many are virtually identical to pieces recovered during our excavations. Kroeber noted the presence of stone architecture and burning on the part of Huaca Larga which we call Platform 2 and considered that these features might date to the Colonial Period; Alfredo Narváez has shown this suggestion to be partly true (see Chapter 4). Kroeber described Huaca Larga as 'a vast raised burial platform,'[66] a designation which was not borne out by Alfredo's excavations. Indeed, 25 years after Kroeber's visit, Schaedel recognized that the subdivisions on top of Huaca Larga were rooms, not graves.[67]

In 1936, another American archaeologist, Wendell C. Bennett (1905–1953), was the first to carry out archaeological excavations at the site. Bennett excavated nine test pits on the eastern side of the central mountain, La Raya. Although these pits were mostly devoid of cultural remains, they did demonstrate that the platforms built against the mountain were largely made of rubble fill. In two of the pits Bennett recovered a few poor graves dating to the Late Horizon, leading him to characterize the site as belonging to the 'Inca-influenced Chimú period'. He also excavated four test pits at the Huaca del Pueblo and in one found two graves. As Bennett's major objective was to develop a ceramic chronology for the north coast, his report is largely descriptive and he does not interpret the site of Túcume.[68]

During the late 1940s US geographer Paul Kosok (1896–1959) and US archaeologist Richard P. Schaedel (1920–) worked at Túcume as part of Kosok's study of ancient irrigation systems on the Peruvian north coast. Kosok noted that Túcume occupied a 'powerful and strategic position' relative to the ancient Taymi Canal system, and he characterized the site as '*the most impressive architectural group of*

32 Panoramic view of the monumental sector of Túcume taken from the West Spur of La Raya Mountain in 1926 by Alfred L. Kroeber. (Courtesy of the Field Museum of Natural History.)

pyramids in the Lambayeque Complex' (italics in original). Kosok believed that Túcume began as a ceremonial center during the 'Middle Period' (between Moche and Chimú) and grew larger through time. He recognized a Chimú occupation in Túcume's 'potsherds and its general layout,' and suggested that the site 'may well have been one of the leading Chimú strongholds in this valley, if not the leading one'. Kosok was also aware of the Inca occupation from Bennett's work.[69]

In the posthumous publication of his research, Kosok included a number of oblique and vertical airphotos of Túcume and discussed the site in relation to the ancient irrigation system and in terms of the Naymlap myth. Schaedel published a vertical airphoto and a map of the site; the map was drawn from the airphoto and presumably field-checked as well.[70] We still use Schaedel's map as the base for our own site plan (*ill. 33*).

Schaedel drew on his familiarity with Túcume in formulating his ideas about the evolution of urbanism in ancient northern Peru. He classified Túcume as an 'urban elite center', which he defined as being 'composed of a series of extensive walled compounds and terraced buildings with complicated internal subdivisions, as well as numerous minor structures, cemeteries, etc.'[71] Our research suggests that Schaedel's definition of an urban elite center fits Túcume in some ways better than he may have realized: excavations in the non-monumental sector of the site revealed that the amorphous mounds on the west and southwest sides of the site are elaborate structures with complex internal subdivisions, different in scale but not in elegance from the larger, monumental structures (see Chapters 5 and 6). However, Túcume did not acquire this urban aspect until after the Chimú conquest.

In contrast to the urban elite centers, Schaedel's 'lay centers' 'are characterized by extensive and dense accumulation of house foundations, large refuse deposits, and occasional structures of high grade construction, but generally inferior to the architectural elegance characteristic of the urban elite centers.'[72] Schaedel saw the lay centers as primarily defensive sites where the population of the region would seek refuge during times of trouble, or where army units would be stationed. Our work indicates that the central mountain at Túcume was fortified, so Túcume has at least one of the functions attributed to the urban lay centers. Indeed, Schaedel himself considered that one of the functions of the structures on the mountain was defense.[73]

Schaedel made several other important observations about Túcume. In terms of chronology, he attributed the 'main buildings' of the monumental sector to the 'Middle Period' between the Moche and Chimú empires; he noted a Chimú presence in the materials excavated by Bennett and the presence of walled compounds, which he viewed as intrusive; and he saw Inca influence in the stone-faced structures on top of La Raya Mountain and characterized the buildings there as 'observatories'. Schaedel suggested a relation between the walled palaces at the Chimú capital of Chan Chan and Huaca Larga, in the 'principle of room subdivisions' and the restricted access. He noted that the function of the surrounding walls of the Chan Chan palaces was fulfilled by the elevated base of Huaca Larga. However, he believed that the Túcume pyramids represented an earlier, intermediate form in the evolution of urbanism in northern Peru: 'These large pyramids . . . are transitional building types between the solid pyramids of the earlier Mochica period and the later truly urban compounds . . . It is likely that they were palaces housing several families of the ruling class, along with servants and craftsmen.'[74]

In 1953, looters working on Platform 2 of Huaca Larga exposed part of the trichrome bird murals that adorn the pre-Inca Bird Temple (see Chapter 4). Fortunately, local archaeologists Oscar Lostenau and Oscar Fernández de Córdova and German archaeologist Hans Disselhoff visited the site five days later. They and other visitors took several photographs of the exposed mural paintings, which were recently published by Duccio Bonavia.[75] Although the exposed paintings have since been destroyed, Alfredo Narváez was able to uncover a continuation of the same wall with identical tricolor birds (see Chapter 4). Bonavia assigns the murals to the Late Intermediate Period Chimú style, which is in substantial agreement with Alfredo's analysis and our radiocarbon dates.

German archaeologist Hermann Trimborn (1901–1986) worked at Túcume for several seasons in the 1960s and 1970s. Trimborn and his team made a sketch map of the monumental sector of the site, although they did not excavate. They were able to remove samples from wooden stakes sticking out of the sides of several of the huacas at the site and thus acquired the first six radiocarbon dates for Túcume. These dates (Table 1) range between about AD 1000 and AD 1300, early in the Late Intermediate Period, during Shimada's Late Sicán phase. Although most archaeologists recognized that the site continued to be occupied during the Chimú and Inca Periods (later LIP and Late Horizon), Trimborn's dates suggested that the apogee of the site was during the early part of its history.[76]

Like most observers of Túcume, Trimborn was impressed by the scale of the site and concluded that 'it must have been . . . in its time an important center of regional power, as well as the seat of a dynasty and of an upper class, with all that corresponds to it.'[77] Like Kosok, Trimborn believed in the historical basis of the Naymlap legend, including the dynastic succession which placed Naymlap's grandson Cala as the first lord of Túcume.

During the 1980s, Walter and Susana Alva directed a clean-up operation at Túcume, constructed a stairway and observation platform on the west spur of the mountain, and commissioned a topographic map of the site.[78] In 1987, Thor Heyerdahl first visited Túcume, as he describes in Chapter 2, and the Túcume Archaeological Project got under way in late 1988 under his general coordination. Initially, the Project was co-directed by Walter Alva and Arne Skjölsvold (of the Kon-Tiki Museum), with Peruvian archaeologist Hugo Navarro running the excavations (Alfredo Narváez assisted in drafting the permit proposal but had other obligations at the time and was unable to remain with the Project when excavations began). I joined the Project at the start of 1989 to take charge of work in the non-monumental sectors and remained on site through 1991, returning in subsequent years to work with the remains. Archaeologist Peter Kvietok also joined the Project for several months in 1992. In 1990, Alfredo Narváez replaced Hugo Navarro as the Peruvian co-director. Field work at Túcume continued through 1993, while lab work continued through mid-1994.

The chronology of Túcume

Our research indicates that the occupation of Túcume consists of three major periods: the Lambayeque Period (c. AD 1000/1100–1350); the Chimú Period (c. AD 1350–1470); and the Inca Period (c. AD 1470–1532). There is also an ephemeral, Early Colonial Period occupation at the site, but all construction seems to have ceased after the Conquest, and Cieza reports that the site was abandoned in 1547 when he passed by. The chronological boundaries and cultural descriptions of the periods were defined by combining the analysis of excavated materials with the available radiocarbon dates (Table 1), previous studies of regional archaeology, and available ethnohistoric data.

The Lambayeque Period corresponds to the middle part of the Late Intermediate Period, contemporary with Shimada's Late Sicán. At this time, Túcume was apparently first constructed as an independent center. The Chimú Period corresponds to the time when the

Lambayeque Valley fell under Chimú domination. The Inca Period is when the Inca controlled the north coast of Peru.

As a final note on chronology, each part of the site has its own sequence of construction and occupation. In the text, the divisions of these sequences are referred to as Phases and are designated by a letter prefix indicating sector and a numerical suffix indicating order, with lower numbers being earlier. To keep this alphanumeric soup straight and to relate the phases to the major occupation periods, Table 2 lists the phase sequences and the corresponding periods. The one exception is Huaca Larga, which has a named, three-part sequence.

Context	Period from Context	Sample #	Uncalibrated	Calibrated 1s
Huaca I		Bonn-1141	660 ± 60 BP; **1290**	
Huaca I		Bonn-1142	680 ± 50 BP; **1270**	
Huaca las Estacas		Bonn-1143	940 ± 50 BP; **1010**	
Huaca Larga		Bonn-1144	690 ± 50 BP; **1260**	
Huaca del Pueblo		Bonn-1955	790 ± 70 BP; **1160**	
Huaca del Pueblo		Bonn-1956	900 ± 70 BP; **1050**	
Huaca Larga	Inca	BGS-1604	455 ± 70 BP; **1495**	1434(1457)1624
Rectang. Compound	Chimú	BGS-1619	525 ± 70 BP; **1425**	1406(1434)1458
Huaca las Balsas	Intrusive from Chimú or Inca?	BGS-1612	555 ± 70 BP; **1395**	1399(1423)1445
West Mound	Late Chimú/Inca	BGS-1616	560 ± 70 BP; **1390**	1398(1421)1444
Huaca las Estacas	Chimú?	BGS-1615	575 ± 70 BP; **1375**	1324(1413)1440
West Mound	Late Chimú/Inca	BGS-1617	595 ± 70 BP; **1355**	1312(1406)1435
La Raya East Spur	Late Chimú/Inca	BGS-1618	600 ± 70 BP; **1350**	1310(1405)1433
Huaca I	Late Lambayeque/Chimú	BGS-1608	600 ± 70 BP; **1350**	1310(1405)1433
Huaca Larga	Late Lambayeque/Chimú	BGS-1605	610 ± 70 BP; **1340**	1307(1403)1431
Huaca I	Late Chimú	BGS-1607	610 ± 70 BP; **1340**	1307(1403)1431
Huaca I	Late Chimú	BGS-1611	625 ± 70 BP; **1325**	1303(1399)1424
Huaca I	Late Lambayeque/Chimú	BGS-1610	630 ± 70 BP; **1320**	1302(1398)1421
Stone Temple	Chimú	BGS-1613	630 ± 75 BP; **1320**	1301(1398)1424
Huaca Larga	Chimú	BGS-1606	645 ± 75 BP; **1305**	1297(1325,1336,1394)1416
Huaca I	Late Lambayeque/Chimú	BGS-1609	705 ± 70 BP; **1245**	1285(1301)1397
West Mound	Late Lambayeque/Early Chimú	BGS-1620	770 ± 95 BP; **1180**	1227(1286)1382
South Cemetery	Lambayeque	BGS-1614	960 ± 70 BP; **990**	1025(1064...1159) 1218

Table 1 Radiocarbon dates from Túcume. (Calibration according to Stiver and Pearson 1993.)

PERIOD / SITE	Lambayeque 1050-1350	Chimú 1350-1470	Inca 1470-1532	Early Colonial 1532-1570
Stone Temple	ST-1	ST-2, -3?, -4?	ST-5	—
Huaca Larga	Green Phase	Tricolor Phase	Stone Phase	Final Fill
Huaca 1	H-1, -2, Pre Huaca	H-2, -3	H-3	—
Rectangular Compound	RC-1?	RC-2		RC-3
West Mound	—	WM-1	WM-2	—
Funerary Platform	FP-1?, -2?		FP-3	—
Huaca Las Balsas	HB-1-7?	HB-8?		
Huaca Facho	HF-1?		HF-2	—
South Cemetery	SC-1	SC-2	SC-3	
La Raya	—	—	LR-1	—

Table 2 Chronology of Túcume: correlation of phases from different sectors of the site. Question marks indicate uncertainty in period assignment.

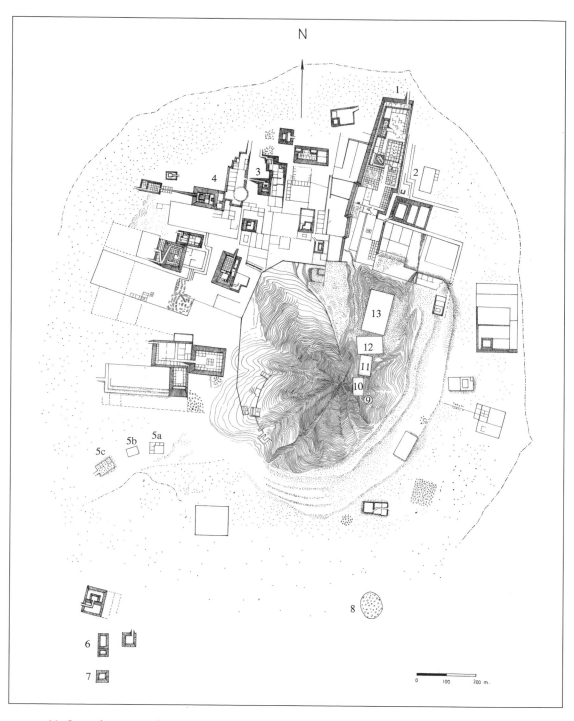

33 General site map of Túcume, showing the principal archaeological features. (Modified from Schaedel 1951: 23.) 1 Huaca Larga; 2 Temple of the Sacred Stone (U-shaped structure below and left of number); 3 Huaca Las Estacas; 4 Huaca 1; 5a Sector V, Rectangular Compound; 5b Sector V, West Mound; 5c Sector V, Funerary Platform; 6 Huaca Las Balsas; 7 Huaca Facho; 8 South Cemetery; 9 White Cave; 10 East Spur Sub-Sector I; 11 East Spur Sub-Sector II; 12 East Spur Sub-Sector III; 13 East Spur Sub-Sector IV. The Monumental Sector is the northwest quadrant of the site, from Huaca Larga (1) counter-clockwise to just north of Sector V (5a/5b/5c).

Alfredo Narváez

The Pyramids of Túcume

The Monumental Sector

THE NORTH AND NORTHWEST quadrants of Túcume contain the greatest concentration of pyramids at the site, so we refer to it as the Monumental Sector (*ill. 33*). It is the buildings in this sector which make Túcume the largest pyramid center in Peru. Our excavations here have concentrated on three structures: Huaca Larga, a 700-m (2300-ft) long raised platform pyramid; the Temple of the Sacred Stone, a small, U-shaped structure just east of Huaca Larga; and Huaca 1,[1] the tallest of Túcume's man-made pyramids. We also excavated test pits in several other parts of the Monumental Sector, such as the plaza to the east of Huaca Las Estacas.

Work in the Monumental Sector began in late 1988 under the direction of my colleague Hugo Navarro, who excavated in the plazas adjoining the north and south sides of Huaca 1, including the Annex on the southeast of Huaca 1. I joined the Túcume Project in 1990, replacing Hugo; since that time, I have directed all the work in the Monumental Sector, including continued work on and around Huaca 1 with my colleagues Alfredo Melly, Marili Apa, César Cornelio, Pablo Carlos de la Cruz; and the Annex with Bernarda Delgado as assistant archaeologist. In Huaca Larga I worked with Jorge Rosas and Marili Apa, and with Bernada Delgado in the Stone Temple, and in Huaca Las Balsas.

Huaca Larga
Huaca Larga measures about 700 m (2300 ft) long (north–south) by as much as 280 m (910 ft) wide (east–west) (*ills 34–35, 41*). The average

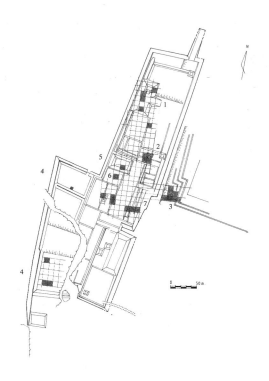

34 Plan of Huaca Larga. The darkened grid squares represent the 10×10 m excavation units. 1 Platform 1 (left of number); 2 Platform 2 (below number); 3 The Temple of the Sacred Stone (above number); 4 West Enclosures (right of numbers); 5 Sunken Depression (right of number); 6 Kitchen Area; 7 Benched Corridors (left of number).

35 (opposite above) Aerial photo of the central portion of Huaca Larga; the reed-mat roof is just to the lower right of Platform 2. Note the Temple of the Sacred Stone, prior to excavation, in the upper left corner between Huaca Larga and the walled roadway.

36 (opposite below) Aerial photo of huacas in the Monumental Sector.

elevation above the surrounding ground level is about 20 m (65 ft), with an additional 10 m (50 ft) or so at Platform 1 and Platform 2. Access to the top of Huaca Larga was gained via a ramp on the north face of the mound. Ramps are an old north coast tradition, but unlike the more common zigzag ramps seen at the other Túcume pyramids and elsewhere in the region, the Huaca Larga ramp is short and straight. A ceremonial walled roadway approaches Huaca Larga from the east, turns a corner by the Temple of the Sacred Stone, and runs north along the side of the pyramid until it disappears. This roadway apparently once continued to the base of the Huaca Larga access ramp. Unfortunately, construction in the modern village of La Raya has removed any obvious traces of the road in the area nearest the ramp.

The top of Huaca Larga has a number of major subdivisions. Near the northwest end is Platform 1: a long, high mound reached by a short inclined ramp on the east side. To the south of Platform 1 is a plaza area surrounded by walls with niches. Continuing south along the west side of Huaca Larga, we find a huge, sunken depression. On the northeast side, opposite the depression, is Platform 2 (ill. 37). Immediately southwest of Platform 2 is an area which was found to be a prehispanic kitchen, while south of the platform is a large, niched plaza flanked by compounds divided into many smaller rooms. Finally, as Huaca Larga continues south on to the lower slopes of La Raya Mountain, the subdivisions of the larger compounds become harder to discern.

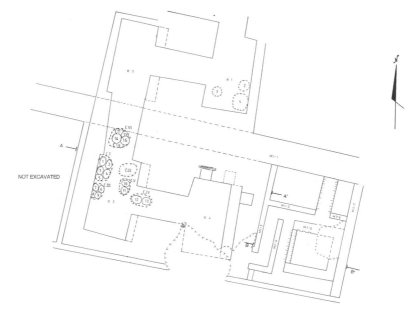

37 *Plan of Platform 2 of Huaca Larga showing the structures of both the stone building (Stone Phase/Inca Period) and the Temple of the Mythical Bird (Tricolor Phase/Chimú Period). The four numbered rooms of the stone building with the locations of the weaving women burials (Room 3) and the mummy bundles (Room 1) are shown.*

NOT EXCAVATED

Excavations on Huaca Larga began in 1990 (*ill. 38*) and continued through 1992. On the basis of this work, three major phases of construction and occupation have been identified: the Green Phase (early); the Tricolor Phase (middle); and the Stone Phase (late). These three phases appear to correlate in turn with the local Lambayeque culture, Chimú domination, and Inca domination. At the end of the Stone Phase, the central Inca building on Platform 2 was deliberately covered with a special fill and the southern rooms were destroyed. This final fill took place at the very end of the Inca occupation at Túcume, probably in the first years of the Spanish Conquest (*c.* AD 1532 to 1540).

38 *The start of excavations on Huaca Larga in 1990. Evidence of intensive burning dating to early in the Colonial Period was found in the form of reddened adobes.*

Although we necessarily dug from the top, or latest, deposits down, in the following sections I will start at the beginning and follow the development of Huaca Larga through time. With each succeeding phase, an increasing amount of information is available.

The Green Phase
The Green Phase is known mostly from fragments of structures found underlying the later Tricolor deposits, and we have little direct evidence for the form of the Green Phase structures. On Platform 2, under what became the Temple of the Mythical Bird, or Bird Temple, during the Tricolor Phase, we found three burnt posts dating to the Green Phase. A radiocarbon date from one of these posts yielded a date of 610 ±70 BP (BGS-1605), or a calibrated range of AD 1307 to 1431 with a mean of AD 1403. This range could correspond to either late Green Phase or early Tricolor Phase.

Whatever form the Green Phase Huaca took, it was certainly much smaller than the later versions, and it was not attached to La Raya Mountain – the sections extending the south end of Huaca Larga to the slopes of the mountain were built in the Tricolor Phase. One possibility is that the original building was a pyramid, like most of the monumental constructions at Túcume. However, if it was a pyramid, then the top must have been removed during the Tricolor remodeling. Perhaps a stronger possibility is that the original building was a low platform. In any case, the Green Phase building was an isolated, free-standing structure.

The Tricolor Phase
At the start of the Tricolor Phase a total remodeling took place and Huaca Larga assumed its final general form, with plazas, patios, and the two platforms. The southernmost sections of the Huaca, which connect it to La Raya Mountain, were built in a single construction episode at this time. The buildings of this phase all had red, white, and black painted decoration, hence the Tricolor denomination. Under these structures were the buildings with unpainted, greenish plaster of the Green Phase. The three posts in Platform 2 may have continued in use during the occupation of the Bird Temple in the Tricolor Phase, and it is possible that they were burnt when that Temple was buried by the Incas.

In addition to plano-convex adobes, flat-rectangular and flat-square adobes were also used in the Tricolor Phase. Flat adobes are known from the main huaca of the Late Chimú administrative center of

39 One of the Tricolor Phase burials found on Huaca Larga, Platform 1 (Chimú Period). As these burials formed part of the construction process and were not intrusive they may have been sacrifices.

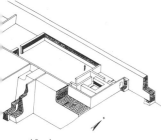

40 An isometric reconstruction of the Temple of the Mythical Bird on Platform 2, Huaca Larga during the Tricolor Phase (Chimú Period).

Pacatnamú in the Jequetepeque Valley,[2] supporting a Late Chimú date for these adobes. However, at Chan Chan flat adobes date to earlier periods and are not found in Late Chimú palaces.

Platform 1, built during the Tricolor Phase, is now very eroded and we found only a few fragments of floors and plastered walls with red, white, and black paint. A single, short, straight ramp leads from the east to the middle of the Platform, which seems to have had a ceremonial function (see ill. 34).

Six burials were encountered sealed under a floor of Platform 1 (ill. 39). These interments were part of the construction process, not intrusive, and were probably sacrifices (like the young woman buried next to the architectural model in the West Mound of Sector V: see Chapter 6). Two of the individuals were adults – a man and a woman – and the other four were children. Like the Temple of the Mythical Bird and other rooms on Platform 2, Platform 1 floors were very clean.

On Platform 2, the Temple of the Mythical Bird dates to the Tricolor Phase (ill. 40). Its central chamber has mural paintings of the Lambayeque diving bird in red, white, and black paint. These paintings were first discovered by looters in 1953; fortunately, archaeologists visited the site shortly after the looters and took photographs.[3] Although the section of mural exposed in 1953 has long since been destroyed, we were able to uncover undamaged paintings on a continuation of the same north–south wall and around a corner on a second, east–west wall (ills 44–45). The north–south wall has a series of inset squares alternating with raised squares in a checkerboard

pattern, with small versions of the diving bird painted on the squares. This pattern of raised and sunken squares also occurs in the late palaces at Chan Chan,[4] the Chimú capital, dating to the Late or Expansive Chimú Period.

The Temple of the Mythical Bird has numerous interconnected rooms to the east and west of the central chamber, with the western area smaller than the eastern area (see *ill. 40*). The rooms were reached via ramps on the southeast of Platform 2. The floors of the Temple and its connected rooms were clean of midden, but food preparation probably took place in the kitchen area located just below Platform 2 on the south. The rooms may have been the residence and center of operations of the ruler; such maximum or paramount lords were considered semi-divine, so the presence of a temple in the middle of a palace is not inconsistent with this hypothesis. In contrast to the private nature of the Temple and associated rooms, the plazas to the north and south of Platform 2 must have been used for more public ceremonies.

41 A general view of Huaca Larga, looking north-northeast, with Thor Heyerdahl and Arne Skjölsvold in the foreground.

42 *An adobe structure with a checkerboard pattern of inset and salient squares, east of the Temple of the Mythical Bird (Tricolor Phase, Chimú Period) at the start of excavation.*

We found two Tricolor Phase burials in Platform 2. One was under the floor of what became Room 1 of the Inca Stone Structure, while the other, an incomplete skeleton, was recovered under the floor in Room 2. These interments lacked offerings and were probably sacrifices like the burials on Platform 1.

The area to the east of the Temple is reached through a door in the north–south wall and along a corridor. There was at least one wall here, with alternating inset and raised squares, but no traces of paint were found (*ill. 42*). It is a U-shaped area and without niches. At Chan Chan, there are several U-shaped structures in the late palaces, although most such structures do have niches. However, no niched U-shaped structures dating to the Late Chimú Period are known north of the Jequetepeque Valley.

Platform 2 can be interpreted as a dividing point in terms of the major functions of Huaca Larga. Only ceremonial activities would have taken place to the north of Platform 2, where Platform 1 and the large plazas are located. To the south of Platform 2, we found evidence for service and production: a large kitchen and enclosed workshop areas with small mounds probably involved in the control of the different activities carried out in each enclosure.

To the southeast of Platform 2 is an area of parallel corridors (see *ill. 34*). The effects of erosion in this sector led Schaedel[5] to show the Benched Corridors as aligned rooms, like storerooms, in his map of Túcume. Our excavations have shown that the original configuration was quite different. Each corridor consisted of large benches on either side of a central dividing wall. The benches had two rows of columns to support short roofs which would have covered the benches but not the corridors. Such relatively narrow, enclosed spaces are not appropriate for meetings or public events, and one explanation for this sector is that it was a residential area. A more likely interpretation, however, is that this was a sector of workshops for highly specialized artisans, like the high-status workshops known as SIAR (Small, Irregularly Agglutinated Rooms) at Chan Chan.[6] The unroofed corridors would have let in light for the workers. Unfortunately, the severe erosion has removed all evidence of production, leaving only fragments of floors and benches and a few preserved columns.

The general layout of the benched corridor sector recalls a scene of weavers on a Moche pot, which shows two classes of weaving women, columns with roofs, and a man seated on a raised bench by a wall receiving something from a figure from a lower area in front of the bench (*ill. 43*). At Chan Chan, evidence for weaving was found only in a late palace (Tschudi), in a similar benched corridor complex associated with storerooms and *audiencias* (administrative structures).[7]

43 A Moche fineline drawing of a textile workshop. (Redrawn from Hocquenghem 1987: figs 37a and 37b.)

A small mound in the southwest corner of the Benched Corridor sector was perhaps for the control of the workshops. We did not excavate this mound, but cleared a similar one on a patio to the west of the niched plaza, itself west of the Benched Corridors and directly south of the kitchen. This mound, lacking ornamentation, has a single room, with a door in the northwest corner leading to a level space occupying the north third of the room. In the southern two-thirds is a raised bench. This layout recalls the bench in the Moche weaving scene.

The kitchen to the southwest of Platform 2 began to function in the Tricolor Phase. A radiocarbon assay of material from the Tricolor Phase remains yielded a date of 645 ± 75 BP (BGS-1606), calibrated to AD 1297 to 1416. This range covers most of the time span assigned to

44 (above) Remains of the mural of diving birds on the wall of the Temple of the Mythical Bird (Tricolor Phase, Chimú Period). A section of this mural had been uncovered by looters in 1953 and photographed by visiting archaeologists.

45 (below) Wall paintings in the Temple of the Mythical Bird.

the Chimú occupation of the Lambayeque Valley and supports the identification of the Tricolor Phase on Huaca Larga as Chimú in date.

The presence of a sizeable kitchen suggests that some people resided on Huaca Larga, probably elites, and indicates a need to feed large numbers of people. Andean lords traditionally had an obligation to offer food and drink to their subjects and subordinate lords on particular occasions, especially when soliciting their labor.

The food remains from the Tricolor Phase kitchen are still being studied but show a predominance of marine species, especially *Donax* (a small surf clam) and various species of fish. Fruits were also common and included avocados (*Persea americana*), *pacay* (*Inga feuillei*), and soursop (*Annona muricata*).

Attached to the west side of Huaca Larga is a large, enclosed compound with massive, high, rubble-cored adobe walls (*ill. 46*). We made a small test excavation in this area against one of the walls, and found internal architecture dating to the Tricolor Phase. The pit was too small to give much idea of the overall layout. However, we did find a section of well-preserved floor joined to a very narrow (12-cm (5-in) wide) wall, separated by a narrow space from another narrow wall. On the floor was midden containing food remains and ash.

Considering that the Tricolor Phase probably dates to the Chimú occupation of Túcume, one explanation of the radical remodeling of Huaca Larga at this time is that it was done to convert the Huaca into something like a Chan Chan palace. Both this idea and my dating of the Tricolor Phase contradict Schaedel's hypothesis that Huaca Larga was an antecedent to the Chan Chan buildings.[8]

In the palaces at Chan Chan are corridors which go around the important interior structures in the central nucleus to reach the southern, rear areas where the overlord's support personnel lived and worked.[9] We found the same pattern on Huaca Larga: a walkway leads around the walls from the top of the access ramp in the northeast corner along the west wall, bypassing Platforms 1 and 2 to reach the kitchen and workshop areas to the south. In contrast, on the pyramids at Túcume, the ramps are zigzag and lead directly to the most important huaca-top chambers.

46 *Thor Heyerdahl inspecting the enclosure on the west side of Huaca Larga.*

There are two major differences between Huaca Larga and the Chan Chan palaces. First, Huaca Larga lacks one of key features which defines a palace as a center of power – it has no funerary platform. Second, Platforms 1 and 2 have no parallels in the Chan Chan palaces, although similar structures are found outside the palaces. Platforms are a particularly Lambayeque feature related to the display of power, functioning on the concept that higher is more powerful. We are dealing with two regions and different people to be ruled, and it is likely that the Chimú adopted the local tradition to make a more effective demonstration of their power.

The Lambayeque region lacks obvious Chimú structures such as those found in other valleys. Túcume was the major Lambayeque center of the pre-Chimú period, and this is probably the reason the Chimú chose it for their center of control (as the Inca did in the next period). The major modifications to Huaca Larga in the Tricolor Phase were intended to create a Chan Chan-like structure suitable for Chimú needs. The elongated architecture and short, straight ramp of Huaca Larga are thus intrusive in the pyramidal tradition of Túcume monumental architecture, with its zigzag ramps. The only other similar structure at the site is the Secondary Platform of Huaca 1, which has the same low form, north–south orientation, and straight ramp on the northeast end.

The Stone Phase

When the Inca conquered Túcume, they established Huaca Larga as the focus of their occupation. The ceremonial walled road which apparently led to the Huaca Larga access ramp passes by the Temple of the Sacred Stone, where important Inca offerings were made by visitors to the site (see below). Furthermore, the road enters the site from the east and points directly at the nearest stretch of the Capac Ñan, the royal Inca highway. On top of Huaca Larga, the Tricolor Phase adobe Temple of the Mythical Bird on Platform 2 was covered with an Inca building made of large stones set in mud mortar, the Stone Structure (*ill. 47*). Apart from several Inca tombs in Huaca Facho (see Chapter 7) and the constructions on La Raya Mountain, probably also built by the Inca (see Chapter 8), this is the only use of stone for building at Túcume. The rest of the site is made of mud – sun-dried mud bricks, adobes, set in mud mortar and covered with fine mud plaster (*ill. 48*). The use of stone is an intrusive element at the site and a good indicator of the Inca presence.

The Temple of the Mythical Bird on Platform 2 must still have been

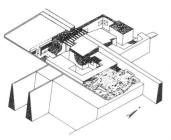

47 An isometric reconstruction of the stone building on Platform 2, Huaca Larga during the Stone Phase (Inca Period).

48 *Adobes – simple, sun-dried mud bricks – form the basic building block for Túcume's monumental pyramids. Here they are exposed in a huaca wall in the Monumental Sector.*

in use when the Incas conquered Túcume. The Inca Stone Structure directly covers the bird murals on the walls of the Temple (see *ills 44–45*). The paintings themselves were severely damaged by the stones of the Inca building, which had been thrown against the murals with no particular care. However, they were not affected by weather, indicating that the murals had not been exposed to the elements before burial under the stone structure. At the same time, the Incas probably burnt the posts dating to the Green Phase which had been reused in the Temple. Those parts of the Temple of the Mythical Bird that lay outside the walls of the new stone building were covered with a fill of adobes. The Inca decision to cover the Temple so completely may represent a deliberate, symbolic destruction and replacement of the earlier temple while at the same time showing respect for it. This sort of behavior would accord well with what we know about Inca policies of conquest and rule.

In the southwest corner of Huaca Larga, we excavated a stone plat-form, 1.66 m (5½ ft) high and 5.2 m (17 ft) square, with 10 columns on top. The associated floor shows traces of a sequence of episodes, begin-ning with torrential rainfall, followed by a fill layer, then burning, and finally erosion. This platform dates to the Inca Stone Phase. Its pattern of rainfall, fill, and burning must be related to the events in the Benched Corridors and the Stone Structure (see below). In the Benched Corridors, we discovered a sequence of burning/destruc-tion, fill, rain, and erosion, while in the Stone Platform we found

49 (above left) Burials of weaving women, or acllas, found in Huaca Larga, Platform 2, Room 3, dating to the Inca Period. These women may well have been sacrificed to accompany the high-status burial found in Room 1 of the same building (ill. 54).

50 (above right) One of weaving women burials was accompanied by this small aryballoid pot (see ill. 51).

51 The Inca Period North Coast-style aryballoid vessel from one of the weaving woman burials (ill.50).

ceremonial burning, fill, rain, more fill, and intense burning followed by erosion. The rainfall on the Stone Platform's floor may date to the final abandonment of Huaca Larga (and of Túcume in general) and is the same rainfall which affected the other two areas during the fill process.[10] When did this rainfall take place? Probably in 1532, the year of the Spanish Conquest.[11] Such a date would reinforce the idea that the abandonment of Túcume is related to the events of the Conquest, as suggested by the presence of early Spanish artifacts in the Stone Platform fill (see below, section on the Final Fill).

The Stone Structure and the Stone Platform in the southwest corner are the only Inca modifications on Huaca Larga: the rest of the Tricolor Phase buildings remained in use throughout the Stone Phase. The Stone Structure consists of four chambers (see *ill. 37*), in the northeast (Room 1), northwest (Room 2), southwest (Room 3), and southeast (Room 4). Wide corridors connect Rooms 1 and 2, 2 and 3, and 3 and 4; 1 and 4 are not connected. We identified two construction sub-phases in this building, marked by architectural changes. In Sub-phase 1, large niches were set into the walls of the four rooms. A sample from Sub-phase 1 provided a radiocarbon date of 455 ± 70 BP (BGS-1604), or AD 1434 to 1624 (calibrated) with a calibrated mean of AD 1457. Within the precision possible for radiocarbon dating, this result corresponds well with the Inca age of the Stone Structure. In Sub-phase 2, the niches were covered and the rooms became smaller. This Sub-phase probably dates to the abandonment of Huaca Larga; otherwise I doubt that the niches would have been covered.

Floors in the Stone Structure were clean and well-preserved, except where burials cut through them. When the Sub-phase 2 structure was abandoned, 22 burials were cut into the floors and covered with fill. Another burial was found in Room 1, but it dated to the Tricolor Phase. The burials occur only in the southwest room (Room 3) and northeast room (Room 1). The burials include 19 weaving women in Room 3 (one in a mummy bundle) (ill. 49) and three males in mummy bundles in Room 1. The weaving women were buried in groups, while the mummy bundles were interred individually.

52 An Inca Period pottery vessel with a modeled animal, from one of the weaving women burials.

The weaving women of Room 3 were mostly young. Buried with them were many weaving tools (spindles, spindle whorls, balls of thread, needles, loom boards, chalk, etc.), often in covered, rectangular reed baskets. Pottery included Provincial Inca and north coast Inca style vessels as well as other pots in the Chimú style. Inlaid wooden earspools are another Lambayeque element found with these women (ills 50–53).

The Stone Structure is the most elaborate Inca building at Túcume, and it was almost certainly the core of the Inca administrative center for the region. Given this context, the weaving women must have been acllas, or chosen women. The Incas cloistered acllas in their major centers, where they worked to produce special crafts, particularly fine textiles, for the Inca or for use as gifts of state. The layout of the Stone Structure on Platform 2 is well set up to maintain the privacy of its occupants.

As highly qualified artisans working directly for the state, the acllas were accorded high status in the Inca Empire. The quality of the personal adornments (bracelets, necklaces, inlaid earspools) and offerings (fine cloths, decorated tools) of the Room 3 weaving women confirms their high status.

Of the Room 1 mummy bundles, all have been X-rayed and two have been unwrapped. Sonia Guillén, a physical anthropologist, and María Luisa Patrón, a textile expert, carried out the bundle openings. The first to be unwrapped was the bundle with the least number of offerings inside, according to the X-rays. No offerings were found in the pit with this bundle. The body was a 32-year-old male, wrapped in 12 layers of textiles, of which 10 were decorated. The sternum was found upside down, suggesting that the bundle may have been moved some time after death.

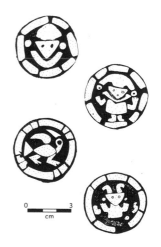

53 Shell-inlaid wooden earspools from the weaving women burials, with designs of birds and animals.

The offerings found inside the first bundle were organized by quadrants within the bundle. In the northeast quadrant were two wooden goblets covered with gourd bowls. The southwest quadrant had a packet of gourd bowls wrapped in cloth (not yet opened) and a ceramic bowl with an uneaten guinea pig (it still had fur) covered with a gourd

54 The high-status
mummy bundle found in
Room 1, Platform 2,
Huaca Larga. This was a
male of about 35 years old.
The quality of the
accompanying grave goods
and the presence nearby of
the weaving women
burials, possibly sacrificed
to accompany him in
death, suggest that the
burial was that of the last
Inca governor of Túcume.

55 Arne Skjölsvold,
Öystein Johansen, Thor
Heyerdahl, and Alfredo
Narváez inspecting the
feather cloak from the
high-status burial. It was
made of white and green
feathers, with geometric
designs in orange and
green.

lid. In the northwest quadrant we found only a large clam shell by the
left knee and a badly preserved, cylindrical wooden object on the
thigh. Finally, in the northeast quadrant, on the shoulder of the individual was a copper *tumi* (ceremonial knife with a half-moon blade)
placed on an unpolished, rectangular stone plaque.

The second bundle to be opened was the richest according to the
X-rays. In the burial pit (*ill. 54*) were two pyroengraved and shell-
inlaid gourds with feline motifs, eight undecorated gourds and a
wooden spoon with bird designs. Five pots were also found: one
stirrup-spout blackware bottle; one black aryballoid; one neckless
olla with strap handles; and two unused, carinated-rim *ollas*. The

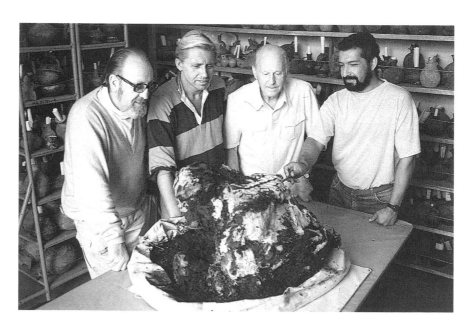

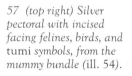

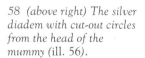

bundle was wrapped in 16 layers of textiles, of which 14 were decorated (ill. 55). Amongst these was a fabulous feather cloak of white and dark green feathers with geometric designs of orange and green. This individual was a 35-year-old male wearing a red, padded hat with a red and yellow tassel dangling from the left side (ill. 56). Unlike the first bundle, all the offerings were in the center, on the body. On the right pelvis was a metal *tumi*, and in front of the *tumi* were three silver objects:[12] a pair of tweezers and two earpicks (ill. 59). One earpick takes the shape of a long-necked bird and has two fine, cylindrical, polished beads connected by a cord which passes through the eye of the bird. The second earpick is also a bird, but more like a hum-

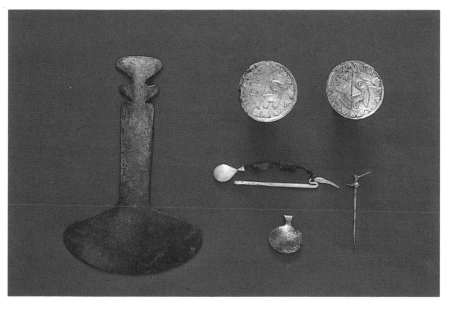

56 (above left) The head of the mummy, still wearing a red padded hat with a red and yellow tassel, such as is described by Inca chroniclers. Around the head was a silver diadem and still in place were two silver earspools.

57 (top right) Silver pectoral with incised facing felines, birds, and tumi symbols, from the mummy bundle (ill. 54).

58 (above right) The silver diadem with cut-out circles from the head of the mummy (ill. 56).

59 (left) A copper tumi knife, silver earspools, silver earpicks, and copper and silver tweezers, found with the mummy bundle (ill. 54).

60 Two pairs of early Colonial glass earrings from the final fill in Platform 2 of Huaca Larga.

mingbird in flight. In addition to the red hat, the head was adorned with two silver earspools still in place (*ills 56 and 59*), and a silver diadem with cut-out discs tied around the head (*ill. 58*). Tied around the neck was a crescent-shaped, silver pectoral with incised facing felines, birds, and *tumi* symbols (*ill. 57*). Dangling from holes punched in the lower edge of the pectoral were 4-cm (1½-in) long strings of beads ending in silver cones. The points of the pectoral joined behind the neck and had 16 strings of *Spondylus* shell beads, each ending in a silver cone. On the left side of the body at the base and by the right knee were groups of *amala* seeds. In front of the body was a thin, pointed wooden tool of unknown use.

The tassel on the hat is particularly interesting, as the chroniclers tell us that the Inca wore a distinctive tassel of these same colors.[13] The earspools show that he was an *orejón* or 'longears', as the chroniclers referred to the Inca nobility, because only lords were allowed to enlarge their earlobes to wear earspools. Given that the Huaca Larga mummy bundle is buried in the center of Inca power at Túcume, he may well have been the last Inca governor of Túcume, who controlled the entire Lambayeque region. The other, less elaborate bundles and the weaving women were probably sacrificed to accompany him in death. A local lord would not be accompanied by Inca *acllas* in an Inca building, supporting the identification of this individual as the Inca governor.

Why were the women buried in Room 3 and the men in bundles in Room 1? These rooms may have had different functions in some way related to the offices of the people buried in them. As we will see below, the fill over the burials was also differentiated by room. When were the burials in Rooms 1 and 3 made? It must have been at the end of the Inca Period, as the Stone Structure was filled in immediately after the burials (see below, section on the Final Fill). The Incas performed human sacrifices at times of great disorder, known as *pachacutis*.[14] The Spanish Conquest would have been such a time. Indeed, the fill above the Stone Structure contains two pairs of European glass earrings, indicating an early Colonial date (*ill. 60*).

The kitchen continued to function in the same place as previously during the Stone Phase. The Tricolor Phase kitchen was buried with fill similar to that which covered the Temple of the Mythical Bird, and a new, Inca Period kitchen began functioning immediately above it. In the later kitchen, camelid and guinea pig bones and chilli pepper predominate in the midden. Relatively few fish and shells were found, although the same fruits were present as in the earlier kitchen. Perhaps the excavated area was a sector specializing in the preparation of meats; there is a large unexcavated portion which could contain areas for preparing other kinds of foods. In any case, the evidence we have contrasts with the earlier, maritime focus of the Tricolor Phase, Chimú Period Kitchen.

The benched corridors to the southeast of Platform 2 continued in use during the Stone Phase. Then, late in the history of Huaca Larga, the posts were broken and burnt, the walls were knocked down, and the area leveled. If this was a textile workshop used by the Inca *acllas*, then everything must have happened at once: the benched corridors were destroyed, the weaving women were sacrificed and buried in the Stone Structure, and that building was filled in. There are traces of a strong rainfall immediately on top of the destruction level in the benched corridors, and similar evidence was found after the first episode of fill in the Stone Structure.

The Final Fill

Shortly (perhaps immediately) after the burials in Rooms 1 and 3, the Stone Structure was covered with a fill full of special items (*ills. 60–68*). Textiles were burnt just above the floors of the rooms, when the process of filling had barely begun. Two sub-phases of filling are distinguishable. First, the rooms were partly filled when it rained; then, after the rainfall, fill continued with the same types of materials. After the fill was completed in the second sub-phase, a series of very intense burning episodes took place. Fuel was placed in holes in the fill and different levels of burnt fuel show multiple burnings. The fires were so intense that the underlying structures and fill were reddened down to a depth of 2 m (6½ ft). All four rooms of the Stone Structure are equally affected.

The second burning must be early Colonial Period in date, as we found two pairs of European glass earrings in the underlying fill. There is an oral tradition in Túcume which says that the Spaniards burnt great fires at the site to convince the natives that it was the entrance to hell, where they would go if they did not convert to Christianity (see Chapter 10). This tradition must be the origin of the alternative name of El Purgatorio (Purgatory) for the site. The multiple burning episodes above the fill lend credence to this story.

Each room had a different fill. In Room 1, where the mummy bundles were found, the fill was very diverse, with many *crisoles* (finger pots, often unfired),[15] wooden artifacts, camelid bones, and a large pot in the form of a four-legged, spotted animal (*ill. 61*). Fragments of this

61 (right) Alfredo Narváez holding a feline-shaped pot from Huaca Larga.

62 (above) A carved wooden bird with a shell beak, from the final fill of Platform 2, Huaca Larga.

pot were found scattered throughout Room 1, showing that it was broken *in situ*. Room 3 contained the majority of textile implements found in the fill – this is also the room where the weaving women were found (*ill. 49*). The fill of Room 3 also included the bones of many disarticulated individuals, suggesting that the artifacts came from earlier burials which had been dug up and thrown into the fill. These burials must have been of high status individuals, given the fine artifacts found in the fill and presumably coming from the same graves. They may well have come from tombs such as those salvaged on Huaca Facho (see Chapter 7).

In general, the fill includes many tools, some of unknown function as well as weaving implements, and there certainly seems to be a strong connection with artisans' workshops. We know from many other sites as well as ethnohistoric documents that Inca administrative centers and other state facilities usually included workshops.[16]

63 (left) An Inca Period pottery vessel in the form of a modeled bird, from the final fill of Platform 2, Huaca Larga.

64 (right) An Inca 'censer', a form which is only rarely found outside Cuzco. This example came from the final fill of Platform 2, Huaca Larga, and was certainly imported from the Inca capital.

The pottery in the fill includes north coast, Chimú-related vessels, such as a polished blackware stirrup spout bottle in the form of four *lucuma* fruits; north coast Inca pottery, such as stirrup-spout vessels with Inca-related decoration and small aryballoid pots; imported pieces such as a classic Cuzco Inca censer (of which very few are known outside Cuzco; John Hyslop, personal communication) (*ill. 64*); and a redware cup with black painted decoration which must come from the area around Lake Titicaca in extreme southern Peru (*ill. 65*). Potsherds include pieces with the fern pattern known as Cuzco Polychrome A decoration,[17] which turns up in Inca sites throughout the Andes. One unusual piece is a white, kaolin-ware vessel representing a Chimú-style corn-man; in this area, kaolin wares are usually thought to come from Cajamarca, although Walter Alva told me of a kaolin source in the Lambayeque region.

65 An Inca Period redware pottery vessel, probably imported from the altiplano region around Lake Titicaca and found in the final fill of Platform 2, Huaca Larga.

We recovered over 3000 *crisoles* from the fill, of two basic types. First, an Inca type, large (up to 10 cm (4 in) tall), with a long body, everted rim, and animal head appliqué on the shoulder; and second a small, presumably local type measuring 1 to 3 cm (⅖ to 1⅕ in) high, with a straight rim and no decoration. The largest *crisoles* were found only in Huaca Larga, while small to medium specimens were also recovered from burials in the rest of the site. Based on ethnographic evidence, I have suggested that *crisoles* were used to heat *chicha*, the corn beer essential to any Andean ceremony or festival (see Chapter 7 for further discussion). If this idea is correct then the larger *crisoles* from Huaca Larga may reflect the larger amount of *chicha* to be heated for the public ceremonies there, in contrast to the private needs of the commoner individuals buried in the other parts of the site.

The fill also contained various metal objects. Gold disks with holes may have been bangles or sequins. One gold, one silver, and several copper and silver-copper rings were found; the silver ring had incised birds on it. One large piece of silver consists of a rectangular sheet with many attached long strips. Gold, silver, and nacre bracelet ornaments have inlaid *Spondylus* shell and green stone. The gold and silver ornaments are shaped like panpipes, while the nacre ones are square or in the form of a fish or a bird. Copper items include a bell, a point, and a knife or money ax.[18]

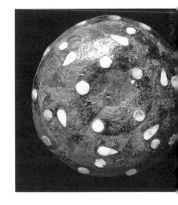

66 Pyroengraved and shell-inlaid gourd with designs including a row of birds, from the final fill of Platform 2, Huaca Larga.

Wooden and gourd artifacts include four bowls of a polished, hard wood with pyroengraved triangles on the rims – a typical Inca decorative technique. One well-preserved gourd bowl is decorated with birds made by a combination of pyroengraving and shell inlaying (*ill. 66*). The bird represented on this gourd is different from other birds found

in Túcume art, and may be the sacred Inca bird called the 'core-quenque' (*Phalcoboenus algobularis*), also known as 'china linda' or 'guaraguau cordillerano'.[19] If this identification is correct, this high-status Inca symbol would support the importance of Huaca Larga in the Inca Period at Túcume.

Among the wooden tools are Y-shaped sticks called *ruecas*, used to hold thread while spinning. Today, the *rueca* is a highland trait which allows the spinner to walk while working. On the coast, spinners work sitting down. Some of the Túcume *ruecas* have carved decorations such as a face of a god in the Lambayeque tradition (*ill. 67*). Many wooden spindles were also recovered, some with both ends pointed and others with one end pointed and the other cut or worn flat. Spindles are usually decorated with paint or pyroengraving. We also found many spindle whorls.

Wooden loom boards are also common. These boards run from warp to warp, and the size of the board determines the size of the cloth to be produced. We found different sized boards, from ones small enough to make ribbons to others large enough for cloaks and blankets. The loom boards from the fill have carved decoration on the ends, usually showing animals such as felines, birds, or fish (*ill. 68 a–b*).

In addition to the artifacts, the fill contained plant and animal remains, including three bird skulls. I believe that this is not ordinary midden, but rather very specially selected. This supposition will be tested in the future by analyzing a sample of midden from the fill from each of the four rooms.

Two alternative hypotheses can be put forward to explain the filling of the Stone Structure. First, the fill may have been part of the same process which led to the burial of the mummy bundles and the weaving women. This process would have included sacrifices and the abandonment of the building in response to the great disruptions which occurred on the arrival of the Spaniards, such as the capture and death of the Inca ruler Atahuallpa. The differentiation of the contents of the fill by room, like the differentiation of the burials, suggests that the burials and the fill are linked, supporting this first hypothesis.

The second hypothesis is that the fill was deposited early in the Colonial Period as an act by the local residents to symbolize their rejection of the Incas, once the Spanish invaders had conveniently removed the threat of Inca reprisal. According to the ethnohistoric sources (see Chapter 3), Túcume had been an ally of the Chimú and thus an unhappy subject of the Incas. The multiple burning episodes on top of the fill may also represent local peoples' rejection of Inca

67 (above) A carved wooden weaving implement (rueca) from the final fill of Platform 2, Huaca Larga. Numerous tools connected with weaving were found in this area, which may have been a state-run workshop.

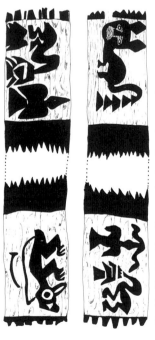

power and its most important center, rather than Spanish proselytiz-ers creating an artificial hell. In the Ica Valley on the south coast of Peru, Dorothy Menzel[20] has found a similar process, in which early Colonial pottery returns to the local styles prevalent before the Inca conquest of that valley.

69 *The Temple of the Sacred Stone near the end of excavation in 1991.*

Excavations in the Temple of the Sacred Stone

The Temple of the Sacred Stone (also called the Stone Temple) is located just east of Platform 2 on Huaca Larga, in a space defined to the west by the edge of the Huaca, to the south by a stepped mound running perpendicular to Huaca Larga, and on the east and north by a walled ceremonial roadway which makes several right-angle turns around the area of the Stone Temple (see *ill. 34*). Within these general limits, low walls enclose the area most closely associated with the Temple. The Temple itself is a small, adobe, U-shaped structure with an upright rock in the middle (*ills 69–73*). I began work there in 1991 because the U-shape was reminiscent of the *audiencias* at the Chimú capital of Chan Chan and other Chimú administrative centers.[21] In these Chimú sites, the *audiencia* is thought to be the seat of imperial bureaucrats, and I hoped that studying such a structure would help define the nature of Chimú control over Túcume. Much to our

68 *(opposite) Carved wooden loom boards from the final fill of Platform 2, Huaca Larga. The undecorated middle sections are not shown.*

surprise, the excavations revealed that the structure was not an *audiencia* at all, but rather a small but extremely important temple full of valuable offerings.

The Temple of the Sacred Stone is strategically located at what must have been the principal entrance to Túcume. One end of the walled roadway which passes the Temple points due east across the valley floor, directly at the closest point on the Inca road (which no doubt was a major thoroughfare in pre-Inca times as well). Unfortunately, centuries of agriculture in the valley have erased the intervening sections of the Túcume branch road beyond the margins of the site. The other end of the existing section of the walled roadway follows the side of Huaca Larga north until it disappears under the buildings of La Raya village but heading straight towards the Huaca Larga ramp.

In its final configuration, the Temple of the Sacred Stone measures 7.5 × 8 m (25 × 26 ft) (*ill. 70*). The walls are made of plano-convex adobes and are aligned with the cardinal directions. Sixteen regularly spaced columns formed of plastered wooden posts in four rows of four supported a roof over the central chamber, which housed a thick, flat, upright stone[22] or *huanca* (*ill. 71*).[23] Such stones were worshipped throughout the Andes, and it is not surprising to find one as the focus of this important temple. Still, it is the first one found on the north coast of Peru. The Túcume *huanca* leans at a noticeable angle towards the north, where the entrance is located. When we began excavations, one of my workmen told me that he had once tried to remove the stone to use in construction, but found that it was too hard to get it

70 General plan of the Temple of the Sacred Stone. The dashed lines mark the edges of 10×10 m excavation units, with unexcavated baulks between; white areas between solid lines are walls. The scale pattern represents prepared clay floors.

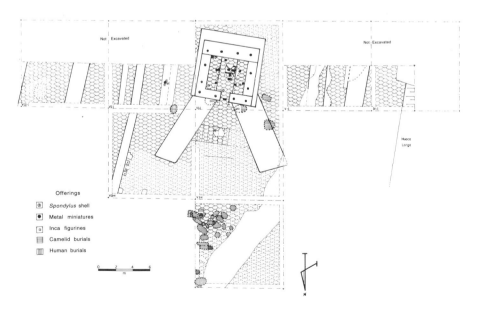

Offerings

⊙ *Spondylus* shell
● Metal miniatures
□ Inca figurines
▤ Camelid burials
▥ Human burials

71 Interior view of the Temple of the Sacred Stone from the entrance, with the sacred stone (huanca) and the altars in front of it visible.

out. I assumed that the angle of the stone was due to his efforts, but as excavations progressed we were able to determine that this angle was original and intentional.

A doorway in the front (north) wall gives access to the central chamber, which had low benches along either wall (see *ill. 70*). The *huanca* is aligned with the doorway and is in the middle of the sunken central corridor between the low benches. In front of the *huanca* are three altars dating to different construction phases (*ill. 71*). Behind the *huanca* in the south wall are two small niches.

Two wide, low benches run diagonally northeast and northwest from the front of the Temple of the Sacred Stone, partially enclosing the flat patio area to the north of the structure (*ill. 73*). Narrower flat areas are found at the sides and back of the Temple. The flat areas surrounding the Temple are enclosed by low walls which define the sacred precinct.

Throughout the use of the Temple of the Sacred Stone, numerous offerings were made in and around the central structure. These offerings included potsherds, miniature metal objects, *Spondylus* shells, figurines of both silver and *Spondylus* with fine clothes and other accouterments, sacrificed llamas, and human burials.

Construction and use of the Temple of the Sacred Stone
Five phases for the construction and use of the Temple of the Sacred Stone have been defined. *Phase ST-1* is known only from the first floor,

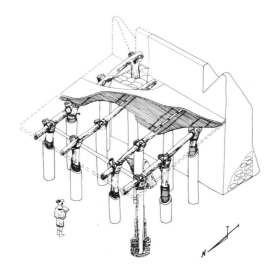

72 A reconstruction of the Temple of the Sacred Stone during Phase ST-1. The huanca, *or sacred stone, that gives the temple its name, was deliberately set up at an angle.*

the south wall to which the floor is joined, and the *huanca*. The east and west side walls appear to have been added later; at this early stage, the side walls probably consisted of posts, as on various Lambayeque ceramic models (*ill. 72*). The south wall has a triangular cross-section, also like the pottery models. I suspect that the form of the south wall is related to the shape of the Sicán Lord head; the Sicán Lord[24] is the principal icon of the Lambayeque tradition, and is best known from the Huaco Rey pots (see Chapter 7). In ceramic representations of Lambayeque buildings, there is generally a seated figure where the *huanca* is located in the Temple of the Sacred Stone. The similarity between the Lambayeque pottery building models and the initial phase of the Stone Temple, with the possibility that the south wall deliberately invokes the Sicán Lord, all indicate that the Stone Temple is part of the local tradition and may well date to Middle Sicán times (*c.* AD 900 to 1100) or at least prior to the Chimú conquest of the region around AD 1350.

When we excavated in the court to the east of the temple we found a wall built on sterile soil which was later dismantled and its destroyed base covered with other constructions. This wall must belong to Phase ST-1 and may have been part of an enclosing wall defining the sacred precinct around the temple. In later phases, the sacred precinct became larger.

When we removed the Phase ST-1 floor, we found that the natural ground surface was quite irregular and had been leveled with an incredible number of pottery sherds. We removed over 1800 from a pit measuring 1 sq. m in front of the *huanca*, and at least 3000–4000 sherds underlay the whole building. Under the sherds and imme-

73 Hypothetical
reconstruction of the
Temple of the Sacred
Stone.

diately on sterile soil were the earliest of the metal miniature offerings from the Temple of the Sacred Stone. These included a double-
spout-and-bridge vessel with a low pedestal base, which would fit
Shimada's Middle Sicán style,[25] supporting the suggested date for
Phase ST-1. This miniature metal pot appears to have been cast in two
parts, rather than made of sheets and soldered. Other metal miniatures from this context include a high-neck jar, two plates, round
bangles covering (but not attached to) a crescent-shaped headdress,
and other pieces of unknown function. The headdress ornament was
made of sheet metal, while the plates were cast and hammered. Cotton
textile remains on top of the plates suggest that they were originally
placed in a bag.

Phase ST-1 was affected by rainfall, most likely associated with an
occurrence of the Niño phenomenon. The temple was then remodeled, giving rise to *Phase ST-2*. In this phase, there is a formal change
in the architecture. The east and west side walls were built, as were the
partial walls on the north defining the narrow doorway. The lateral
walls are straight, lacking the triangular cross-section of the earlier
south wall. The columns and benches were also added at this time. A
wooden door frame was installed: a post was placed on either side of
the door and a wooden trough to receive the door was laid across the
threshold. The outside of the temple was coated with fine gray plaster.

Without the adobe side walls, the *huanca* was visible from outside during Phase ST-1. In Phase ST-2, the sacred stone was enclosed and hidden, made into a mysterious object of greater power and prestige. This transformation represents the greatest change in function during the history of the Temple of the Sacred Stone.

Our one radiocarbon date from the temple comes from a Phase ST-2 post, which might have been reused from Phase ST-1. The result of the test was 610 ± 75 BP (BGS-1613), calibrated to AD 1301 to 1424 with a mean of AD 1398. This date fits well with a Chimú Period assignment of Phase ST-2.

Excavations on the west side of the temple revealed a north–south wall which defined one side of the newly enlarged sacred precinct around the Temple; although built in Phase ST-2, it continued in use throughout the subsequent phases.

The floors built above the Phase ST-2 structure are poorly preserved, so it is difficult to determine the association of the different offering pits cut into the interior of the Temple of the Sacred Stone. All the pits cut through the first floor on the side benches, but it is not always clear whether they also cut through any of the overlying floors. Of eight pits, three were definitely covered by overlying floors and thus must have been made in Phase ST-2 when the benches were functioning. The offerings in these three pits consist mainly of *Spondylus* shells (*ill. 74*). Pit 8, in the southeast corner, contained a miniature crown of gilded copper, a fish carved of *Spondylus*, and four *Spondylus* shells in two groups of two (*ill. 75*).

Phase ST-2 ended with another rainfall episode, leading to the remodeling of *Phase ST-3*. A new floor was built over the benches. A square stone altar (Altar 1) was placed in front of the *huanca* and filled with offerings: gilded and silvered copper miniatures (see *ills 84–85*);

74 (left) Spondylus *shells from offering pits around the Temple of the Sacred Stone.*

75 (right) Whole and carved Spondylus *shells, and a miniature golden headdress found in a pit inside the Temple of the Sacred Stone.*

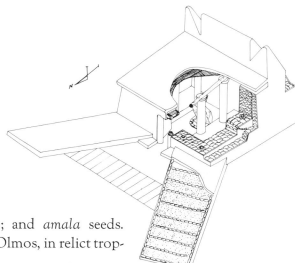

76 A reconstruction of the
Temple of the Sacred
Stone during Phase ST-5.

whole, broken, and powdered *Spondylus* shells; and *amala* seeds. *Amala* is a tropical species which also grows near Olmos, in relict tropical forests on the western slopes of the Andes.

Another rainfall event required further remodeling: *Phase ST-4.* A new adobe altar (Altar 2) was built between the *huanca* and the stone altar, connected to both of them. Like Altar 1, the new one contained offerings of metal miniatures and *Spondylus* shells, as well as red, green, blue, and white powders.[26] A new facing was added to the outside of the lateral walls, covering the fine gray plaster. In the Phase ST-4 additions, white adobes predominate and are visibly different from the gray mortar used to join them. White adobes had been present, but not common, in the previous phases. During Phase ST-4, a series of seven adjoining rectangular boxes were lightly carved into the floor of the courtyard in front of the Stone Temple. To the east, the carved lines go under the diagonal bench and there must be one or more boxes we could not uncover. Each of the boxes measures 0.58 × 1.92 m (2 × 6¼ ft), for a total exposed area of nearly 6 sq. m (64 sq. ft).

Following yet another rainfall event, the final modifications of the Temple of the Sacred Stone resulted in the *Phase ST-5* structure (*ill. 76*). A new, oval, adobe altar (Altar 3) was built in front of the *huanca*, partly cutting Altar 2, and associated with it were the same kinds of offerings as the previous two. The previous floor remained in use in the sunken central corridor, but new floors were built over the lateral benches. The two low, diagonal benches radiating out from the front of the temple were built either at the beginning of this Phase or towards the end of the preceding Phase ST-4. These diagonal benches focus on the doorway in the front of the temple.

Phase ST-5 dates to the Inca period at Túcume. On each side of the doorway and in the center of the courtyard (cutting the Phase ST-4 rectangular carved boxes) are offering pits containing Inca figurines. The courtyard pit had a single, 17-cm (7-in) high, silver figurine wearing a

77 (left) The head of an Inca silver figurine wrapped in a cloak fastened with a copper tupu (pin), found in a pit in the courtyard in front of the Temple of the Sacred Stone.

78 (below) Two Spondylus figurines, one male and one female, were discovered in an offering pit located outside and to the east of the entrance of the Temple of the Sacred Stone (front and side views). They are shown here without the textiles that originally clothed them (ills 79 and 80).

79 (bottom left) Inca male figurine carved from Spondylus shell and wearing woven clothes, tied with a belt, and a headdress. This figurine was found in the same pit as a female figurine (ill. 80).

80 (bottom right) Inca female figurine of carved Spondylus shell, also dressed in woven clothes.

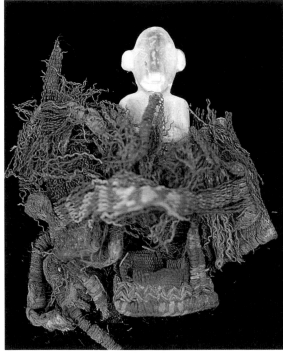

plaincloth cloak fastened with a copper *tupu* (Inca cloak pin) (*ill. 77*). The pit to the east of the doorway had two *Spondylus* Inca figurines with embroidered shirts and woven hats. One figurine was found higher in the pit than the other; it measured 6.4 cm (2½ in) high, had a small wooden rod and a textile belt, and was male (*ills 78 (left) and 79*). It had better preserved clothing than the lower, female figurine, which measured only 5.4 cm (2 in) high (*ills 78 (right) and 80*). Gender was easy to distinguish, both from the genitals and the hairstyles.

In the pit to the west of the doorway were two other Inca-style figurines wearing feather headdresses and clothed in embroidered wool cloaks. The lower, and less well-preserved specimen was of *Spondylus*, had a white feather headdress, and was sewn to a small log. This specimen has not been unclothed yet. The upper figurine is one of the most important objects found at Túcume: it has a perfectly preserved, red feather headdress, is made of silver,[27] and is female (*ills 81–82*). The polychrome cloak (probably of alpaca wool) is fastened with a silver *tupu*. This figurine is identical to others found in high altitude Inca

81–82 Inca silver figurine with a splendid feather headdress, silver tupu *(pin), and polychrome woven cloak. One of the most spectacular finds from Túcume, it came from one of the offering pits just west of the entrance to the Temple of the Sacred Stone. (Front and back views.)*

83 Some of the 31 llama burials found north of the Temple of the Sacred Stone.

shrines in the southern Andes, such as Cerro del Plomo in Chile, and Pachacamac.[28] The Túcume specimen was probably imported from elsewhere. Nevertheless, the half-moon shape of the feather headdress is a north coast trait, not a highland one, even though the figurines found in the high altitude shrines have the same headdress.

The location of the other figurines similar to that from the west pit shows the high status of these artifacts in the Inca Empire. Such figurines were placed as offerings only on very special occasions: the death, or its anniversary, of an Inca, or the accession to the throne of a new Inca. These facts highlight the importance of the Temple of the Sacred Stone as an Inca sanctuary, placing it in the category of sites such as Pachacamac. The Stone Temple must have enjoyed great prestige due to the religious and/or ideological power of the *huanca*. This idea fits with the notion of Túcume as the successor to Batán Grande as the religious center of the northern north coast.

The pits on either side of the doorway cut through the diagonal benches, supporting the notion that these walls date to Phase ST-4. During the pre-Inca phases (1–4), two adult llamas had been buried on the west side of the temple, probably during Phase ST-3, if the Phase ST-4 attribution of the diagonal benches is correct – one of the llama burials was later covered by the northwest diagonal bench. During Phase ST-5, more llamas were buried on the north side of the court in front of the Stone Temple (*ill. 83*); some of these llama burials cut pre-Inca human burials (see below).

When the Temple of the Sacred Stone was abandoned at the end of Phase ST-5, the tops of the walls were knocked over, the central chamber was filled, the *huanca* covered, and the columns were burned. Seen as reddening of the surrounding clay as well as carbonization of the wooden post at the core of each column, the effects of the fire reached as far down as the lateral benches. This deliberate destruction may have taken place at the same time as the destruction and first burning of the bench/corridor area and Platform 2 on the adjacent Huaca Larga; if so, that would date the abandonment of the Temple of the Sacred Stone to the very last years of the Inca Period or the very first years of Spanish rule.

To summarize the chronological data for the Temple of the Sacred Stone, it seems quite likely that it was in use over a very long period, certainly from before the Inca Period. From at least Phase ST-2, the temple was linked to the outer, east wall of Huaca Larga built during the Chimú Period Tricolor Phase of that Huaca. The following tentative identifications can be made: Phase ST-1 of the Stone Temple dates to the Lambayeque Period at Túcume, Phases ST-2 to -4 date to the Chimú Period, and Phase ST-5 dates to the Inca Period.

The metal miniatures

During Phases ST-1 to -4, the primary offerings were metal miniatures (*ills 84–85*). These show a uniformity in terms of types and technology – most are made of copper-silver alloy sheet metal, recalling traditional north coast metallurgy. Analysis of the miniatures has revealed three key characteristics. First, the miniatures appear in groups, either in pits

84 (below left) Metal miniatures were the most frequent offerings at the Temple of the Sacred Stone. Some, as here, were found still in the Spondylus *shell they had been offered in.*

85 (below right) The metal miniatures offered at the Temple were mostly made of copper-silver alloy and represented a great range of themes and objects, both natural and man-made. Here they include: a hammock or litter (upper right), a headdress and birds (second row) and plants. In the bottom left corner are pieces of sheet metal left over from cutting out the figures.

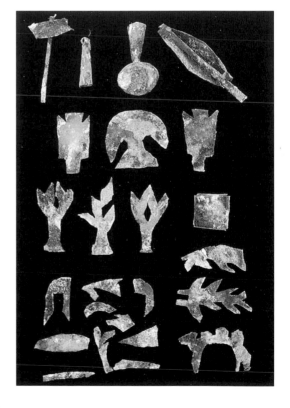

or in articulated *Spondylus* shells. Second, they represent varied themes: flora, fauna, ornaments, musical instruments, tools, pottery vessels, and miscellaneous objects. Ornaments consist of crowns and earspools. Among the musical instruments are trumpets, flutes, panpipes, and drums. The miscellaneous objects include hammocks, umbrella-like shades, and a boot. Both the miscellaneous objects and the tools and pots are items used by high-status individuals. Third, gold and silver (usually as alloys of copper) and copper are found in the same offering group. These metals are associated with high-status individuals, not commoners; it must have been these high-status people or their emissaries who deposited the offerings in and around the Temple of the Sacred Stone.

There was probably a primary connection between Huaca Larga and the Stone Temple: those who were entering Huaca Larga via the walled roadways for certain ceremonies could have made offerings in the Temple as the first step in advancing into the Huaca.

The easternmost of the walled roadways must relate to the final phase of the Stone Temple. Earlier roads would have existed closer to the temple structure but were later destroyed to give more room to the sacred precinct. The walled roads are more worn in the center than on the sides, indicating that they were, indeed, used as pathways. Camelid excrement was found in the roadway, indicating that llamas as well as humans walked this route.

The burials in the temple's sacred precinct
Both humans and llamas were buried in the sacred precinct around the Temple of the Sacred Stone. As mentioned above, two adult llamas were buried on the west side of the Temple prior to the Inca Period, but the majority of the llamas and all the humans were found in the area to the north of the Temple (see *ill. 83*). In this area, we excavated a total of 11 human and 31 llama burials.

Two types of human interments were found. First semiflexed, lying on the back with the legs crossed and the head slightly raised on a support; and second extended, lying on the back. The two types are contemporaneous, as semiflexed burials occurred both above and below extended burials. All human burials were oriented east–west with the face looking west.

Humans and llamas were sometimes buried in the same pits (*ill. 86*). For instance, in Pit 8, the burial sequence began with a small llama at the base, which was disturbed later by two overlying extended human burials, which in turn were disturbed by an overlying, single, semi-

86 A detail of a llama burial to the north of the Temple of the Sacred Stone. A human skeleton is flexed underneath that of the llama.

flexed human. Unfortunately, subsequent disturbance and erosion make it impossible to relate Pit 8 to the building sequence of the Temple of the Sacred Stone. In the same area, however, some of the llama burials can be dated to the Inca Period, Phase ST-5. These cut through the latest floor and either occur alone or else above and cutting human and other llama burials.

Another important feature of the burials at the Temple of the Sacred Stone is the similar treatment of humans and llamas – both could be disturbed by later burials of either species. This fact, plus the presence of secondary human burials (two skulls, one with two cervical vertebrae still attached, in a pit on the east side of the Temple entrance – (ill. 87)), indicate that the human burials were offerings. The skull with attached vertebrae may be from a decapitated individual. Thus, the sacred precinct of the temple was not a simple cemetery, but rather was dedicated exclusively to ceremonial rites and offerings.

87 A detached skull buried in the front wall of the Temple of the Sacred Stone.

The Temple of the Sacred Stone was clearly a religious building, and one that was probably used by high-status individuals visiting Huaca Larga to participate in important ceremonies. Its location must have been particularly important, not only as the final stage in approaching Huaca Larga, but also for its proximity to the Stepped Mound just to the south of the temple. This mound has three platforms which rise to the west, with a high, sheer wall on the west end opposite Huaca Larga, from which it is separated by a narrow channel. Stepped platforms are a common symbol in local iconography. More significant, the Stepped Mound is covered with whole, broken, and fragmentary Spondylus

shells, especially on the upper platform. Like the Temple of the Sacred Stone, the Stepped Mound must have been an important religious place within Túcume.

In Inca times, priests could be either male or female. However, the Inca Period figurines from the Temple are either of *Spondylus*, which comes from the sea or *mamacocha* (mother of waters in Quechua), or silver, which was also considered feminine. Thus, the Inca Period Phase ST-5 Temple was probably tended by priestesses and dedicated to female deities and rites. The same may be true of the pre-Inca phases as well, given the predominance of *Spondylus* and silver among the earlier offerings.

A final question about the Temple of the Sacred Stone concerns its construction around the sacred, unmodified stone or *huanca*. At first I considered that this was just an Inca practice, and that the entire Temple must have been built during the Inca Period. Then I recalled that the early 17th-century chronicler Father Calancha[29] talked of stones that were worshipped in Chimú temples. Also, in the Naymlap myth, the founder's last descendant Fempellec brought about terrible disasters by attempting to remove the sacred green stone from the temple. From an archaeological point of view, there are several other pre-Inca temples known from the coast which contain unmodified stones in central locations (for instance, Huaca Carquín and Huaca Bacín de Oro).[30] Thus, the *yungas* or coastal peoples had the same tradition of worshipping sacred stones as did the Incas.

Huaca 1

Huaca 1 is located in the northwest corner of the Monumental Sector, just west of Huaca Las Estacas (*ill. 88*). The first excavations of the Túcume Archaeological Project took place in the south plaza of Huaca 1 in 1988, and work continued on and around this mound through the 1992 field season. Huaca 1 is the tallest of the man-made Túcume pyramids, measuring over 30 m (98 ft) above current ground level – and excavations showed that the ground level at the time of construction was as much as 5 m (16 ft) lower, adding that amount to the original height of the mound.

Built of plano-convex adobes, the main structure is a high platform oriented east–west and supporting a series of rooms and other features on top (*ills 89–90*). Access to this structure was a long, high, adobe ramp running from west to east up to the body of the pyramid, when it makes the first of several right-angle turns. A lower, secondary platform connects to the east end of the main structure, running north to

89 Aerial photo of Huaca 1. Note the excavations in the South Plaza (center right to bottom) and in the North Plaza (center left). This photograph was taken in early 1990 and excavation of the Annex (center right, above) had not advanced far.

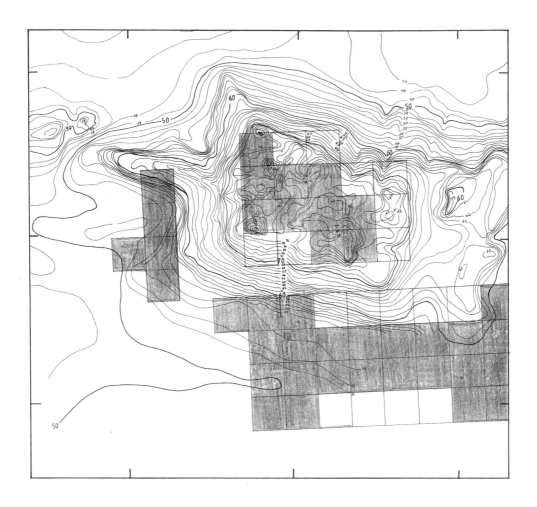

90 *Topographic plan of
Huaca 1 with the
10×10 m excavation grid
superimposed and contours
marked at 1 m intervals.
The darkened areas are
excavated units.*

91 *Archaeological plan of
Huaca 1.*

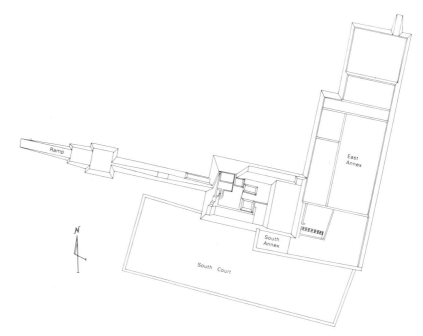

form an L-shape. In the angle of the L, north of the main structure and west of the secondary platform, is the North Plaza. The South Plaza is located to the south of the main structure and is enclosed by a large adobe wall. This plaza measures 78 m (256 ft) north–south by 210 m (689 ft) east–west. In the South Plaza and attached to the southeast part of Huaca 1 is the Annex, a rectangular structure which will be described in detail below.

During the five seasons of field work at Huaca 1, excavations took place in the South Plaza, the North Plaza, the Annex (*ill. 91*), on top of the main platform, and at the base of the ramp. The following sections summarize our current understanding of the growth and development of Huaca 1, based on the various excavations there.

The Pre-Huaca Phase

Before the construction of the pyramid, there was a non-monumental occupation of *quincha* (cane and mud) structures. In the excavation near the ramp, at the southwest corner of Huaca 1, we found the remains of *quincha* rooms containing midden and domestic pottery, including vessels with *paleteada* (paddle-stamped) decoration.

From this pre-huaca phase came an infant burial associated with two pots. One is an *olla* with two modeled animals connecting the shoulder to the rim. The other is a blackware, stirrup-spout vessel representing a ray (*ill. 92*). The spout is round and has a monkey at the base. The style of the ray pot identifies it as Middle Chimú Period, which dates to *c.* AD 1200 to 1300, before the Chimú Empire conquered Lambayeque. Thus the presence of a Middle Chimú vessel *under* Huaca 1 does not mean that the Huaca was built after the Chimú conquest of Túcume. In fact, there is plenty of evidence for significant interaction between the Lambayeque and Moche Valleys from the beginning of the Chimú sequence, around AD 850. For instance, the friezes at Chotuna in the Lambayeque Valley are clearly related to those at Huaca Dragón in Moche.[31] In Túcume itself, a Tricolor style Early Chimú vessel came from a Lambayeque Period grave in the South Cemetery (see Chapter 7).

As part of our program of making stratigraphic cuts throughout the site, we also found domestic occupations under Huaca Las Estacas, to the north of Huaca 1 (*ill. 93*), and under a small huaca to the north-northeast of Huaca Las Estacas. It seems, therefore, as though there was a pre-monumental phase in the northwest quadrant of Túcume, where the majority of the site's large pyramids are now found. However, it is possible that these domestic occupations are associated

92 A blackware stirrup-spout vessel representing a ray, found under the main ramp of Huaca 1. This Middle Chimú pot was found in the Pre-huaca Phase of Huaca 1 and thus dates to the Lambayeque Period.

93 Aerial photo of Huaca las Estacas, part of Huaca Larga, and La Raya mountain, looking southeast.

with the first phases of the huacas and were covered by later additions as the huacas grew laterally and vertically. The levels excavated below the outer edge of Huaca Las Estacas yielded a radiocarbon date of 575 ± 70 BP (BGS-1615), which calibrates to AD 1324 to 1440 with a mean of AD 1413. Surprisingly, this date is very similar to our dates for Phases H-2 and H-3 on Huaca 1 (see below).

Following the pre-huaca phase at Huaca 1, the subsequent constructions can be divided into three major phases. Phase H-1 belongs to the Lambayeque Period, Phase H-2 to the late Lambayeque and Chimú Periods (the Chimú probably arrived towards the end of Phase H-2), and Phase H-3 to the Chimú and Inca Periods.

Phase H-1

Evidence for *Phase H-1* was found at the bottom of our excavations in various parts of Huaca 1, but we do not have sufficient data to define the form of the pyramid in this Phase. The available evidence does suggest strong continuity from Phase H-1 to Phase H-2. A test pit under the Phase H-2 structures in the Annex uncovered a wall and associated floor built on a fill of stones over sterile gravel. The wall is parallel to, but stratigraphically earlier than, the south wall of the

Phase H-2 Annex. The fill over Phase H-1 floors on top of the Huaca is like the fill used in the Annex at the end of Phase H-2.

Phase H-2
By *Phase H-2*, the structures associated with Huaca 1 in the South Plaza were monumental in scale and type: large rooms, clean floors, fine plaster, and so on. These rooms were built on top of sterile sand and gravel with no indication below them of earlier structures dating to Phase H-1. During Phase H-2, Huaca 1 was smaller than the final pyramid visible today and the early South Plaza rooms were probably connected to this initial structure.

On top of the Huaca, Phase H-2 is represented by the earliest exca-vated structures (*ill. 94*), which have the same characteristics as the South Plaza rooms: clean floors, fine plaster, and large walls. There are traces of red, yellow, and possibly black paint on some of the plaster. Phase H-2 has several sub-phases, but the same general design is main-tained until Phase H-3.

During Phase H-2, access to the top of Huaca 1 was via the ramp on the west side of the mound. Once the ramp reached the body of the pyramid, a series of zigzag ramps began (*ill. 95*). On one ramp we found the framework for a door, consisting of two posts and a wooden trough across the threshold, just like the door frame into the Temple of the Sacred Stone. There was no alternative route to reach the rooms on top of the Huaca: anyone entering the pyramid-top chambers had to pass

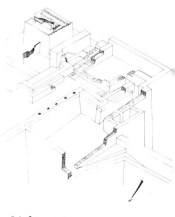

94 *Isometric reconstruction of the top of Huaca 1 during Phase H-2 (Lambayeque to Chimú Periods).*

95 *The west side of the top of Huaca 1, with a zigzag access ramp dating to Phase H-2, Lambayeque to Chimú Periods.*

through the narrow doorway. Clearly, the inhabitants of Huaca 1 were deeply concerned with controlling access to their inner chambers.

Once past the door, the ramp continued south until reaching a corridor which led east into the rooms on top of Huaca 1. The first floor of this corridor dates to Phase H-2. Like the south face of the Huaca and the Annex at this time, during Phase H-2 the east–west corridor was plastered with greenish mud, similar to the Green Phase on Huaca Larga.

The area on top of Huaca 1 can be divided into three major sections (see *ill. 94*): smaller rooms to the west; a sunken Central Chamber; and the Niched Platform to the east. Food remains occurred in the Central Chamber and the smaller rooms.

The Central Chamber contained a number of interesting architectural elements, including benches on the south and west sides, box niches set into the walls, and a stepped structure in the east wall. In a later sub-phase of Phase H-2, the box niches and stepped structure were covered over, possibly indicating the end of the phase. The Central Chamber must have had a residential character – it is the only Phase H-2 room on top of the pyramid where we recovered hearths and food remains, including shells, guinea pig bones, corn cobs, and so on, in addition to potsherds both on top of and stuck to the floor. The pottery types include fugitive black on polished redware. A radiocarbon date from the Central Chamber came out at 630 ± 70 BP (BGS-1610), calibrated to AD 1302 to 1421 with a mean of AD 1398. This result fits the assignment of Phase H-2 to the late Lambayeque and Chimú Periods.

Once past the Central Chamber, the east–west corridor connects with a ramp leading to the Niched Platform. In this area, we excavated a sequence of 22 floors separated by fill and midden levels. The first five floors (18–22) belong to Phase H-2. An algarrobo log from the base, which may predate the Niched Platform, was radiocarbon dated to 705 ± 70 BP (BGS-1609), which calibrates to AD 1285 to 1397 with a mean of AD 1301. This date fits well with the late Lambayeque Period or the early Chimú Period, so the log could relate to either Phase H-1 or Phase H-2.[32]

The Niched Platform on the east side of the top of Huaca 1, at the end of the east–west corridor, is the highest point on top of the Huaca. During Phase H-2, the Niched Platform consisted of a raised, walled, rectangular room with two rows of boxed niches on the interior of the south wall. The upper row was slightly later than the lower row, but still belonged to Phase H-2.

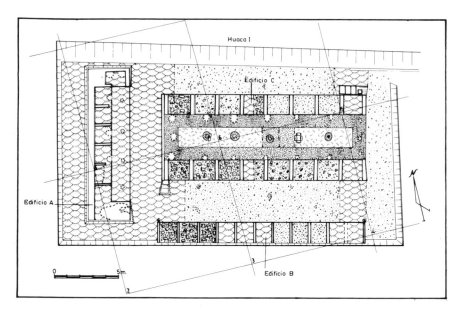

Huaca I

Edificio C

Edificio A

Edificio B

0   5 m

96 Plan of the Huaca 1
Annex during Phase H-2,
showing the Bell-Shaped
Building (Edificio A), the
Central Building (Edificio
C), and the niched south
wall (Edificio B). The
10×10 m excavation grid
is superimposed on
the plan.

97 (below left) Huaca 1
Annex, the southwest
corner of the Bell-Shaped
Building when first
exposed by Hugo Navarro
in 1989.

98 (below right) Isometric
reconstruction of the
Huaca 1 Annex during
Phase H-2 showing the
Bell-Shaped Building
(right) and the Central
Building (center). The
strange Bell-Shaped
Building has no known
parallels in Andean
architecture.

In the Annex, the earliest structure also dates to Phase H-2, consisting of an enclosed rectangular patio with the long dimension oriented north–south (*ills 96–98*). The plaster of the Phase H-2 Annex has
the same greenish tint as the Lambayeque Period architecture on
Huaca Larga and Huaca Las Balsas. Two structures on the patio, separated from each other and from the external walls of the Annex by a
finely plastered floor, are the Central Building and the Bell-Shaped
Building. Facing the patio along the south wall is a row of large, evenly
spaced niches measuring about 1.25 m (4 ft) wide and separated by 22-
cm (8½-in) wide dividers (Edificio B). In front of the niches are posts,
also evenly spaced at intervals of 2.30 m (7½ ft). The difference in
spacing of the posts and the niches resulted in some posts being placed

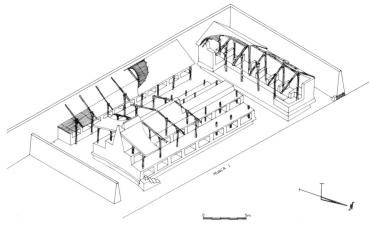

HUACA I

0   5 m

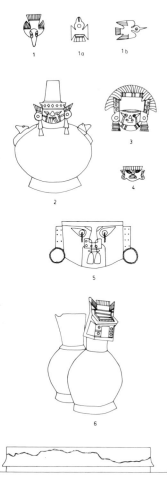

in front of and blocking the niches, while others were aligned with the dividers. Each niche was closed on top, so the posts must have supported a roof attached to the south wall of the Annex and covering the tops of the niches. This roof was quite narrow, as we found a dripline on the Annex floor only 1.25 m (4 ft) in front of the niches.

In the middle of the Phase H-2 Annex is the Central Building (Edificio C), a low, rectangular structure measuring 7 × 15.5 m (23 × 51 ft) and containing rows of eight niches on the north and south sides, slightly larger than those along the south wall of the Annex. Three north–south rows of seven columns run down the middle of the Central Building and must have supported a roof. Attached to the northeast and southwest corners are small, clay steps, like the stepped symbol so common in Lambayeque iconography, and also like the shape of the Stepped Mound east of Huaca Larga and south of the Temple of the Sacred Stone. The steps in the northeast corner are more finely made than those in the southwest, a difference reflected in the distribution of offerings in the first of the Huaca Larga mummy bundles (see above).

At the west end of the Phase H-2 Annex is the Bell-Shaped Building (Edificio A) (*ill. 97*), a rectangular structure with its long axis oriented east–west, at 90 degrees to the Central Building. The outer wall of this building curves outwards from top to bottom until it is about 55 cm (14 in) above the floor when it stops abruptly, creating an overhang and producing the bell shape visible at the corners. Some of the clay below the overhang had fallen off and we could see that the projecting bulk of the wall was supported by a mesh of canes over parallel algarrobo logs – the same construction technique used for the main mound of Huaca 1 (see below). On top of the Bell-Shaped Building are six 1.25-m (4-ft) square niches along the center portion of the west side, which open to the east, towards the patio. The northwest and southwest corners have solid square blocks the same height as the niches but of slightly smaller dimensions. The northeast and southeast corners have small, niche-like rooms, with doors opening towards the center of the building. The east central portion of the Bell-Shaped Building is open towards the patio, with a series of postholes. Evidence for a roof is provided by a dripline in the floor between the Bell-Shaped Building and the west wall of the Annex. Both walls and floors of the Bell-Shaped Building are quite worn, showing that the structure was heavily used.

The curved overhang which gives the Bell-Shaped Building its distinctive form is a unique architectural feature in Andean archaeology. The intention of the architects was perhaps to create a 'winged

99 Winged motifs found in various materials and forms: the diving bird and variants (1, 1a, 1b); classic Huaco Rey with wings as ears (2); a headdress with wing (sides) and tail (top) symbolism (3); masks also include wing (sides) and tail (top) motifs (4 and 5); vessel with an architectural element in which the roof represents the wing (top, sides) and tail (top, center) motifs (6). The projecting overhang of the Bell-Shaped Building at Túcume, can also be seen as symbolizing the wing motif (7).

100 A Moche fineline drawing of a lord or deity receiving offerings. This scene may represent activities similar to those carried out in the Huaca 1 Annex during Phase H-2. (Redrawn from Hocquenghem 1987: figs 17 and 18.)

pyramid', similar to the form seen on a gold *kero* (drinking vessel) from the Lambayeque region. This strange shape is itself a version of the most important emblematic symbol of Lambayeque – the diving bird. I also see the pointed 'ears' on the side of Huaco Rey heads (see Chapter 7) and on the sides of temples (both the Stone Temple and ceramic models) as the wings of the diving bird (*ill. 99*).

A strong formal correspondence exists between the architectural design of the Bell-Shaped Building and a Moche pattern shown in various fine-line drawings (*ill. 100*): in particular, the location of the posts and the presence of two levels above the external floor in the left-hand building in the Moche scene. The same scene also shows rows of pots apparently sitting on the different levels of a structure like the Central Building. The presence of the stepped symbol in the Central Building is also interesting; on the Moche scene it appears behind the left-hand building that I compare to the Bell-Shaped Building. The winged edge of this Building must be a peculiarly Lambayeque feature, as it does not appear in the Moche scene.

A radiocarbon date was obtained for the Phase H-2 Annex, of 600 ±70 BP (BGS-1608), calibrated to AD 1310 to 1433 with a mean of AD 1405. This date is similar to the other definite Phase H-2 date from the Central Chamber.

Phase H-3

Following Phase H-2 major changes took place both in the South Plaza and on top of the pyramid. The early Bell-Shaped and Central Buildings in the Annex were partially destroyed and then buried, as were the monumental rooms in the South Plaza proper and the structures on top of Huaca 1. However, this destruction was not accompanied by burning or by evidence of rainfall or any other natural catastrophe. After the earlier structures were buried, the entire area was remodeled, giving rise to *Phase H-3*.

On top of Huaca 1, the Phase H-2 system of ramps and accessways was covered with fill and a new system of ramps and rooms was constructed (*ill. 101*). Parts of the Phase H-2 rooms were destroyed in the process, and pieces of the broken buildings were found in the fill covering Phase H-2 and forming the base for Phase H-3.

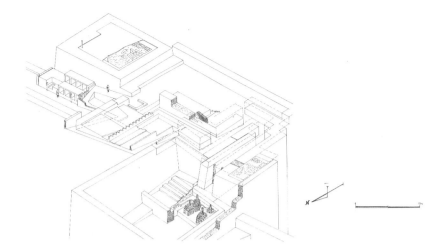

101 Isometric reconstruction of the top of Huaca 1 during Phase H-3 (Chimú to Inca Periods).

During Phase H-3, floors and rooms seem to have had a more residential use than the preceding phase, with many superimposed floors and more primary midden. This midden includes hook-rim plate sherds, dated by Donnan[33] to the Inca Period in the Lambayeque Valley. Inca influence is also apparent in the neck of a Chimú–Inca blackware bottle from a primary deposit and in a high incidence of everted rims.

Architectural ornamentation appears on top of Huaca 1 at this time. Several walls are topped with stepped ornaments, and one diagonal wall has friezes of seabirds on both faces (ill. 102), very reminiscent of Chimú friezes at Chan Chan. The Huaca 1 friezes date to the earliest sub-phases of Phase H-3, and they were broken and covered by floors of the later sub-phases. I would tentatively suggest that Phase H-3 began in the Chimú Period and continued through the Inca Period. If this is correct, the extensive remodeling of Huaca 1 at the beginning of Phase H-3 would be related to the Chimú conquest of Túcume. However, there are some contradictory data, discussed below.

During Phase H-3, the Niched Platform on the east end of the huaca top was modified. The rectangular room was filled in and two rows of

102 Seabird friezes found on top of Huaca 1, Phase H-3 (Chimú Period). These are in the Chimú style and comparable ones were found at the Chimú capital of Chan Chan.

large niches were built on two steps on the north outer face of the Platform. The upper row was added slightly later than the lower one, but still during Phase H-3.

At the end of the east–west corridor, Floors 17 to 1 date to Phase H-3. Floor 12 yielded a radiocarbon date of 625 ± 70 BP (BGS-1611), which calibrates to AD 1303 to 1424 with a mean of AD 1399. Ceramic indicators date Floor 12 to the Chimú occupation, just prior to the Inca arrival, consistent with the radiocarbon assay. One of the most common ceramic indicators of the Inca Period in the Lambayeque region is the hook-rim plate.[34] We found sherds of hook-rim plates on Floors 1 to 10. Stirrup-spouts, a probable Chimú indicator, occur on Floors 1 to 14, while another Chimú indicator, goose-flesh or stippled decoration, occurs on all the floors (1–17). Fugitive black decoration on polished redware also appeared on all Phase H-3 floors. Another ceramic style known as Coastal Cajamarca shows up only on the upper floors, from 1 to 6.

In the Annex, the Niched/Stepped Structure of Phase H-3 is symmetrical in form, with two long steps oriented north–south on either side of a central wall (ill. 103). The steps support rows of niches measuring about 60 × 30 cm (24 × 12 in). Below the lowest step on each side is a wide floor; to the north, the floor ends with the wall of Huaca 1, while to the south it ends with the outer wall of the Annex. Driplines on these floors show that the Niched/Stepped Structure had a roof, though no roof posts were found.

Underlying the Niched/Stepped Structure and covering the buildings of Phase H-2 was a fill containing numerous potsherds. Among the pottery types represented are Coastal Cajamarca, Casma Serpentine Appliqué,[35] polished redware with fugitive black decoration, polished redware with white decoration, and fine blackware including Huaco Rey fragments (see Chapter 7). Fragments of plaster with red paint on one face and cane marks on the other were also found in the fill, clearly the remains of some earlier structure, as were two knotted cords, reminiscent of the Inca *quipu*. This was a complex set of knotted cords used as a mnemonic device by Inca accountants to record information of various types. Some pre-Inca *quipus* are also known.[36]

The fill of the Niched/Stepped Structure was placed around a grid of cylindrical adobe columns spaced about 1.7 m (6 ft) apart, some filled with small stones only, while others had a central vertical log (ill. 104). There were five rows of columns running east–west and three rows running north–south; the columns continued above the fill into

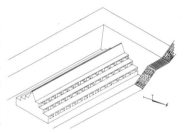

103 Isometric reconstruction of the Huaca 1 Annex during Phase H-3 (Chimú to Inca Periods), showing the Niched/Stepped Structure.

104 Adobes of the Niched/Stepped Structure of Huaca 1 Annex, Phase H-3 (probably late Chimú Period). Note the grid of cylindrical columns (here excavated flush with the adobes), which in some cases still had the central wooden post intact.

the adobe courses of the structure. I call this technique 'Column and Fill', to distinguish it from the more common 'Chamber and Fill' construction technique known at Túcume and elsewhere in the Lambayeque region. Three of the log columns and one of the simple stone columns had burnt textiles on top.

Above the fill, the Niched/Stepped Structure was built of super-imposed courses of adobes. In each course the adobes laid around the columns break the pattern of the rest of the course with a noticeable preference for placing marked adobes in circular or subrectangular rings around the columns, both in the adobe courses of the structure and in the underlying loose fill. The adobes around the columns tended to have different makers' marks in a particular level or course.

One of the logs from the Niched/Stepped Structure yielded a radiocarbon date of 610 ± 70 BP (BGS-1607), which calibrates to AD 1307 to 1431 with a mean of AD 1403. The log may have been reused from the Phase H-2 buildings, but the date is still consistent with the postulated beginning of Phase H-3 during late Chimú times.

South of the main ramp on the west face of the pyramid, we excavated many layers of mud for construction dating to Phase H-3, along with dirt which would make good mud mortar. The mud is full of plant remains and was probably intended for roofing: at Chan Chan, only roof mud has plant parts, and this custom is still observed in the Túcume area today. While excavating the mud deposit, we found many mixing pits, footprints of workers, and even tool marks. Also, a big, Y-shaped post, such as were used to support roofs, was found on top of the mud layers (*ill. 105*).

105 Thor Heyerdahl and
Öystein Johansen (right)
inspect a Y-shaped
algarrobo post. In the
background are more
algarrobo logs forming the
base for the last addition to
Huaca 1.

Mud for roofs, for mortar in adobe walls, or for wall plaster must be mixed close to where it is to be used, otherwise, it dries before it is applied. In contrast, adobes can be made anywhere and brought dried to the construction site. The mud mixed at the southwest corner of Huaca 1 is different from that of the nearby South Plaza structures; only small amounts were found in mortar of the Phase H-3 Niched/Stepped Structure in the Annex. Given the location near the main ramp, the mud must have been used for the roofs of the elite structures on top of Huaca 1.

The South Plaza and the Annex yielded other evidence for the process of constructing the Huaca 1 complex. Along the south wall of the South Plaza and outside the outer wall of the Annex, we found large quantities of llama dung, while llama tracks were uncovered in the mud mortar of the Phase H-3 Niched/Stepped Structure in the Annex. In a few cases we even found a child's footprints next to the llama tracks – possibly belonging to children who led the laden llamas. The animals would have been kept in the South Plaza (hence the large amount of excrement there) and used to carry building material on to the construction site.

More evidence for the construction techniques came from the

southwest corner of Huaca 1, by the ramp, where we found a horizontal layer of algarrobo logs which underlay the final addition to the south face of the mound.[37] Above the logs but under the adobes was a mesh of canes. Whatever its function, this log and cane construction technique was widely used at the site. A similar technique was used in the overhang of the Phase H-2 Bell-Shaped Structure in the Annex, and rows of logs are visible in the sidewalls of many of the large pyramids at Túcume. As suggested above, these logs probably were used to create projections which converted the huacas into winged pyramids.

At the beginning of Phase H-3, about 25 small, informal structures were established in the South Plaza, mostly averaging 1.20 by 1.60 m (4 ft by 5¼ ft), though some are larger and have hearths and benches. Their bases were frequently outlined by adobes, but all were made of *quincha*. Many have midden, textile tools, such as needles and spindle whorls, and sherds with copper adhering to their surfaces; Hugo Navarro even found part of a *tuyère* (a tube used in smelting metals). The area may have been an artisans' center. Underlying the rooms were ash deposits, brought from elsewhere as the surrounding clay is not reddened, which contained only small clam shells (*Donax obesulus*), some plant parts, and animal bones. Although it has been suggested that this ash is from human cremations, there is no evidence to support this idea. Nevertheless, the effort involved in building a base for the informal structures out of special ash does suggest some ceremonial purpose.

These structures may originally have housed the construction crews working on Phase H-3 (even as the pre-huaca phase *quincha* houses may have been used by the crews that built Phase H-2 of the Huaca). Later, the same South Plaza rooms may have sheltered pilgrims who came to attend rituals at Túcume. The large, enclosed South Plaza makes most sense as a place for spectators and participants in rituals carried out on Huaca 1.

Whether Phase H-3 of Huaca 1 dates to pre-Inca or Inca times, it was probably built by *mit'a* labor. *Mit'a* is an Andean system of labor tax by which communities or other social groups subject to a particular lord provide a certain number of person-days of work per year on a rotating basis.[38] Workers would thus have rotated through temporary camps such as the rooms of the South Plaza. The presence and distribution of marked adobes in the structures throughout Túcume provide further indications of *mit'a* labor. Such marks are generally thought to indicate the person, workshop, or social group responsible for making the adobe. Charles Hastings and Michael Moseley[39] were

106–108 Late Lambayeque-style pottery vessels from a burial on top of Huaca 1, probably dating to the Chimú Period.

the first to suggest that the same mark concentrated in a single section is probably an indication a particular group made the adobes, brought them to the site, and built the wall – as one would expect under the *mit'a* system. Although Cavallaro and Shimada[40] found that adobes with the same mark did not tend to cluster together in mounds at nearby Batán Grande, in Huaca 1 the same mark sometimes predominates in a section of building. This pattern is most notable in the lower courses of adobes in the Niched/Stepped Structure of the Annex.

The Secondary Platform on the east side of Huaca 1 (see *ill. 91*: East Annex) has not yet been excavated and there is no direct information about its chronology or function. However, the form of this Platform provides useful hints. It is the only long, low monumental platform at the site other than Huaca Larga, with which it also shares a nearly identical, north–south orientation and a short, straight ramp in the northeast corner. If the similarities arise from a common period of construction, then the Huaca 1 addition would date to the Chimú and/or Inca Periods at Túcume, that is, the latest occupation at the site, represented by Phase H-3 of Huaca 1.

Chronology of Huaca 1

As outlined above, Phase H-1 and part of Phase H-2 date to the Lambayeque Period, while the Chimú Period covers the transition from Phase H-2 to Phase H-3 and the Inca occupation begins part way through Phase H-3. The radiocarbon dates and pottery sherds discussed in the text fit these assignments in general terms and there are other sources of chronological information for Huaca 1.

On top of Huaca 1 a burial contained three Late Lambayeque-style pots, apparently dating to the transition between Phases H-2 and H-3 (*ills 106–108*). Unfortunately, the overlying Phase H-3 floors had been eroded in this area, and there is a slight chance that the burial may be Phase H-3 or later. The pots include polished redware with black painted decoration, like the style from Batán Grande which Shimada labels Late Sicán and dates to the period preceding the Chimú conquest of Lambayeque.[41] However, the same pottery types continued to be manufactured through the Inca Period.

The bird friezes made at the beginning of Phase H-3 are Chimú in style, and I suspect that this phase begins with the Chimú conquest of Túcume. However, I also date the Tricolor Phase of Huaca Larga to the Chimú Period; and whereas the Tricolor Phase makes extensive use of flat adobes, Huaca 1 is built entirely of plano-convex adobes. Phase H-3 of Huaca 1 definitely continues through the Inca Period and there are no major breaks or remodelings in the sequence of subphases. The presence or absence of flat adobes may be due to different functions: Huaca Larga may be seen as the seat of foreign power at Túcume, and flat adobes as intrusive. Huaca 1, on the other hand, was a center of local power, probably the residence of one of the native lords of the site, so 'foreign' flat adobes would have been deliberately rejected.

During the Expansive or Late Period of the Chimú sequence, when that empire was conquering territories up and down the north coast, the only sites with flat adobes were Pacatnamú, a major Chimú administrative center in the Jequetepeque Valley, and Huaca Larga at Túcume. This distribution strengthens the hypothesis that flat adobes were an element brought by the Chimú invaders. Flat adobes were not used at this time at the Chimú capital of Chan Chan, and they may therefore be a local, Jequetepeque trait – perhaps the Chimú imported workmen from Jequetepeque to build Huaca Larga. By the Inca Period, it was a common state practice to transfer workers from place to place within the Empire, either on a rotating basis as *mit'a* or on a permanent basis as *mitmaq*.

Alfredo Narváez

The Maritime Connection

Huaca Las Balsas

EARLY IN 1992, excavations began on the Huaca Facho tombs as part of our program of stratigraphic testing throughout the site (see Chapter 7). We had decided that a second section was needed in the same general area, and I was looking for a place where erosion or looting had exposed a deep profile. A local farmer told me about a small huaca in the southwest part of the site where there were walls with beautiful 'drawings' that looters had exposed in two large pits. He took me there, and I began to sort through the looters' backdirt. Within 10 minutes, I had discovered fragments of mud friezes in high relief. Bringing a workman to the small mound, we immediately began formal excavations. More frieze fragments soon appeared as we worked through the backdirt, all of a greenish tint like the earliest phase of Huaca Larga.

Before we started, I asked Teodoro Sandoval, the workman, to clean back the spiny branches of two small algarrobo trees growing in the center of the looters' pit. When he did so, he found that one tree had the form of a cross. Cross-shaped trees are considered sacred by the local farmers, and Teodoro immediately got out the tea he had brought for lunch and offered it to the tree, saying 'Cruzecita bendita, que haya trabajo, que haya trabajito, muéstrenos los secretos de la huaca, que encontremos cosas muy lindas' ('blessed little cross, let there be work, let there be a little work, show us the secrets of the Huaca, let us find very beautiful things'). Within a week, we had our first view of the fantastic balsa raft frieze preserved on a long segment of original wall (*ill. 111*).

Huaca Las Balsas (or Mound of the Rafts) is located on the south-western edge of the site, in the only group of large pyramids outside the Monumental Sector in the north (see *ill. 33*). Huaca Los Gavilanes (Mound of the Crows) is slightly north and west of Las Balsas, while Huaca Las Abejas (Mound of the Bees) lies to the east. Unlike these two large pyramids, Huaca Las Balsas is a small, low mound (*ill. 112*), as is Huaca Facho to the south, where the Inca tombs were found. Were it not for the looters' discovery of the friezes, there would have been nothing to distinguish Las Balsas from several dozen other low, amorphous mounds in the southwestern and southern sectors of Túcume.

However, the excavations of Huaca Las Balsas have shown it to be one of the most important structures yet uncovered at Túcume. Eight construction phases have been distinguished (*ill. 113*), seven of which have associated friezes. All phases were made of plano-convex- (or breadloaf-) shaped adobes.

109 Huaca Las Balsas. In this phase (Phase HB-2) the relief was of a row of crouching birdmen with half-moon headdresses, holding round objects in their hands. Above them the wall was cut out in a series of wave motifs.

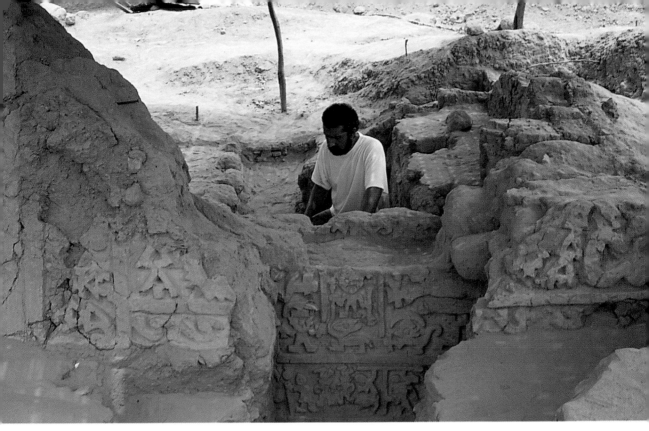

110 (above) Alfredo Narváez examining the reliefs exposed by a looters' pit in Huaca Las Balsas. The pit had cut the Balsas Frieze to the right (north) of the main panel. In the center the Frieze of the Rite is visible.

111 (below) The Balsas Frieze of Huaca Las Balsas (Phase HB-4, probably Lambayeque Period). One of the most extraordinary finds from Túcume, the central panel of the relief shows two reed rafts with two birdmen on each. The rafts are set in a field with diving birds and fish, and the whole is surrounded by a border of the anthropomorphic wave motif.

112 *Plan of excavations in Huaca Las Balsas. The large squares are the 10×10 m excavation grids. The plan is superimposed on a topographic map of the mound.*

The discovery of the friezes

During the 1992 excavations, we found a hearth at the base of the looters' pit with no associated architecture. Nevertheless, this hearth must have been part of an elaborate structure, as one side was made of adobe covered with plaster of the same greenish color as the later mud friezes. Above the hearth is fill. A radiocarbon assay of charcoal from this hearth yielded a result of 555 ± 70 BP (BGS-1612), which calibrates to AD 1399 to 1445 with a mean of AD 1423. The hearth is probably intrusive, but the fill in which it was found forms the base for the first construction phase of the mound.

Phase HB-1, with a bench and an associated floor is constructed over the fill. The base ('zócalo') of the bench is decorated with mud friezes showing a line of mythical birds wearing half-moon headdresses. Another wall rises behind the bench, but it was covered with later friezes so we could not expose it.

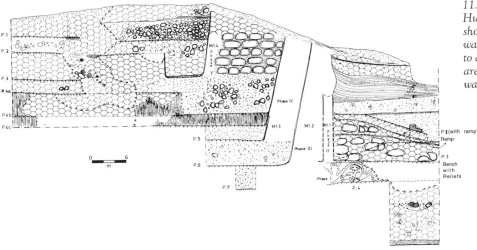

113 *South profile of Huaca Las Balsas, showing superimposed walls and floors belonging to different phases. P 1–7 are floors; M denotes a wall.*

A fill covering the Phase HB-1 bench formed the base for *Phase HB-2*. This phase has an inclined, east–west wall decorated with a frieze of a row of birds with half-moon headdresses, each holding a round object in front of its body. Above the birds is a series of cut-out stepped crests connected on top by a clay rail, like a banister (*ill. 109*); between each stepped crest is open space, producing a lattice-like effect. On the other side of the banister is an inclined ramp, which turns at right angles at the top of the crested wall to run north as a level corridor. Friezes on the east wall of the corridor show a wave motif with a bird perched on top of each wave. In a second sub-phase of Phase HB-2, the wave-bird frieze was covered and a ramp added to the south of the inclined, crested wall.

To build the *Phase HB-3* structure, the Phase HB-2 crested wall and associated ramps were covered with a fill of loose earth in small, crudely made chambers of adobe and mortar. In some places, broken stepped crests from the Phase HB-2 friezes were used instead of adobes. Much of the Phase HB-3 structure within the excavated area had been destroyed by looters, while other parts are covered by later friezes and could not be exposed. However, on the east face of one north–south wall we found the Frieze of the Rite (*ill. 110*). The upper part of this frieze shows a priest inside a roofed structure; he holds a line attached to a llama-like animal in one hand and a rod ending in a half-moon form in the other. To one side is a geometrical symbol which may be an attempt at a three-dimensional representation of a structure with corridors, a door, and exterior walls decorated with stepped temple symbols, in other words a typical Lambayeque

building similar to Huaca Las Ventanas at Batán Grande.[1] Separated by a raised line, the lower section of the Frieze of the Rite shows several figures in dance-like poses and with birds on their heads. In the background is a large vessel, similar to those depicted in fineline scenes on some earlier Moche culture pots; jars of similar form are still used today to hold *chicha* (corn beer), an essential ingredient in all indigenous rites and festivals today as in the past. On one side of the lower section is a crane-like device from which another figure is suspended by the waist.

In *Phase HB-4*, a new north–south wall was added in front of the Phase HB-3 wall, covering the Frieze of the Rite. Originally, this wall was plastered but lacked reliefs, and a floor was built in front of it. When a second floor was placed on top of the first floor, the *Balsas* or *Rafts Frieze* was added to the east face of the wall (*ills 111, 114–115*). At this time, low benches were built along the sides of the room, creating a sunken chamber in front of the Balsas Frieze. The wall directly opposite the Frieze has not yet been excavated; it may also be decorated.

The Balsas Frieze

The Balsas Frieze is one of the most extraordinary finds at Túcume. The central panel, measuring 2.20 × 1.60 m (7 × 5¼ ft), shows two reed boats or rafts, each with two figures holding oars or paddles; one has a human body and the head of a bird and the other is a mythical bird. On each raft, one birdman has a half-moon headdress while that of the other consists of two stepped structures shown in profile and joining in the center at the lowest step (*ill. 114*). Within the same central space as the rafts are more figures, representing fish and diving birds. Around the edges of this central panel are borders containing a figure known as the 'anthropomorphic wave' (*ill. 115*) which can be traced back at least to late Moche times.[2] I have noticed that this figure also has avian characteristics and could more correctly be called the 'anthropoornithomorphic wave' were that not such an awkward term.

To the north of the main panel is an area deliberately left clear of decoration. Some piece of movable art (such as a decorated textile or a carved wooden panel) may have been placed in this space; Dan Sandweiss found a similarly shaped space in one wall of the West Mound in Sector V (see Chapter 6). Further north, the Balsas Frieze wall was destroyed by the looters (*ill. 110*), exposing the Frieze of the Rite of Phase HB-3. To the north of this gap is a small, poorly preserved section of frieze which must be a continuation of the Balsas

114 (opposite above) Close-up of the right-hand raft of the Balsas Frieze.

115 (opposite below) A detail of the anthropomorphic wave motif from the Balsas Frieze.

Frieze. All that remains is part of a flexed figure with a long headdress, reminiscent of the anthropomorphic wave in the border around the raft scene. This figure holds a round object, like the birds in the Phase HB-2 frieze.

During Phase HB-3 or HB-4, postholes were cut through the Phase HB-2 walls, presumably to support a roof which would have covered the decorated chamber in one or both of these phases. It seems likely that both the Frieze of the Rite and the Balsas Frieze were protected from the elements by such a roof. The fine preservation of both friezes argues in favor of this idea – without a roof, the constant winds, seasonal drizzle, and occasional torrential rains associated with El Niño would surely have damaged the delicate mud designs. Instead of such environmental deterioration, most of the damage to the friezes was caused by later construction or by the looters. Where the loose fill of a later phase lay against the friezes, the designs are well preserved. Where the mud mortar of an overlying wall was in direct contact with the friezes, preservation is worse.

In *Phase HB-5*, the Balsas Frieze was covered with another plastered but undecorated wall. This wall and its associated floor and corridor were built on a thick layer of fill containing pieces of the earlier friezes, as does the wall itself. In fact, the looters' pit had exposed much of the Phase HB-5 wall, and the fragments of frieze reused as adobes provided some of the first clues to the contents of the mound. During Phase HB-5, friezes were placed on the east wall of the main chamber, opposite the now-covered Balsas Frieze. So far, we have seen only traces of these friezes and cannot yet describe them.

Our most recent excavations demonstrate that Phase HB-5 is associated with a system of access ramps from the west side of the mound. These ramps also have decorated walls along their upper sections at the top of the Huaca. The reliefs consist of repeated pairs of diagonally opposed stepped symbols alternating with wave-like volutes arranged across the opposite diagonal – a motif known throughout the Andean region since the Formative Period (Late Preceramic – Early Horizon).

Later, the Phase HB-5 floor was covered with fill and two superimposed floors were built over it. These floors represent *Phase HB-6* and *Phase HB-7*. Despite destruction by looters, we have found walls, benches, and ramps associated with these phases of Huaca Las Balsas.

During Phase HB-6, a complex of interconnected rooms was built against the east wall of Huaca Las Balsas. One room was clearly a kitchen, entered by a narrow door on the south. The eastern side is occupied by a low platform and a carefully made, square hearth was built of modeled mud against the side of the platform; when we dug it, it was full of ash. Large quantities of food remains were stuck to the floor: corn cobs, charred corn kernels, camelid and guinea pig bones, crab carapaces, shells, fish bones, and pods from the *pacay* fruit (*Inga feuillei*).

The walls of the kitchen and connected rooms had been painted a reddish color, now badly eroded and faded. The one exception is the west wall of the kitchen – the outer wall of the huaca – which was greenish. A short ramp from the northwest corner of the kitchen led to a corridor to the main entrance to the Huaca, which from at least Phase HB-4 through Phase HB-6 was located on the northeast side of the mound. The ramp on the north side provided a secondary entrance to the Huaca; during Phase HB-6, the Phase HB-5 friezes along this ramp were partly covered by the remodeled ramp but still visible.

To the east of the kitchen, we found a room full of llama dung. Clearly, this space was a corral of some kind, perhaps for the llamas eaten in the kitchen. Another possibility is that the llamas were to be sacrificed, as in the Frieze of the Rite (see above) or as the llamas buried around the Stone Temple in the Monumental Sector.

Following Phase HB-6, the kitchen, associated rooms, and the northeast entrance were filled and sealed. During Phase HB-7, the final face of Huaca Las Balsas was added to the north side of the mound, covering the northeast entrance. At this time, the west ramp must have become the principal entrance. The upper parts of the Phase HB-5 friezes in the west ramp continued in use throughout Phase HB-7. The final phase, *HB-8*, is poorly preserved and represented only by a few floor fragments of fine gray plaster and a series of postholes, all found on top of the south end of the Huaca.

Chronology of Huaca Las Balsas

In terms of chronology, I initially believed that Huaca Las Balsas was built, enlarged, and then abandoned in a relatively short span of time prior to the Chimú conquest of the Lambayeque Valley. This hypothesis would place the date of the mound sometime around AD 1200, the period of local, Lambayeque control of the site and the region. Given that the one radiocarbon date available for Huaca Las Balsas comes from a hearth which may predate construction of the mound and falls between AD 1399 and AD 1445 (calibrated), I must now reconsider my original estimate. Perhaps the hearth is intrusive and belongs to a later period, or it is possible that the Huaca itself is later. In that case, it would provide evidence for the remarkable vitality and continuity of the Lambayeque cultural tradition even under foreign domination by the Chimú and later Inca empires.

Interpretations

Regardless of the absolute date and span of Huaca Las Balsas, one of the most striking features is the continuity displayed throughout the entire sequence of phases. With one possible exception, it seems clear that we have here the product of a single, long-lasting cultural tradition: the Lambayeque Tradition. All construction phases employed the same, plano-convex adobes – the type characteristic of late prehispanic architecture in the Lambayeque Valley. The growth of the Huaca resulted from the deposition of fill and the construction of parallel, superimposed walls. All the plaster from Phases 1 to 7 shows the greenish tint characteristic of the Lambayeque (pre-Chimú) structures on Huaca Larga; the gray plaster found on Chimú and Inca period buildings in the rest of the site occurs only in fragments of a floor dating to the final phase, HB-8.

Finally, with the exception of the Phase HB-3 Frieze of the Rite, the iconography of the friezes shows considerable formal coherence. The reliefs found in Phases HB-1, -2, and -4 all have a strictly maritime theme: rafts, fish, seabirds, shells, anthropomorphic and 'natural' waves, and so on. In contrast, the Frieze of the Rite shows dancers and priests with llamas. Surely this scene represents the celebration of a religious ceremony. There is no evidence that this ceremony was related to the sea, but given the theme of the earlier and later friezes, I suspect that this is the case. It may be that the Frieze of the Rite shows a ritual related to the moon or another of the coastal gods (in *muchik*, the native language of the north coast, the word 'si' means both moon and sea).[3] The animal wearing a half-moon headdress is a descendant of the Moche moon animal.

In the Lambayeque iconographic tradition of AD 1000 to 1600, repetitive or stereotypical elements predominate, as in the contemporary Chimú tradition further south. The Frieze of the Rite is an anomalous element in the late Lambayeque tradition in which religious scenes are scarce. It is more like scenes represented in the fine-line drawings on earlier, Moche culture vessels, and I see a Moche spirit behind the conception of this relief. Indeed, at Túcume a strong Moche tendency is detectable, more like the revival of an old and revered tradition than a simple archaism.

A similar return to things Moche may be involved in the continued use of extended burials at Túcume, instead of the more 'modern' flexed burials. In sites such as the nearby Batán Grande, or Chan Chan in the Moche Valley, the later Middle Horizon (c. AD 850 to 1100) saw an ideological change inspired largely by external influences and expressed in part as a shift from extended to flexed burials and a predominant use of blackware pottery as burial offerings. In Túcume, this change is not so clear – extended burials continue. However, I should note that we do not have any evidence for a Middle Horizon occupation at Túcume, and Shimada reports that extended burials do return to Batán Grande in the periods succeeding the Middle Horizon.[4] We may be witnessing a generalized return to pre-Middle Horizon, local traditions.

Prior to our project at Túcume, few modeled mud friezes were known from Lambayeque – the most important examples are those found by Christopher Donnan at Huaca Gloria in the Chotuna complex. The Chotuna friezes are clearly a copy of those found in the Moche Valley at Huaca Dragón; the Chotuna version lacks a proper style and it is obvious that the artists had no clear idea of what they were representing.[5] This situation contrasts markedly with the mastery of execution of the Huaca Las Balsas friezes, where the artists show a fully developed conception of their subject matter.

Donnan argues that the Chotuna friezes end the relief tradition in Lambayeque, and that no further development takes places in the region. He suggests that Lambayeque lacked a local relief tradition and tried to import one from the Moche Valley (witness the Chotuna friezes), without great success.[6] Our discoveries at Túcume provide evidence that this is not so: the Huaca Las Balsas friezes and the Chimú-period frieze on Huaca 1 (see Chapter 4) demonstrate the continuation of a long, local tradition of mud reliefs. This tradition coexisted with a Lambayeque mural painting tradition known from sites such as Ucupe[7] and Huaca Pintada of Illimo,[8] and continued with the vibrant bird paintings in the Temple of the Mythical Bird on Huaca Larga at Túcume (see Chapter 4).[9]

Daniel H. Sandweiss

Life in Ancient Túcume

Sector V

THE INITIAL PLAN for field work at Túcume called for simultaneous excavations in two areas of the site: at one of the pyramids in the Monumental Sector; and at some part of the supposed residential area. The head Peruvian archaeologist (first Hugo Navarro and then Alfredo Narváez) was placed in charge of the Monumental Sector, while the residential area became my responsibility.

After walking over the non-monumental parts of the site with Walter Alva, we chose an area to the south of the Monumental Sector and to the west of La Raya Mountain. This area, which we call Sector V (see *ill. 33*), combines most of the features found in the non-monumental areas of Túcume: a large, rectangular compound; several small, amorphous mounds (including the West Mound); a heavily looted, low mound (the Funerary Platform); and flat, intermediate areas with evidence of midden or midden fill in exposed looters' pits. Two large *quebradas* (gullies or ravines) originating on the bedrock face of La Raya Mountain flank the north and south sides of the area, while the east end abuts the mountain and the west end terminates where the *quebradas* meet just beyond the Funerary Platform. *Quebradas* had marked major divisions in the earlier site of Pampa Grande,[1] upvalley from Túcume; if the same were true here, it would lend greater coherence to the area chosen for study.

Work in this sector was designed to contrast the residents housed there and the activities they carried out with those of the monumental precinct, where my Peruvian colleagues have been working. I expected to find an area of craft specialists and other support personnel for the site's elites, comparable to what John Topic[2] identified in the lower-class sectors of Chan Chan, the Chimú capital in the Moche Valley. Evidence for shell-bead manufacture in the Rectangular Compound and metallurgical (and possibly ceramic) production just south of Sector V supported this expectation, but the West Mound proved surprising.

During the 1989 season, work concentrated on the Rectangular Compound, although we also dug in the Intermediate Area between the Compound and the West Mound and began work on the West Mound itself. During this first season, I was assisted by a number of Peruvian archaeologists and archaeology students as well as our local crew. In 1990 and 1991, excavations in Sector V focused on the West Mound, with smaller units opened across the southern *quebrada* in 1990 and in the Funerary Platform in 1991. Peruvian archaeologist Diana Flores D. worked with me on the West Mound excavations in the 1990 and 1991 seasons, while Peruvian archaeologist César Cornelio Lecca joined us in 1991 to work on the Funerary Platform.

Excavations in the Rectangular Compound

The Rectangular Compound is a large, almost square enclosure measuring about 44 × 42 m (144 × 138 ft) (*ill. 116*). Surface inspection indicated that the Compound consisted of six large rooms of various sizes and proportions, labeled A to F.[3] Excavations showed that each of the large rooms was divided into a warren of smaller spaces and that other walls adjoined the outer perimeter of the Compound. In many of the rooms we cleared, wall fall or deliberate fill lay directly on the floor, leaving few clues as to the rooms' functions. However, in a few cases, significant remains were found *in situ* on the floors as evidence of the activities carried out there. Erosion was also a problem: two small *quebradas* cut the Compound from north to south, joining the large *quebrada* that defines the southern edge of Sector V.

Exterior and interior walls were made of loaf-shaped adobes set in mud mortar. Adobes in alternating courses were set at right angles, in a pattern known as runner and header. Small rocks set between adobes served as chinking. A curious feature of the adobes in the Rectangular Compound and elsewhere at Túcume is the use of different colors, ranging from grays and tans to oranges and greens. Each color may have come from a different workshop using a different source of clay and other material, and perhaps each color represented that workshop for accounting purposes, like the makers' marks found on other

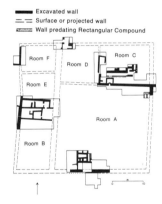

116 *Plan of the Rectangular Compound in Sector V, showing the excavation areas (inside solid black lines), excavated walls, and projected walls (often visible on the surface).*

adobes (see below). The use of colored adobes was not for decorative purposes, as the adobes were never meant to be seen – wherever preservation was good enough, we found that the walls were covered with a fine, gray, mud plaster.

In the Rectangular Compound, I identified three major phases of construction/occupation: RC-1 (Lambayeque Period?); RC-2 (Chimú and Inca Periods); and RC-3 (early Colonial Period). The Compound was built and used during RC-2, over some pre-existing RC-1 deposits. Although there is no evidence that the Compound was used after the Spanish conquest, people occasionally buried artifacts in the abandoned rooms during RC-3.

Except for the northeast corner of Room A, the Rectangular Compound was built directly on sterile soil or on fill laid down to level the uneven ground. The exterior walls and the major interior walls that divide the Compound into the six principal rooms were all put up during a single construction episode, showing that the Compound was a planned structure. In contrast, the subdivisions within the major rooms had generally been modified several times.

Room A is the largest room in the Rectangular Compound, measuring 28 × 30 m (92 × 98 ft). In the northeast corner, we found several levels and associated walls underlying the Compound (*Phase RC-1*). Immediately below the Compound walls was an ash level, probably fill used to level the surface for the later construction. Cut into the fill and partly below one of the Compound walls was a hearth which had been emptied and then refilled with two large potsherds and many unburned plant parts in an ashy matrix. Perhaps this deposit was an offering made just before construction began, to ensure the success of the building. One of the sherds is from a highly polished blackware bowl with stippling on the exterior. Dr Carol Mackey identified this piece in the field as a Late Chimú type. Under the ashy fill, we uncovered several walls from an earlier structure. On the north side of one wall was a thick deposit of camelid dung. This area was apparently a corral; bunches of plant remains were mixed with the excrement and presumably were part of the animals' fodder. Below the corral and associated walls, the irregular natural surface had been leveled with a fill of midden mixed with gravel.

In the opposite, southwest corner of Room A, we defined three phases of architecture associated with the Rectangular Compound; all are sub-phases of *Phase RC-2*. The lowest, earliest sub-phase included an eastern sector with at least seven sub-rectangular cells without entrances and one larger chamber, and a western sector consisting of one long room. Except where fill was needed to level an irregular ground surface, the structures of the earliest sub-phase rest directly on sterile soil. At this time, the larger chamber on the eastern side was connected to the western sector via a doorway. The sub-rectangular cells may have been storerooms, but they were clean except for the fill that covered them during the next phase. The western sector, however, had a series of floors and midden deposits that contained abundant evidence of shell-bead manufacture (*ill. 118*). Tools included several polishing stones, one made on an ammonite fossil. The entire shell reduction sequence was present – from whole shells, to cut shells, to perforated, square shell disks awaiting the final step of grinding into a circular shape, to finished beads (*ill. 117*). Among the whole shells were valves of the scallop *Argopecten purpuratus*, and many of the beads were made from a similar kind of shell. Another whole shell was the rayed clam *Chione subrugosa*, which today is found only in the warm waters from Tumbes north into Ecuador. Like the *Spondylus* shell commonly found at Túcume, the *Chione* valve demonstrates that Túcume participated in an exchange network which reached as far north as the Ecuadorian coast. A radiocarbon date from the earliest level of the Shell-Bead Workshop gave a date of 525 ± 70 BP (BGS-1619), AD 1406 to 1458, with a mean of AD 1434. This date suggests that the Rectangular Compound was built during the Chimú Period at Túcume; indeed, the Compound itself calls to mind the craft work-shops at Chan Chan, the Chimú capital, where sumptuary goods were also produced.[4]

During the occupation of Room A, the inhabitants had thrown rubbish over the south wall into the *quebrada*, including shell beads in the process of manufacture. While the deposits in the southwest part of Room A included many finished beads of stone and copper as well as shell, all 15 beads excavated in the *quebrada* behind Room A were made of shell and unfinished. Other unfinished beads appeared sporadically throughout Sector V, and another concentration occurred in the Intermediate Area between the Rectangular Compound and the West Mound.

On the side of the *quebrada* behind Room A, under the midden level with the unfinished beads, a wide, shallow pit had been excavated into sterile soil. The pit was lined with the remains of the same fine gray mud used for plaster throughout Sector V, and both human and dog foot-prints were impressed in the mud. The builders of the Rectangular Compound must have used this pit to mix plaster for the walls. We found a similar pit at the base of the excavation in the Intermediate Area.

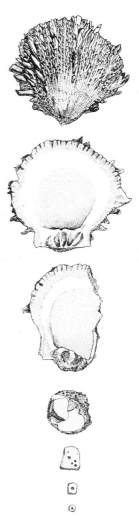

117 The sequence of manufacture of a shell bead, based on finds in Room A of the Rectangular Compound, Sector V.

Although we excavated large areas in Rooms B and C and uncovered extensive subdivisions with several stages of remodeling (see *ill. 116*), few of these rooms had primary midden and thus did not offer many clues as to their function. A few pieces of Chimú–Inca pottery indicate that the Compound continued in use through the Inca Period at Túcume.

Similarly, our research provided little information on patterns of movement between the major rooms of the Compound. No doorways were visible on the surface. Excavations revealed only one, a sunken passageway between Rooms C and A that was later covered over and converted into a niche on the Room A side. However, we did find an entrance into the Compound in the northwest corner of Room D, a sunken passageway with niches on the northwest and southeast, a low platform along the east side, and a large boulder forming the corner of the southeast niche. At a later time, perhaps after the entire Compound had been abandoned, this entrance was covered over and a structure made of posts built in the same place.

Just outside the Compound on the north side, we cleared an apparent storage unit in Area G (see *ill. 116*). This small structure consisted of three rectangular chambers, two on the north side measuring about 0.6 × 0.8 m (2 × 2½ ft), and a larger one on the south measuring 1.0 × 1.2 m (3 × 4 ft). Between the large chamber and the two smaller ones low dividers about 50 cm (20 in) high give the smaller spaces the appearance of bins. All three chambers had a level of waterlaid sediment just above the floor, presumably from El Niño rainfall. After the rain, the storage unit had been filled with loose material.

The floor under the rainfall sediment was clean in the south and northwest chambers, but in the northeast bin we found some of the original contents on the floor: animal bones; four articulated fish vertebrae; shells; corn cobs; and an egg-shaped, smooth green stone similar in size and shape to one of the polishing stones in the Shell-Bead Workshop.

The interior of the bins was covered with the same fine gray plaster as the Compound and they are probably contemporary. The exterior was unplastered, showing that the whole storage unit had been cut into the surrounding deposits. The lowest of these deposits was fill, covered by a thick midden layer. At the base, the midden consisted of ground algarrobo (*Prosopis chilensis*) leaves, perhaps the remains from making algarrobo *chicha* (beer). Above that was a thick level of dense, mixed midden composed primarily of plant remains, especially stalks, inflorescences, and cobs of maize, but including other botanical ele-

ments. This level also contained camelid and other animal bones, yellow and green feathers, camelid dung, vegetal cordage, potsherds, and some pieces of metal. The upper levels of the midden consisted almost exclusively of animal dung. It may be that this area was the original trash dump for the Rectangular Compound, or perhaps for the people living in the area before the Compound was built.

We do not know exactly when the Rectangular Compound was abandoned, but it seems likely that it happened at the same time as the West Mound was filled in, at or near the end of the Inca Period at Túcume. After abandonment, the various rooms of the Compound were filled in either deliberately or through natural processes. Later, a variety of unusual objects was buried within the rooms of the Compound (*Phase RC-3*); the general outline of the rooms has remained visible right up to the present, and whoever buried these objects deliberately placed them within the abandoned structure. In each case, the objects were placed in pits that cut through the sediments overlying the Compound, and in some cases through the original walls. In Room B, we found a carefully formed, loaf-shaped block of diatomaceous earth (natural chalk). Pieces of this material were found with the burials of the weaving women on Huaca Larga as well as in some of the South Cemetery graves. Even today, local weavers use chalk when spinning thread. In Room C, we uncovered two pits. One contained a sooted, carinated-rim *olla* decorated with the reticulated paddle-stamped design. This small cooking pot was covered with an upside-down gourd bowl and accompanied by seven pairs of identical, upside-down gourd bowls. The second pit in Room C contained two large tassels made of red, yellow, and dark wool yarn with cotton cores; originally the two tassels were connected by a cotton rope. Under the tassels was a wooden object, 1.1 m (3½ ft) long, with a short, squared-off handle and a long, rectangular blade. Although a large

118 (above left) Polishing/grinding tools and raw material from the Shell-Bead Workshop. Top: flat, rectangular polishing stone. Bottom, left to right: ammonite fossil with extensive wear; uncut scallop (Argopecten) shell; cut fragment of false abalone (Concholepas) shell; uncut rayed clam (Chione) shell from tropical waters.

119 (above right) A wooden object, probably a steering board for a small raft, found in the Rectangular Compound, Sector V.

crack runs halfway up the blade from the base, the object is complete. The end of the blade shows no sign of wear, so it is unlikely to be a digging implement. As Thor pointed out when he saw the object, it bears a strong resemblance to the steering boards used on balsa rafts through the early part of this century (*ill. 119*).[5]

Excavations in the Intermediate Areas

When we began work in Sector V, looters had recently dug a few pits in the area between the Rectangular Compound and the West Mound. We cleaned and expanded these pits, establishing the following sequence. At the base was a large depression with tool marks, probably used to mix mortar or plaster for either the Rectangular Compound or the West Mound. Above the depression were several levels of primary midden, similar to that found on the north side of the Compound. A use-floor with many postholes lay on top of the midden; apparently, a building of perishable material was built over this trash dump. An ashy fill lay over the use-floor, capped by two superimposed, more formally constructed clay floors associated with

120 The empty tomb chamber, beginning of Phase WM-1 of the West Mound, Sector V, after excavation (1991). Note the three raised niches on either side of the central chamber (two on the east side were only partially excavated). The hole in the floor was presumably made by the people who emptied the tomb, ensuring, no doubt, that there was nothing underneath.

several walls of adobes and cobbles set in mud mortar. The increasing formality of the architecture through time parallels what happened in the West Mound prior to the Inca arrival (see below).

Excavations in the West Mound

The West Mound is a low, amorphous mound similar to many others found in the west and southwest sectors of Túcume. Extended excavation, however, revealed a sequence of complex, finely plastered structures which had been deliberately buried. The building sequence can be divided into two major phases: Phase WM-1 (early); and Phase WM-2 (late). Each has a series of sub-phases.

Phase WM-1

The earliest construction in the West Mound was a sunken chamber cut into the sterile deposits underlying the site. The central chamber is aligned roughly north–south and measures 1 × 2.75 m (3 × 9 ft). On either side of the central chamber is a row of three raised niches, each measuring just under a square meter (*ill. 120*). When excavated, this structure was empty except for fill from later construction and the sherds from several large storage jars called *porrones*. However, the form – a sunken chamber with raised niches on either side – is that of the elite tombs of the Lambayeque burial tradition going back at least to Sipán,[6] and I am certain that this was a high status tomb. Most of the lower status extended burials excavated in Túcume have the same north–south orientation as the sunken chamber, and flexed burials tend to be seated with the legs crossed, looking north (see Chapter 7).

Beyond the form, however, there is a significant divergence from the local tradition: the West Mound tomb was not buried. Rather, it was kept open, or possibly covered with a removable roof. An inclined ramp on the west side of the tomb provided access to the top of the chamber. When first built (*ill. 121*), a structure made of posts was located to the north of the tomb. The entire area may have been enclosed by a low wall; we found such a wall in a test pit several meters north of the main excavation. Through time, the structures associated with the tomb became increasingly complex, with the addition of platforms, ramps, and massive adobe walls (*ill. 122*). The accumulation of primary midden throughout the Phase WM-1 occupation suggests that people were living within the enclosing building. However, although the food remains in the midden indicate domestic activities, the presence of a copper *tumi* (ceremonial knife) suggests that rituals were also performed here.

121 Isometric reconstruction of the initial Phase WM-1 (late Lambayeque or early Chimú Period) structure in the West Mound, Sector V, showing the tomb – which would have been occupied and probably covered with a removable roof – associated structure, and entrance ramp. An earlier excavation to the north uncovered a segment of the wall here shown as enclosing the tomb precinct.

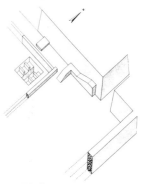

122 Isometric reconstruction of the terminal Phase WM-1 (Chimú Period) structure in the West Mound, Sector V, at which time the tomb would still have been occupied and probably covered. The enclosed area around the tomb is larger and more monumental than at the start of the phase (ill. 121), extending into unexcavated areas to the west and south.

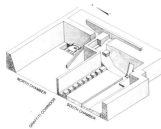

123 Isometric reconstruction of the initial Phase WM-2 (Inca Period) structure in the West Mound, Sector V, showing the complex entrance path via passages and ramps. (Note that the perspective has shifted 90 degrees from ills 121 and 122.)

124 The north face of the Graffiti Corridor (east-west), Phase WM-2 (Inca Period). The lower drawing shows the entire exposed wall, which took the form of crenelated benches later joined together. The upper drawing shows the panels with graffiti, perhaps scribbled by people waiting in the corridor.

Phase WM-2

After years of steadily accumulating midden and gradually increasing architectural complexity, something happened. The contents of the tomb were removed, the associated structures were leveled to a certain height and covered with fill (except the largest adobe wall, on the north side, which was reused), and an entirely new structure with a different design and, presumably, a new function was built over the now-buried tomb (ill. 123). The new, Phase WM-2 building consists of two large, rectangular rooms. The North Chamber measures 13 × 21 m (43 × 69 ft) and seems to have been the inner sanctum. Access to this room was gained by a series of sunken passages and zigzag ramps. The visitor entered the West Mound at the southwest corner and passed through a narrow channel about 30 cm (12 in) lower than the floor of the South Chamber. This room has the same orientation and approximately the same dimensions as the North Chamber, though separated from it by a high wall. A narrow passageway called the Graffiti Corridor ran between the wall and a long, low bench in the South Chamber (ills 123–124), which originally consisted of isolated, solid, square boxes like sawed-off columns, separated from each other by crenelations. At this time, graffiti was incised on panels on the corridor side of the bench. Most of the carvings are simple cross-hatched lines, with no apparent order or meaning. Among the few representational signs are a helmet with crescent headdress on Panel 5 and a design on Panel 3 which looks inexplicably like a Chavín mouth band.[7] Thinking about the contexts in which much graffiti is scrawled today, I suspect that the West Mound incisions were carved by bored people forced to spend a long time in the Graffiti Corridor, perhaps guards controlling access to the North Chamber, or bureaucrats receiving tribute.

After the graffiti were drawn, the isolated boxes were joined together into a continuous bench by filling in the crenelations; some

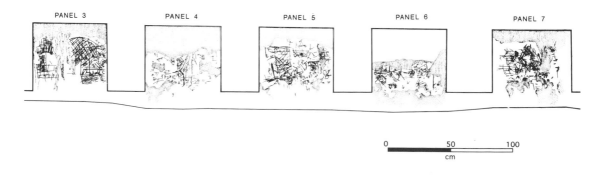

time later, a heavy rain damaged the bench and the resulting erosion was repaired. The rain must represent an El Niño event, and it may have happened fairly early in Phase WM-2: we found raindrop marks on the original floor of the North Chamber, water tracks on the north wall of the North Chamber down to the first WM-2 floor, and a series of footprints made in wet mud at the top of the ramp leading into the North Chamber. Several later floors were built after the rains.

Once a visitor had passed along the Graffiti Corridor, he or she went up three successively smaller ramps, each at right angles to the other; crossed back and forth on top of the east wall; and descended a straight ramp into the North Chamber (ill. 125). This complex entry system shows a deep concern for controlling access to the chamber. Inside this room, the first construction sub-phase included a clay architectural model built against the east wall (ill. 129) representing a two-level, trapezoidal, stepped platform with a ramp on the south side. The top had been damaged by later construction, but we could see that a series of rooms had originally stood on the upper platform. Although I studied the plans of the existing platforms at Túcume with care, none showed more than generic similarity to the West Mound prototype. Only later did I find a building which could have been a copy of or from the model: the Inca administrative structure at La Centinela, in the Chincha valley nearly 1000 km (620 miles) to the south.[8]

A 12–15 year old woman[9] was buried next to the architectural model (ill. 126), presumably a sacrifice. The body was extended, lying face up

126 Detail of the skeleton of a 12–15-year-old woman buried next to the clay architectural model. Note the small circular wooden beads, many of which are still aligned in their original position, thus preserving the form of the necklace. The jaw was broken when the body was forced into the narrow pit between pre-existing walls.

■ Black

□ White

▨ Red

▨ Orange

▨ Natural

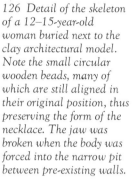

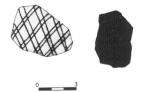

0   3
cm

127 Typical potsherds with painted decoration from Phase WM-2 (Inca Period) primary midden in the West Mound, Sector V.

with the head to the east. The orientation and size of the burial pit were constrained by underlying walls of the Phase WM-1 building, which probably accounts for the unusual east–west alignment. The pit was slightly too small for the body, so it had to be jammed in, breaking the jaw in the process. Although without pottery, the young woman had been wrapped in a fine, decorated cloth and was accompanied by several wooden spindles, a comb or carder, and over 1200 small, disk-like wooden beads which had originally formed a necklace draped in four loops around her neck. Wooden beads are quite rare at Túcume, where shell beads predominate – as they do at most Peruvian sites.

After the sacrificial woman was buried, the North Chamber underwent several slight modifications, culminating in the construction of a new floor over the entire room. The architectural model was damaged by this floor, which covered it. An enigmatic clay object resembling some kind of altar was built in the middle of this last floor. Throughout Phase WM-2, primary midden accumulated in the North Chamber, indicating that people were living there, or at least carrying out a variety of activities that left food remains as well as artifacts (e.g., ills 127, 141, 142 c).

Soon after the 'altar' was built, the entire Phase WM-2 building was deliberately buried. The fill included broken pieces of the building and abundant secondary midden (ills 128, 130, 141 top left and right, 142 a, b); it was contained by the Phase WM-2 walls and by new, unplastered adobe retaining walls built for this purpose using marked adobes. We found no evidence for any later structures built on top of the fill. The largest retaining wall cut the North and South Chambers in half; the outer, west face of this wall was inclined and plastered, giving the buried mound a monumental aspect and suggesting that whatever the reason for burying it, the West Mound continued to be an important place.

There are three radiocarbon dates from the West Mound. A sample of wood dating the start of Phase WM-1 gave an uncalibrated date of 770 ± 95 BP (BGS-1620) calibrated to AD 1227 to 1382, with a mean of AD 1286. This date suggests that construction began either just before or just after the Chimú conquest of Lambayeque around AD 1350. Charcoal samples from close to the end of WM-1 and from the start of Phase WM-2 are largely overlapping: AD 1398 to 1444, with a mean of AD 1421 (BGS-1616, uncalibrated 560 ± 70 BP), and AD 1312–1435 with a mean of AD 1406 (BGS-1617, 595 ± 70 BP), respectively. These dates would place the WM-1 to WM-2 transition just prior to the Inca conquest of Lambayeque, according to the standard chronology for Inca expansion. Other evidence leads me to suspect that these dates are slightly too old[10] and that the WM-1 to WM-2 transition marks the arrival of the Incas at Túcume.

The contents of the midden and the fill provide additional chronological information, as does the architecture. None of the ceramics associated with the Phase WM-1 structure – the empty tomb – show any Inca influence. However, based on our findings elsewhere at Túcume and work in other parts of the region,[11] the diagnostic pottery could have been manufactured any time from the later Late Intermediate Period through the Late Horizon (c. AD 1100 to 1532).

128 A bird carved from bone, from the fill covering the Phase WM-2 structure, West Mound, Sector V. At the base is a circular break, probably indicating that the bird was the head of a tupu (cloak pin).

129 Clay architectural model built on the earliest floor of the Phase WM-2 building in the West Mound, Sector V. This model represents a trapezoidal, two- or more tiered stepped platform with access ramp.

130 Dan Sandweiss examining a net excavated in the West Mound fill, Sector V, 1990.

Some sherds from the fill placed on top of the Phase WM-1 structure to form the base of the Phase WM-2 structure show possible Inca influence, though most of the decorated pottery from the primary deposits found inside the Phase WM-2 building are part of the local, Lambayeque tradition that lasted for at least 450 years (*ill. 127*). Other objects found in the Phase WM-2 primary midden and in the final fill also have motifs in the local style, such as the anthropomorphic wave (*ill. 142*). The trapezoidal form of the architectural model in the Phase WM-2 building is a typical Inca form most often seen in doors, niches, and windows but also occasionally used as the ground plan for buildings and plazas. Examples include the Inca administrative center in Chincha, mentioned above, and the plaza at Tomebamba, the principal Inca site in Ecuador.[12] The fill which covered the Phase WM-2 structure contained a few sherds of clear Inca influence but no Colonial materials.

With these data in mind, it seems likely that the Phase WM-1 structures were built in the later Late Intermediate Period, prior to the Inca conquest of Túcume, and the Phase WM-2 building was constructed after it. The accretional growth of the structures surrounding the tomb indicates continuity throughout Phase WM-1, while the removal of the tomb's contents, the other destruction, and the entirely new plan of the Phase WM-2 building suggest an abrupt change to Phase WM-2. Thus, Phase WM-1 must date to the Chimú occupation of the site during the 120 years preceding the Inca conquest. As I will discuss in detail later, the form of the Phase WM-1 tomb and associated structures presents a striking similarity to the burial platforms of the highest ranking Chimú elite at Chan Chan. Following Shimada's Lambayeque chronology,[13] a Chimú date would place Phase WM-1 between *c.* AD 1350 and 1460/1470. Phase WM-2 would date from AD 1460/1470 to 1532.

The Empty Tomb and its meaning
William H. Isbell has recently argued that mortuary structures can reflect the presence or absence of *ayllu* organization in Andean sites. The *ayllu* was the basic unit of Andean social organization at the time of the Spanish conquest, and continues to exist in many parts of the Andes. Because the ancient *ayllu* focused on the worship of founding ancestors' mummies, the associated mortuary structures should be 'open sepulchers where the bodies could be stored, viewed, visited, and venerated.'[14] By searching the archaeological record for open tombs, Isbell suggests that we can both pinpoint the origin and plot

the spread of *ayllu* organization. Recognizing *ayllu* organization offers potential insight into social structure and the organization of power in the prehispanic Andes.

The burial tradition of the Lambayeque region of the Peruvian north coast can be viewed in terms of Isbell's hypothesis. Thanks to the spectacular archaeology carried out over the last decade by Walter Alva at Sipán,[15] Izumi Shimada at Batán Grande,[16] and Christopher Donnan and Luis Jaime Castillo at San José de Moro,[17] we now know more about the elite burial tradition of this region than any other part of the Andes. The deep tombs at these sites offer several features relevant to this discussion. First, as Isbell points out,[18] such tombs are the antithesis of open, accessible mortuary monuments – the bodies were buried under meters of fill. Second, the chronology of the buried elite tombs is significant: Sipán and San José de Moro are Moche tombs dating to the Early Intermediate Period, while the Batán Grande tombs are Middle Sicán, which Shimada dates to the early part of the Late Intermediate Period.[19] For the succeeding later Late Intermediate Period and Late Horizon, no high-status, buried tombs have been excavated in Lambayeque.

Major changes occurred between the early and late Late Intermediate Periods in the Lambayeque region. Shimada has recently detailed these changes, which affected iconography, settlement pattern, and other aspects of material culture, and which presumably reflect changes in ideology.[20] The pyramids in the Sicán Precinct at Batán Grande were burned and abandoned at the same time that construction of the monumental pyramid complex at Túcume apparently began. During the next four and a half centuries, the Lambayeque region saw successive waves of foreign conquest by Chimú, Inca, and Spanish invaders.

Given the size and complexity of Túcume, it was clearly a major regional center during these final prehispanic periods. Túcume is thus a logical locale to follow the Lambayeque burial tradition up to the Spanish conquest, and our recent excavations at the site do, indeed, shed light on this problem.

Excavations by the Túcume Project have uncovered over 100 burials dating mainly to the Late Horizon Inca occupation of the site (see also chapters 4, 7). A few early Colonial interments have been found, and some burials date to the earlier Chimú and Lambayeque occupations. Although some status distinctions between individuals are clear, based on grave goods and elaboration of the burial chamber, none could be characterized as 'maximum elite'. Unlike at nearby Batán Grande, there is no modern tradition at Túcume of looting rich graves. Where have all the elite burials gone?

The empty tomb offers an answer: the Inca removed them. The chronology is right, and Inca policy certainly included taking ancestral mummies of conquered peoples to Cuzco. An open tomb is an open invitation to loot, if the looter is not part of the mummy's *ayllu*. Those elite, late burials left in Lambayeque by the Inca no doubt disappeared quickly in the early Colonial Period.

The Chan Chan connection

The open tomb at the West Mound is an anomalous structure in the Lambayeque burial tradition. High-status burials of preceding periods are deeply buried, with no post-interment access to the body of the deceased. Contemporary lower-status burials at Túcume and other Lambayeque sites are also underground interments. If the Phase WM-1 structures in the West Mound date to the period when the Chimú controlled Túcume, then we should look first to the Chimú for the source of the new, open tomb pattern. At Chan Chan, the Chimú capital, the most elaborate funerary structures are the nine burial platforms identified by Conrad as the final resting places of the Chimú kings.[21] Conrad describes the Chan Chan structures as:

truncated pyramid mounds containing multiple prepared cells entered from above. Access to the top of the platform, and thence to the cells, is via a ramp or system of ramps along one face of the mound(s). Adjacent to this face is a forecourt that controls entrance to the ramp system. Both the platforms and their forecourts are surrounded by an enclosure wall . . .[22]

Platforms are oriented north–south, as is the main axis of the principal cell; cells are described as 'rectilinear chambers'.[23]

The open tomb at Túcume has many similarities to a Chan Chan burial platform, albeit on a much reduced scale: access to the cell is via a ramp and from above; the chamber is rectilinear and oriented north–south; and there is an enclosed space on the north side of the chamber. At least in a later sub-phase of Phase WM-1 this space was entered from a doorway in the massive north wall. I would argue that Chan Chan and the Chimú are the proximal source for the intrusive ideology embodied in the West Mound open tomb.

The ideology of open tombs and ancestor worship on the north coast

If the open tomb is a Chimú burial pattern, then we must turn to the Moche Valley to understand what was happening at Túcume. Despite differences of opinion on specific interpretations of the Chan Chan burial platforms, current ethnohistorical and archaeological research[24] would support the hypothesis that ancestor worship involving the bodies of the deceased was practiced at Chan Chan for the maximum elite. Although it is not clear whether or not there was direct access to the mummies of high ranking lords interred in the burial platforms, there is no question that these lords maintained high status and visibility after death.[25]

Unlike the elite tombs, lower-status burials in the Chimú heartland are underground interments,[26] as in the Lambayeque region. In contrast, many lower-status, late prehispanic burials in the Cuzco area are in caves, niches, or *chullpas*.[27] Following Isbell, this difference may represent differential acceptance of the ideology of *ayllu* organization in the two areas, perhaps as a function of time, perhaps as a function of elite self-interest. What we certainly see on the north coast of Peru is a new ideology which arrived sometime after AD 1100. This ideology would have provided a potent means of legitimizing rank and privilege and would have had a strong appeal for local elites seeking to increase their power, or for Chimú invaders wishing to control the local lords. Towards the end of the prehispanic period, the invading Inca found this familiar system in place and useful in justifying their own claims to rule.[28] Apparently, they removed the West Mound mummy, and no doubt many others. The empty tomb of Túcume is thus mute testimony both to the mummy's role in Late Lambayeque and to Inca strategies of provincial control.

Excavations in the Funerary Platform

To the west of the West Mound lies a low, looted elevation dubbed the 'Funerary Platform'. Our excavations here revealed that this mound had started out as an adobe structure with fairly massive walls and well-made floors. After two phases of construction (FP-1, FP-2), the building was completely filled in and then used as a cemetery (Phase FP-3). As with many other low mounds in the southwest part of Túcume, looters had been at the Funerary Platform long before we arrived: Schaedel's 1951 map and early airphotos show the Platform pock-marked with pits. On excavation, we found several partially looted burials and a variety of grave goods missed or ignored by the looters.

In one case (PF16), only the lower legs and feet were left, the rest of the body having been removed by the looters. The remaining parts

131 *A broken blackware stirrup-spout vessel representing a reed boat with two crew members facing each other across a mat, from a partially looted burial (PF16) in the Funerary Platform, Sector V.*

132 *A broken blackware stirrup-spout vessel representing a drummer beating a drum, from the same burial as ill. 131. Note the holes in the side of the pot which were made prior to burial, perhaps to 'kill' the pot ritually. (Front and side views.)*

showed that the body, wrapped in a shroud and laid on a reed mat, had been extended with the feet to the west and the head (presumably) to the east. Fortunately, some of the grave goods had been buried at the feet of the skeleton and so were overlooked by the looters. Three clay vessels lay in a row; the largest, to the south, was a redware, sooted cooking *olla* with a reticulated paddle-stamped design. This pot was covered with an inverted gourd bowl. North of the *olla* was a black-ware bottle modeled in the shape of a reed boat with two crewmen seated and facing each other across a mat (*ill. 131*). The third vessel was a blackware, stirrup-spout bottle in the shape of a seated person wearing a cowl and striking a round drum with a short stick (*ill. 132*). Museums in Peru and elsewhere have versions of both the blackware vessels.

All three pots had small holes broken in the side; in each case, the holes faced downward when we uncovered the vessels and so were made before burial. Perhaps the pots were ritually 'killed' to accompany the deceased person in the afterlife.

A second looted burial (PF2) consisted of an individual placed in a circular pit about 1 m (3 ft) in diameter and lined with loaf-shaped adobes; although most of the skeleton was present, only the left leg and lower right leg were undisturbed. The individual had been buried sitting cross-legged and looking north, a common burial position for later interments in the South Cemetery (see Chapter 7). Various offerings were placed around the body: a broken blackware stirrup-spout bottle with a wave design molded around the shoulder (*ill. 133*); a bone needle; a perforated ceramic disk; a possible stone polishing tool; two articulated *Spondylus* shells; a piece of a copper object; textile remains; a deteriorated gourd; and tassels of colored thread.

A frequent item in the looters' backdirt were the small fingerpots known as *crisoles*. *Crisoles* accompany late prehispanic burials in the Lambayeque region, often in great numbers. Alfredo found many in the South Cemetery, and he discusses their possible functions in Chapter 7. Most of the *crisoles* from the Funerary Platform in Sector V were unfired and crudely made of local soil with very coarse inclusions. Clearly, these specimens were expediently made as burial offerings; they could not have held liquid without crumbling.

Another, badly disturbed burial was accompanied by two black-ware, hook-rim plates, an indicator of Inca date in the Lambayeque Valley.[29] We found no Colonial objects in the Funerary Platform, so its use as a cemetery dates to the Inca Period at Túcume and perhaps earlier.

Daily life in Sector V

The excavations in Sector V give us a glimpse of daily life in ancient Túcume. Some of the primary midden (garbage found where it was originally deposited) has been analyzed by specialists to discover what people ate. Study of the artifacts tells us about other activities that the inhabitants carried out and about the objects they used. The activities in Sector V range from the mundane tasks associated with eating and living, through construction and productive operations, to ideologically charged actions in the inner sanctum of the West Mound.

133 A broken blackware stirrup-spout bottle with a wave motif, from partially looted burial (PF2) in the Funerary Platform, Sector V.

Food

To date, Elizabeth J. Reitz and Susan D. deFrance have studied several thousand vertebrate bones from the Shell-Bead Workshop in the Rectangular Compound and from Phases WM-1 and WM-2 in the West Mound;[30] María del Carmen Sandweiss has studied several thousand shells from the same contexts;[31] and Asunción Cano has analyzed over 40,000 plant parts from the Shell-Bead Workshop, from a habitation area to the south of the West Mound, and from Phase WM-2 in the West Mound.[32] Taken together, the results give a picture of diet at the site and also show some differences between structures.

Table 3 lists the edible plant and animal species identified from the midden. Animal protein came principally from camelids (llamas and/or alpacas), and secondarily from guinea pigs and small clams. Many camelid bones had cut marks from butchering, and bones of various species were charred, presumably from cooking. Other animals present in lesser quantities include both cartilaginous and bony fishes, crabs, several small lizards, a few birds, and dogs (which may not have been eaten in this part of the site, but bones with butchering marks came from other areas of Túcume). One deer bone was found, in the West Mound Phase WM-2 deposit. In each of the three areas studied, 'the remains of at least one juvenile, possible newborn, [camelid] individual (< 9 months old)' were found, as were remains of subadults; adults were the least common.[33] This age profile suggests to deFrance that the inhabitants of Túcume were raising camelids, not merely bringing them in either as adult animals or as butchered meat. She also found that the camelid body parts from the midden had more head and feet parts than would be the case if the bones were brought in as *charqui* (dried meat). Our discovery of a camelid corral under Room A of the Rectangular Compound supports the idea that camelids were herded and perhaps bred at Túcume.[34]

ANIMALS			PLANTS	
R = *Rare*; A = *Abundant*			R = *Rare*; A = *Abundant*	
Common name	**Scientific name**		**Common name**	**Scientific name**
Mammals	**Mammalia**		Cherimoya[R]	*Annona cherimolia*
including				
Camelids (llama or alpaca)[A]	Camelidae		Guanabana[A]	*Annona muricata*
Guinea pig	*Cavia porcellus*		Avocado	*Persea americana*
Dog	*Canis familiaris*			
White-tailed deer[R]	*Odocoileus virginianus*		Pacay	*Inga feuillei*
Cartilaginous fish	**Chondrichthyes**		Palillo[R]	*Campomanesia sp.*
including				
Sharks	Cacharhiniformes		Guayaba[R]	*Psidium guajava*
Rays, skates	Rajiformes			
Bony fish	**Osteichthyes**		Lucuma	*Pouteria lucuma*
including				
Shad, herring	Clupeidae		Squashes	*Cucurbita maxima, C. moschata*
Anchovies	Engraulidae			
Peruvian rock bass[R]	*Paralabrax humeralis*		Gourd	*Lagenaria siceraria*
Drums	Sciaenidae, incl. *Cynoscion analis* and *Paralonchurus peruanus*		Peanut[R]	*Arachis hypogaea*
Flounders[R]	Bothidae		Algarrobo[A]	*Prosopis sp.*
Unidentified birds[R]	**Aves**		Maize[A]	*Zea mays*
Lizards[R]	**Reptilia**			
Crabs	**Crustacea**		Algae[R]	*Gigartina chamissoi*
Mollusks[A]	**Mollusca**			
	almost exclusively the small surf clam *Donax obesulus*		Coca[R]	*Erythroxylum sp.*

Table 3 Food remains from Sector V.

Among the edible plants identified in the midden, the most common were the *guanabana* or soursop fruit, maize, and algarrobo (a carob-like tree legume). Maize and probably algarrobo would have been used to make a fermented beverage known as *chicha*. Avocados were fairly common, and various other fruits were eaten in moderate or small amounts. Strangely, we found only one peanut shell among the tens of thousands of analyzed specimens. Peanuts are abundant at other coastal sites of similar age in other valleys,[35] but extremely scarce to absent at Lambayeque sites of any age. Even today, peanuts are rarely grown in the region – perhaps environmental conditions are not favorable for peanuts and they had to be imported from elsewhere. At the earlier site of Sipán (see Chapter 3), peanuts were considered important enough to replicate in gold and silver, perhaps because of their rarity.[36]

Although similar in general outline, there are some interesting differences in the distribution of plant and animal remains between the Shell-Bead Workshop and the West Mound indicative of the status of the inhabitants. The Workshop would have been staffed by artisans, presumably of lower class than the nobles thought to reside in the West Mound. The only deer bone and the few coca remains came exclusively from the West Mound. At the Inca Period fishing site of Lo Demás, in the Chincha Valley far to the south of Túcume, the only deer bone and coca remains also came from the elite sector of the site.[37] Differential access to important resources is the basic definition of social stratification in complex societies;[38] Túcume and Lo Demás offer clear archaeological examples of this principle.

Pottery

The inhabitants of Túcume used a variety of pottery forms for their daily needs (*ill. 134*). The utilitarian pottery described below characterizes the site as a whole, although the specific descriptions are based on the work in Sector V. The inventory of utilitarian vessels is quite similar to that found by Donnan[39] in his Middle and Late Phases at Chotuna and Chornancap, about 25 km (15½ miles) southwest of Túcume; phases which date between AD 1100 and 1600, contemporaneous with Túcume.

Food was served and eaten from shallow bowls or plates of various forms. Most common were crude, mold-made bowls of undecorated brownware with ring bases made from a circular fillet of clay (*ill. 134 a*). In contrast, more finely made, often highly polished blackware bowls are a regular if less common constituent of the deposits (*ill. 134 b, c, d*). These bowls are often decorated with geometric, anthropomorphic, or zoomorphic figures molded on their sides. A common motif is a diamond pattern with variable numbers of dots inside the diamonds (*ill. 134 c*). Frances Hayashida has found a mold for such a pattern at an Inca Period pottery workshop in nearby Batán Grande, which suggests that this pattern may be an indicator of Inca date. Another, firmer indicator of Inca date in the Lambayeque Valley is a bowl form known as the 'hook-rim plate' (*ill. 134 d*);[40] we found several of these plates in the Funerary Platform (see above), and they are found elsewhere in Sector V and throughout Túcume.

The basic cooking vessel was the carinated-rim *olla* (*ill. 134 e, f*), while a slightly less common type was the collared *olla* (*ill. 134 g*). These vessels have the rounded bottoms and slightly constricted necks which are useful features for cooking pots: the first inhibits 'thermal damage and . . . the rounded contours permit greater exposure of the vessel base, walls, and contents to the heat . . . [while] a slight orifice or a low neck helps prevent boiling over and reduces evaporation'.[41] Sherds from carinated-rim and collared-rim *ollas* at Túcume are often sooted on the exterior, confirming their use in cooking.

The Túcume cooking vessels are very frequently decorated with

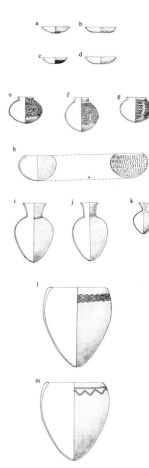

134 Utilitarian pottery forms from Túcume: a–d plates/bowls (c and d are hook-rim plates); e–f carinated-rim cooking ollas with paddle-stamping; g collared-rim cooking olla; h grater; i–k tall-necked jars; l–m porrones with incised decoration (large storage and chicha jars).

paddle-stamped (*paleteada*) designs made by striking the wet clay with a wooden or fired clay paddle carved with a design (*ills 135–136*). Because it is difficult for the stamper to line up each blow of the paddle exactly with the previous one, the overlap between different blows is often visible, demonstrating the size of the design area on the paddle. Paddle-stamping began around AD 700 to 750 in the Lambayeque-Piura area[42] and by the Late Intermediate Period was extremely common on the whole north coast. Paddle-stamped pottery is still made in the region today, and many of the same geometric designs are used.[43]

The paddle-stamped motifs on the cooking vessels are usually geometric and repetitive; most common is simple cross-hatching (reticulation) but we found a great variety of other designs as well. Sometimes a paddle has a single geometric design rather than a repeated pattern (*ill. 136 a–e, g*). Such single designs usually include concentric circles or boxes, often with pendant triangles. Round dots sometimes run between the concentric circles. Like the representational stamps discussed below, the single-stamp geometric motifs are more frequent on La Raya Mountain than in Sector V. Occasionally, a single representational motif such as a double-spout-and-bridge pot or anthropomorphic figure occurs instead of the usual single or repetitive geometric pattern (*ill. 136 f, h, i, j, k*). These designs do not appear on sherds which clearly came from cooking jars; they occur more frequently on La Raya Mountain than in Sector V, so they are discussed further in Chapter 8.

An unusual vessel form at Túcume is that known as the grater (*ill. 134 h*), consisting of a neckless *olla* with rows of deep incisions lining the interior (*ill. 137*). One or both edges of the incisions has a ridge of clay, and a soft object (such as an ear of corn) dragged along them would, in effect, be grated. Unfortunately, we have no direct evidence for the use of these vessels, which are found throughout the region.

Rarer than other utilitarian forms were sherds from a variety of tall-necked jars (*ill. 134 i, j, k*). Such vessels are well-suited for storing liquids and other pourable substances such as grains.[44] The tall neck helps prevent spillage during transport, can serve as a spout for pouring, and is easy to cover.

The final common utilitarian vessel form at Túcume is a large jar known locally as a *porrón* (*ill. 134 l, m*). *Porrones* have thick walls, a thickened, comma-shaped rim, and no neck. Paddle-stamping is rare on *porrones*; when present, decoration usually consists of incised lines around the upper part of the vessel, often with a zigzag or wavy design.

135 Paddle-stamped (paleteada) potsherds from Sector V and the East Spur of La Raya Mountain. These designs are typical of the repetitive geometric motifs of Túcume paddle-stamping. The simple cross-hatching is the most common design at Túcume as at other north coast sites.

Stamped circles made with a cut cane or similar hollow element also occur around the upper vessel, sometimes in combination with incised lines. Although it would be difficult to tie a cloth lid on to a *porrón*, a flat lid could be placed on top as Bankes shows with recent examples;[45] however, we did not find any lids in the excavations. Different sizes and shapes of *porrones* are used today principally in the manufacture of *chicha*,[46] and this was probably one of their functions in prehispanic Túcume. We found many *porrón* sherds with a thick layer of darkened organic matter adhering to the interior, which can occur when a vessel is used repeatedly to produce *chicha*.

In addition to the utilitarian pottery, Sector V yielded sherds from decorated and undecorated finewares, both blackwares and redwares. These fine vessels are part of the same pottery tradition present in the monumental sectors and major cemeteries of the site, but with few exceptions – from the Funerary Platform (see above) – we found only broken sherds and a reduced overall design inventory.

The redwares from Sector V are usually covered with a polished red slip and sometimes contain mica which sparkles in the light. Decoration on redwares includes both modeling and painting. Common modeled figures include animal and human heads or faces and animal appliqués such as frogs. The most frequent painted designs are geometric motifs in fine or thick black lines (see *ill. 127*); although often applied directly on the red slip, the fine lines are sometimes painted on zones of cream-colored slip over the red base. A common motif is a curling wave-like form. This pottery looks very much like the Late Sicán pottery from Batán Grande, which Shimada dates between AD 1100 and 1350.[47] In Sector V, as elsewhere at Túcume, this pottery continues to appear in levels as recent as the Inca Period (*c.* AD 1460/70–1532), such as the Phase WM-2 levels in the West Mound.

Decoration on blackware vessels includes modeling and press-molding. Modeled figures are similar to those on the redware pottery. Common press-molded motifs include the diamond-and-dot pattern, stippling (called the goose-flesh design in Peru), geometric figures such as the step-and-wave, and occasional animal (especially bird and monkey) and human front-face figures.

Construction

The construction material of preference at Túcume was adobe, or sun-dried mud brick. Stone was used only on La Raya Mountain (see Chapter 8) and in the Inca buildings on Huaca Larga (see Chapter 4).

136 Single-image paddle-stamped (paleteada) potsherds from the East Spur of La Raya Mountain (a, c, d, f, g, k) and Sector V (b, e, h–j). These designs are found in greater frequency on La Raya Mountain. Note that some designs are representational, showing a version of the anthropomorphic wave (h), Lambayeque-style double-spout and bridge bottles (j, k), and a geometric wave motif (f, i).

137 Rim sherd from grater – the interiors have clay ridges that were probably used for grating corn cobs. These come from the fill surrounding the West Mound, Sector V.

In Sector V, most adobes were shaped like bread loaves (*ill. 138*). Although this was the most common shape throughout the site, flat, rectangular adobes were also found in the Monumental Sector (see Chapter 4). Size and proportions vary somewhat, but the most common dimensions (Type I) are approximately $35 \times 20 \times 16$ cm ($14 \times 8 \times 6$ in). Adobes were laid in a runner-and-header pattern and set in thick layers of mud mortar. After a wall had been built, it was covered with a fine mud plaster. Pits for preparing mud mortar were excavated in the *quebrada* behind Room A of the Rectangular Compound and in the Intermediate Area.

We found no traces of paint *in situ* on walls in Sector V, although some broken wall fragments in the fill covering the West Mound did appear to have red paint. Other plaster fragments in the fill had cord and cane impressions, suggesting that the upper part of the buildings was made of *quincha* (wattle-and-daub) and/or that the buildings had cane and mud roofs.

Many of the adobes have designs drawn on top when the mud was still wet. These are common on the north coast and are known as 'makers' marks'. As elsewhere at Túcume and in other sites of the region, Sector V adobes have a wide variety of marks, from a simple line to the impression of a foot (*ill. 139*). At Huaca del Sol in the Moche Valley, capital of the Early Intermediate Period Moche culture, Hastings and Moseley found that walls were made of segments, with the same mark predominating in each segment. The excavators interpreted this pattern as showing that some groups in Moche society paid their labor tax by making adobes, transporting them to the construction site, and using them to construct a segment of wall. Each group had its own mark to keep track of their labor contribution. Few of the adobes in any particular wall segment were marked; because the same group that made the adobes laid them in the walls, a few marked bricks sufficed to indicate who had built each section and therefore also made all the bricks.[48]

In contrast, Cavallaro and Shimada found a different pattern in the somewhat later, Middle Horizon, Middle Sicán structures at Batán Grande, near Túcume. There, they found that a greater proportion of bricks have marks and that any particular wall segment has more variety of marks, sizes, shapes, and soils.[49] Cavallaro and Shimada suggest several possible models to explain this pattern,[50] perhaps the most likely being that the makers of the adobes deposited their products in a common pool from which the builders – a different group – took the adobes necessary for construction. Most adobes would need

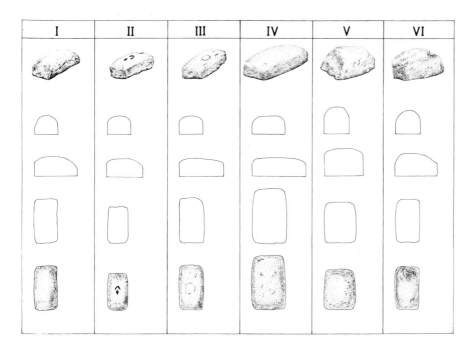

	I	II	III	IV	V	VI

138 The variety of sizes and proportions found in the adobe bricks used in the construction of Sector V. Types I–III are most common.

139 Makers' marks from adobes in the West Mound, Sector V.

140 *A wooden harpoon found in the West Mound, Sector V, and dating to the Inca period.*

to be marked so that each group of makers would get proper credit for its contribution, while the builders would not care whether they mixed marks in construction.

Although more recent in date, the walls at Túcume, and in particular Sector V, show the same basic pattern as Batán Grande. Adobes within a given wall segment vary in size, proportions, soil, and mark, and well over half of the adobes are marked. In Sector V, however, we did not find the same kind of chamber-and-fill construction as Cavallaro and Shimada illustrate for Batán Grande. This may be due to the different kinds of structures involved; Cavallaro and Shimada refer mostly to pyramids. In Sector V at Túcume, the Rectangular Compound was made of free-standing walls, while the West Mound has massive retaining walls holding back the fill which surrounds the sunken central chambers. We did not dismantle these walls so we do not have many details about their construction. However, eroded spots showed that they are made of loaf-shaped, marked adobes laid in the runner-and-header pattern. We did dismantle the retaining walls built to keep fill *in* when the West Mound was buried at the end of Phase WM-2. These show the same pattern of mixed-mark adobes laid in runner-and-header patterns, but were also built in segments.

Artifacts and activities

In addition to preparing and serving food, the artifacts in Sector V demonstrate a variety of other activities carried out in the 'non-monumental' area of Túcume. A shell-bead workshop operated in the Rectangular Compound and a metallurgical (and possibly pottery) workshop functioned in a nearby area to the south (see below). Although spinning and weaving tools were not common in Sector V, the relatively large number of cotton seeds in the primary midden, particularly in the West Mound, suggest some processing of this vegetal fiber. The animal bones show that camelids were bred and raised at Túcume throughout its history, and the corral under the Rectangular Compound indicates that these beasts were kept in Sector V at least at the beginning of occupation. Pawprints in the mud behind the Rectangular Compound and carnivore-gnawed animal bones in the primary midden are testimony to the presence of dogs. The bins found in Area G on the north side of the Rectangular Compound indicate formal storage of foodstuffs and probably tools.

141 *Carved wooden objects from the West Mound, Sector V. The two examples on the left show the anthropomorphic wave motif. The designs are carved on the curved interior of the thin, highly polished pieces of wood.*

Other artifacts found in Sector V may have been produced elsewhere. These include personal items such as a copper depilator or tweezers and a barbed wooden spear point (see *ill. 140*) found in Phase

WM-2 primary midden in the West Mound. One particularly striking artifact type found both in primary and secondary deposits in the
West Mound consists of slightly curved, thin pieces of wood with
complex figures incised on the inside of the curve (see *ill. 141*); the incisions are sometimes filled with red pigment. These pieces are always
broken, so their original form and use are unknown. The most
common design is a version of the 'anthropomorphic wave' which
appears prominently as the border of the Rafts Frieze in Huaca Las
Balsas (see Chapter 5). The anthropomorphic wave has a long history
on the north coast, at least as far back as Moche V times (*c.* AD
600–750).[51] In the West Mound, the anthropomorphic wave also
occurs on a pyroengraved gourd fragment from the late fill, along with
a monkey surrounded by wave-like lines (*ill. 142 a*). The monkey and
waves shows up on another gourd fragment from the fill (*ill. 142 b*), as
does an anthropomorphic wave-like figure with a crescent headdress
(*ill. 142 c*).

Finally, the tomb in the West Mound suggests that the mound was
originally the center for an important noble lineage or *ayllu* at
Túcume, while the Phase WM-2 building was the locale of restricted,
presumably high-status and perhaps sacred activities.

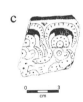

*142 Pyroengraved gourd
fragments from the West
Mound, Sector V,
showing: a the
anthropomorphic wave
motif and a monkey-like
figure; b a monkey-like
figure; c a figure with
headdress.*

Residence

We can point to the places where people ate, worked, and interacted
in Sector V, but there is no direct evidence that people slept there.
Although we did not find anything which resembled a bed, we do not
know what would have constituted a bed for the ancient Tucumanos.
It seems likely that some of the people who carried out the various
activities in this area resided there, perhaps in 'clean' (artifact- and
debris-free) rooms such as the chambers of Room B in the Rectangular
Compound, and in the more ephemeral structures in the Intermediate
Area, as well as in the West Mound. I suspect that the lesser elite of
Túcume society lived in structures like the West Mound, while the
working class lived in the Intermediate Areas between the larger buildings (workshops and elite residences) that they staffed. The presence
of many unfinished shell beads in the Intermediate Area between the
Rectangular Compound and the West Mound suggests that the staff
of the Shell-Bead Workshop lived there. The clean rooms of the
Rectangular Compound (especially Room B) may have housed lower
level bureaucrats overseeing the workshops.

Final observations on Sector V

We began work in Sector V with the assumption that it was a residential area for the urban lower classes who provided support services for the elite residents of the Monumental Sector and perhaps also housed the laborers working the adjacent agricultural fields. The model for this idea was Chan Chan, the capital of the Chimú empire.

That craft production took place in the 'non-monumental' areas of Túcume now seems clear. In addition to the evidence for the manufacture of shell beads in the Rectangular Compound, surface collections from a similar area several hundred meters south of Sector V indicate metal and possibly pottery production in association with a small, amorphous mound like the West Mound. Evidence for pottery working includes a few 'wasters' (potsherds distorted by improper firing) and a fragment of a ceramic mold for a large, basin-like vessel. Evidence for metalworking took the form of abundant charcoal and slag-like material, many small, green drops of oxidized copper or copper alloy, stone tools for grinding ore, and numerous, badly burnt potsherds with oxidized copper adhering to their surfaces. These sherds would have been part of crucibles or smelter linings. The Lambayeque region has a long tradition of copper-based metallurgy, best known from Shimada's work at Batán Grande;[52] the Túcume surface finds fit well into this tradition.

Although craft production did take place outside the monumental core of Túcume, the other features of Sector V do not easily fit a definition of 'non-monumental'. The Rectangular Compound demonstrates a level of formality and organization as great as any in the Chan Chan SIAR, with which it shares the function of craft production. Perhaps a closer comparison for the Compound is the *Spondylus* shell workshop housed in a large enclosure at the base of the Huaca Fortaleza at Pampa Grande[53] (see Chapter 3).

The West Mound exhibits small-scale monumentality in its form and presumed functions, first as an elite mausoleum and later as a special purpose center that housed a clay model of a large stepped platform. The West Mound seems to have been the center for an important personage or family, probably one of the site's lower-ranking lords. The 'non-monumental' sector of Túcume is full of low, amorphous mounds like the West Mound, and all are probably the remains of the palaces, temples, and/or mausoleums of the lesser nobles. In this light, 'non-monumental' is a misnomer and we must revise our image of Túcume's urban organization.

Alfredo Narváez

Death in Ancient Túcume

The South Cemetery and Huaca Facho

A T THE START of the 1991 field season, Dan Sandweiss and I made a tour of inspection around the site, looking particularly for areas exposed by erosion or looting where we could get a quick look at the stratigraphy of the area. I had already used this strategy of using destroyed areas to get a fast and inexpensive overview of site development in the Tschudi Palace at Chan Chan, the Chimú capital in the Moche Valley,[1] and we hoped to repeat this success at Túcume. When we reached the southern extreme of the site, we found a

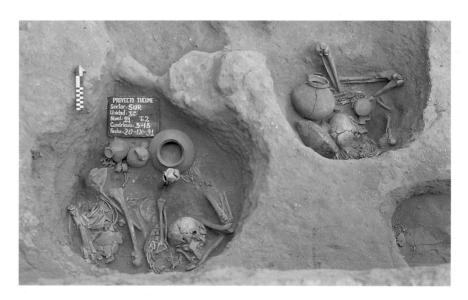

143 Inca Period burials in the South Cemetery. The burial on the upper right includes a North Coast Inca-style fish pot.

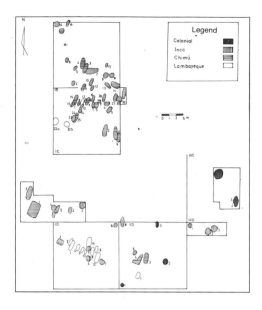

144 *South Cemetery:*
plan of excavated
units and location
and age of burials.

145 *(above right) A*
Lambayeque-style Huaco
Rey pot and an Inca Period
bottle in the same South
Cemetery grave.

146–147 *Lambayeque*
Period pots modeled in the
shape of birds, found
with a child burial in the
South Cemetery.

cemetery in the very process of being looted – not only were several big pits open, but we even found some unbroken utilitarian pots which the looters had left behind. Within a short time I had begun to direct salvage excavations in this area, baptized the South Cemetery (see *ill. 33*) and work continued throughout the rest of the year with my colleague Jorge Rosas as assistant archaeologist.

In 1992, I came upon another area of looted burials, this time on the southwest side of the site, just south of Huaca Las Balsas (see *ill. 33*). Here, in Huaca Facho, we found a different kind of tomb from those elsewhere at Túcume: stone-lined shaft tombs cut into previous architecture and containing individuals associated with Inca-style pottery. In cleaning these looted tombs, we were able to determine the form and construction of the burial chambers and to salvage some of the originally associated material.

In the following sections, I will discuss the results of the excavations in these two southern cemeteries. My work at two other burial areas, on Huaca Larga and in front of the Small Temple, are detailed in Chapter 4 on the Monumental Sector of Túcume. Several other burials were found on Huaca 1 and are mentioned in the same chapter, while Dan Sandweiss found a few burials in Sector V, which he discusses in Chapter 6.

The South Cemetery

By the time excavations ended in the South Cemetery, we had recovered 73 intact burials together with their offerings (*ill. 144*), which

148 (left) A Lambayeque Period vessel found with a redware Huaco Rey pot in a burial in the South Cemetery.

149 (right) The Huaco Rey pot found with an Inca Period vessel in ill. 145.

consisted mainly of pottery but also included shells (especially the ritually important *Spondylus* imported from Ecuador), pieces of natural chalk, copper tools, shell beads, *crisoles* (small finger pots, often unfired), and in the most elaborate tomb, a copper medallion and a gold nose ornament. Based on the styles of the pottery, these burials seem to span the last prehispanic periods, from perhaps as early as AD 900 to the early Colonial Period of the 16th century. Although our work at Túcume has demonstrated that absolute chronology based on ceramic styles in later Lambayeque prehistory is more problematic than most previous investigators had suspected,[2] the one available radiocarbon date for the South Cemetery generally supports the stylistic chronology described below.

The South Cemetery provided a sequence of burial types and offerings. The deepest burials were 13 individuals in an extended position with the head to the south (*ill. 150*), all of which contained Classic Lambayeque Tradition pottery (*ills 146, 147, 148, 151–152, 155*).[3] Eight were found underneath a later wall running east–west across the cemetery. The pottery from these burials can be compared with Shimada's Middle Sicán style from nearby Batán Grande,[4] seen on polished blackware vessels and vessels with black and cream paint on a polished red surface. In one burial, these styles were found associated with pottery in the Tricolor style from the area between the Chicama and Chao valleys to the south of Lambayeque – the same as Early Chimú Red-White-Black,[5] known as Taitacantín in the Virú Valley.[6]

Among the offerings in the 13 'pure' Lambayeque burials were two

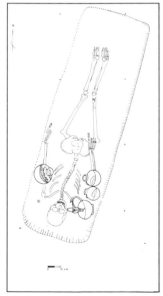

150 A Lambeyeque Period burial in the South Cemetery (Unit ID, Burial 12). At this period the dead were usually buried fully extended, with the head to the south, as here.

151–152 (above) South
Cemetery, Lambayeque
Period vessel (side and
front views).

153 (right) Two North
Coast Inca-style head pots
found in the South
Cemetery.

154 Pottery accompanying an Inca Period burial in the South Cemetery, including a blackware vessel in the form of a Galapagos turtle (lower left). The two blackware vessels on the right are in the form of monkeys, while the one on the upper left represents four fruits, probably lucumas. The redware vessel is a typical carinated-rim cooking olla.

'Huaco Rey' (King Pot) vessels, one of redware and one of polished blackware. These are a very distinct vessel type characterized by the representation of a standardized individual whom Shimada calls the Sicán Lord; according to Shimada, the Sicán Lord is only represented during the Middle Sicán Period, from AD 900 to 1100.[7] However, a second blackware Huaco Rey was found in association with a blackware bottle showing clear Inca influence (ills 145, 149);[8] apparently these offerings accompanied a partially looted, seated and flexed burial found in a different part of the cemetery from the other

155 A Lambayeque Period vessel modeled in shape of a dog, found in a burial in the South Cemetery.

Lambayeque burials and not located under the east–west wall. The majority of seated and flexed burials in the South Cemetery include unmistakably north coast Inca-style pottery among their grave goods.

Shimada's Middle Sicán burials often have a black- or redware, double-bodied vessel associated with the Huaco Rey,[9] and we found the same association in the South Cemetery Lambayeque burials. The double-bodied vessels have two small handles on the shoulders, as do most of the pots in the Lambayeque burials at Túcume.

Within his Middle Sicán Period, Shimada sees an evolution through time of the Huaco Rey: the base gets higher, and the earlier, lower-based examples are of blackware while the later, higher-based examples are redware. The black Huaco Reys have the classic, sharply defined Sicán Lord face, while these characteristics are less well-defined on the redware examples, which are more like a mask than a real face.[10] At Túcume, we have both extremes of the Middle Sicán sequence (early black and late red), but both are from burials under the east–west wall which appear to be roughly contemporaneous.

With the exception of the Inca-period burial with the Huaco Rey, all the burials with Lambayeque-style pottery share many characteristics with Middle Sicán, including the extended position of the body, with the head to the south. The presence of a Tricolor vessel from further south is not surprising, given that this pre-Chimú period was a time of notable interaction between Lambayeque and the region centered around the Moche Valley. Much Lambayeque material is found in the Moche area at this time. The 13 'pure' Lambayeque burials are therefore contemporary with Middle Sicán of Batán Grande and the Tricolor Phase of the Moche area, thus preceding the Chimú conquest of Lambayeque and dating to AD 900 to AD 1100. Our one radiocarbon date for the South Cemetery came from a Lambayeque burial and supports my chronological estimate: 960 ± 70 BP, with a calibrated range of AD 1025 to 1218 (BGS 1614).

Nevertheless, I want to underline the fact that the association of the third Huaco Rey with an Inca-period pot and a flexed burial demonstrates continuity of the Lambayeque Tradition through the Late Horizon. The Sicán Lord of the Huaco Rey is even shown on a green-glazed, Colonial Period pot in the local Brüning Museum. Another Huaca Rey was found in excavations in a late 17th-century church in Trujillo (Manuel Tam, personal communication). Thus, although Shimada may be right that the Sicán Lord is not represented after Middle Sicán in the Batán Grande area, a short distance away at Túcume, the Lambayeque Tradition and its principal icon continued to be expressed despite over three centuries of unabated foreign domination by Chimú, Inca, and early Spanish conquerors.

The 13 pure Lambayeque burials cut through underlying floors of a clearly domestic nature, with hearths, midden, and well-defined post-holes. The earliest of these floors had been constructed on sterile soil. The use of the area as a cemetery must have been contemporary or just following its first domestic occupation. Later floors cover the burials, and it is clear that domestic activity continues after the Lambayeque Period.

Following the Lambayeque Period, the South Cemetery area underwent many remodelings, though remaining fundamentally domestic, probably during the Chimú domination of Túcume. Then, in the Inca Period, came the major use of the area as a cemetery (*ills 143, 156*). Burials at this time include not only those with clearly Inca-influenced material (*ills 145, 153*), but also those with only Chimú-related pottery (*ills 154, 158, 159*). In one burial, only the *crisoles* indicated an Inca date; the rest of the offerings were Chimú in style. Both Chimú and Inca-style pottery are found in 57 burials, while three with Colonial Period glass beads show that the cemetery continued in use in the early years after the Spanish Conquest.

One Inca-style burial cuts the east–west wall, which was made of both plano-convex and flat adobes. This burial contains a seated individual, facing north and accompanied by three blackware head pots as well as other vessels (*ill. 156*). By association with the Huaca Larga architectural sequence and in terms of the stratigraphy of the South

156 An Inca Period burial from the South Cemetery (Unit ID, Burial 3). The deceased was buried sitting upright, with legs crossed, in a custom that was popular under Inca rule.

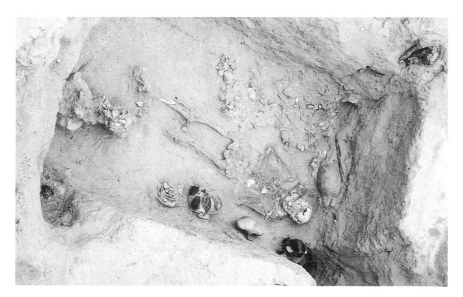

157 Tomb 1 (chamber burial), which probably dates to the Inca Period, but the extended position of the body follows the old Lambayeque tradition, lying on the back with the head to the south. Note the posts in the four corners of the chamber. The remains of a child lie at the feet of the main burial. This is the most elaborate burial in the South Cemetery.

158 (above left) A
Chimú-style vessel in the
form of a bat.

159 (above right) A
Chimú-style vessel from the
Tomb 1 chamber burial,
dating to the Inca Period.

Cemetery, the east–west wall relates to the formalized domestic architecture of the Chimú Period. During the final use of the area as a mass cemetery, this wall and associated features were largely destroyed by burials containing Chimú, Chimú–Inca, and Inca pottery.

In summary, the sequence of the South Cemetery is: Phase SC-1 – a Lambayeque Period domestic occupation, with some Lambayeque burials; Phase SC-2 – a Chimú Period domestic occupation characterized by formal domestic architecture; and Phase SC-3 – an Inca and Early Colonial Period cemetery.

Looking more closely at the types of burials and offerings in the South Cemetery, it is clear that most of the interred individuals were not part of the site's elite. The one exception was Tomb 1, the only chamber burial found in the South Cemetery (*ill. 157*). This tomb cuts the floors associated with the east–west wall, so it must post-date the second phase of the cemetery (SC-2), that of the intense, formal domestic occupation. The pottery in Tomb 1 is Chimú in style. The most diagnostic piece is a duck-shaped blackware pot with a square cross-section stirrup-spout; this vessel is late in the Chimú sequence and could even be Chimú–Inca. (However, it might date to the time of Chimú expansion and conquest.) There were also over 40 unfired *crisoles* in the tomb; some were still wet when deposited, as they became deformed *in situ*.

Archaeologists frequently find *crisoles* in tombs in northern Peru, and we have often wondered what their function may have been. Talking with local residents in the Túcume countryside, I discovered that as recently as 50 years ago, people used *crisoles* to heat *chicha* (corn beer). The *crisol* would be placed in a fire until red hot, then removed with a stick inserted in the finger hole and dunked in a gourd bowl of *chicha*. This hot drink is said to have medicinal properties as well as a restorative effect on cold mornings.

Tomb 1 is rectangular in shape, with the remains of a post in each of the four corners. The principal individual buried in this tomb was clearly an important personage. In addition to a partial llama offering, a child had been placed at his feet, accompanied by an orangeware, stirrup-spout pot with a design in black paint; this piece is reminiscent of north coast Inca pottery identified by Ravines and Bonavia.[11]

Despite the Inca date indicated by the stratigraphy and the child's pot, the Tomb 1 individual was buried in the old Lambayeque Tradition – extended with the head to the south. In contrast, most of the Inca Period burials in the South Cemetery are flexed, seated cross-legged, and facing north. Several clasp a *Spondylus* shell in their hands (see *ill. 156*).

The Huaca Facho shaft tombs

Huaca Facho is a low adobe mound in the southwest corner of Túcume, just south of Huaca Las Balsas (see *ill. 33*). The original structures of this mound were made of both flat and plano-convex adobes with gray plaster, like the Tricolor Phase and later architecture at Huaca Larga. It seems likely that Huaca Facho dates to the same immediately pre-Inca period as the Huaca Larga Tricolor phase. The use of flat adobes and gray plaster contrasts markedly with nearby Huaca Las Balsas.

The Inca tombs in Huaca Facho are intrusive, cutting through the earlier architecture and are constructed as stone-walled shafts and chambers, with niches in the walls and roofs of algarrobo beams. Burials are generally multiple in each chamber, recalling the Inca weaving women buried in Room 3 of Platform 2 on Huaca Larga. Although largely looted, we were able to recover some individuals and whole ceramics from the Huaca Facho tombs. Of the four tombs excavated, two were completely looted, one was partly looted, and one was intact. The two fully looted tombs and the partially looted one still contained the remains of multiple individuals. The intact tomb, however, had only one person buried in it.

Among the pots are several which are Provincial Inca in style; that is, they seem to be local copies of Inca vessel forms, rather than the Inca-influenced vessels of the north coast Inca style found in burials in other parts of the site. The partly looted tomb included two vessels,

160 *An Inca snake-shaped* paccha *vessel, probably used in water rituals, from a partly looted tomb in Huaca Facho.*

each composed of seven globular chambers connected to each other by tubular openings in their sides. These pots are like Inca *pacchas* used in rituals related to water. A piece of another, classic, snake-shaped *paccha* came from the same tomb (*ill. 160*), as did *Spondylus* shells. The association of *Spondylus* and *pacchas* makes perfect sense, as both were important elements in Inca water rituals.

In the intact tomb, the buried individual was seated and flexed, holding a *Spondylus* shell in his or her hands. The pottery in this tomb included a blackware pot shaped like a llama head, a north coast Inca small aryballoid vessel, two blackware stirrup-spout vessels with round spout cross-sections, a Chimú–Inca blackware bottle with a bird head on the neck, a double-bodied, double-spouted redware pot with a bird sealing one spout and an incised bridge connecting the two spouts, and four carinated-rim cooking *ollas* with paddle-stamped decoration.

Burial patterns at Túcume

Our information on burials at Túcume relates to the earliest and latest occupations of the site – Lambayeque and Inca. For the Lambayeque Period, we have only the 13 burials from the South Cemetery, which show a single burial pattern: extended with head to the south. In contrast, for the Inca Period we have well over 100 burials from different parts of the site. There is significant diversity both in burial position (principally seated cross-legged looking north, but also extended with the head to the south) and in stylistic affinities of the grave goods (Lambayeque, Chimú, Chimú–Inca, north coast Inca, and Provincial Inca). These different elements can be mixed in different ways. For instance, one extended burial in the South Cemetery had a blackware north coast Inca aryballoid vessel, while another extended burial had a highly polished, blackware Chimú–Inca pot representing a long-necked bird and also displaying molded stepped waves. There is also the association of a north coast Inca vessel, a Huaco Rey, and a flexed, cross-legged burial.

During the Inca period, the form of the tomb itself varies, from simple pit burials to the rectangular chamber of Tomb 1 in the South Cemetery, from the stone-lined shaft tombs of Huaca Facho to the mummy bundles in the northeast room of Platform 2 on Huaca Larga. Contrasting the Lambayeque and Inca Period burial patterns, it is clear that an epic ideological dislocation took place during the Inca Period at Túcume.

Daniel H. Sandweiss

Peak of the Past

La Raya Mountain

A T THE CENTER of Túcume lies La Raya Mountain, a steep-sided, rocky hill rising out of the flat coastal plain like a giant monument (see *ill. 33*). And, during the Inca Period, it was just that – the largest pyramid of them all, perhaps the biggest in Peru (*ill. 162*). Centuries of El Niño rains have eroded many of the walls and platforms which once adorned the mountain, preventing previous researchers from realizing the extent of construction on La Raya. The ancient architects managed to convert the most outstanding feature of the natural landscape into the most impressive cultural artifact of prehispanic Lambayeque, a massive stepped pyramid which functioned as a temple and as a fortress. However, it appears that the structures on the mountain do not date to the period of Lambayeque autonomy. Rather, the domestication of La Raya took place in the Inca Period for Inca state purposes; this single phase on the mountain is denominated Phase LR-1.

La Raya consists of a central peak elevated some 140 m (460 ft) above the surrounding plain; to the east, south, and west of the peak, the sides of the mountain fall steeply. From these sides, access to the top is difficult except up the South Ravine on the southeast. To the north, a wide ravine splits the mountain into two parts, the West Spur and the East Spur. This North Ravine offers an easy route to the union of the East Spur and the main mountain.

I began field work on the East Spur of La Raya in 1991. At that time, I divided the East Spur into four Sub-Sectors from south to north. Sub-Sector I is the presumed residential/administrative complex where we began excavations (*ill. 161*). Moving north, Sub-Sector II is

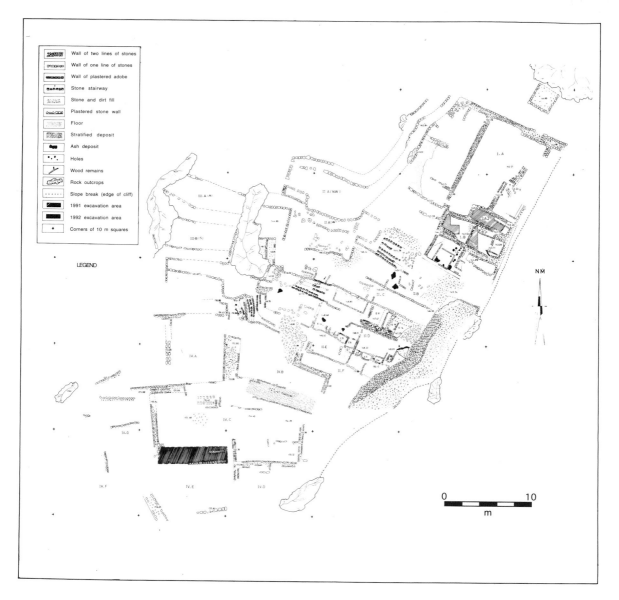

161 (above) La Raya Mountain: plan of architectural features in Sub-Sector I of the East Spur. (From an original map by B. Ojeda.)

162 (opposite) Aerial photo of Huaca Larga and La Raya Mountain looking south. Note the stepped platforms at the end of the East Spur and Sub-Sector I, where the East Spur joins the main mountain.

a high point with a flattened summit and stone-faced sides. Sub-Sector III is an eroded adobe mound. At the north end of the East Spur, Sub-Sector IV looms over Huaca Larga and appears to have been a temple.

In 1991, I also placed several test pits in the White Cave, on the eastern face of the mountain just below the East Spur. That same year, Bernardino Ojeda made a detailed map of all of the structural remains on the mountain (unfortunately, too large and detailed to present in this book). In 1992, D. Peter Kvietok spent several weeks working on the East Spur excavating additional units in Sub-Sector I and clearing parts of several stepped platforms in Sub-Sector IV. During both 1991 and 1992, Peruvian archaeologist César Cornelio Lecca worked with us on La Raya.

The structures of La Raya

The entire mountain is covered with the remains of ancient structures, which can be classified into eight major units: *1* lower stone-faced terraced platforms; *2* massive stone wall-and-tower complexes; *3* adobe mounds; *4* stone-faced stepped platforms; *5* agglutinated stone rooms; *6* terraced stone storage units; *7* stone-faced summit walls; and *8* a circum-Raya pathway. This list shows the overwhelming use of stone for building on La Raya, in notable contrast to the adobe construction in the rest of the site, except the Inca buildings on top of Huaca Larga. Finally, though not a structure *per se*, the White Cave played an important part in the cultural modification of La Raya.

Around the base of La Raya and rising from a third to a half of the way up[1] are rubble-filled, stone-faced, terraced platforms. These terraces are best preserved on the east side of the mountain, and it was here that Bennett[2] began his excavations in 1935 (see Chapter 3). It is not surprising that Bennett failed to note the stone faces of the platforms: they are visible only where recent erosion from the 1982–83 El Niño event has exposed them. Elsewhere, the stone façades have either been covered with rubble fill eroded from above or removed for more recent construction. While mapping the mountain, Ojeda found a well-worn, recent track leading to a half-dismantled terrace facing-wall on the west side of La Raya, and Walter Alva told me that for years the mountain had been marked as a quarry on Highway Department maps.

Both the North and South Ravines are blocked about a third of the way up the mountain by a massive stone wall running from one side to the other. Just upslope from the wall across the North Ravine are the remains of a platform (2.5 m (8 ft) square), while a stone-faced and rubble-cored tower (measuring 5 × 10 m (16 × 33 ft)) is built on the uphill side of the South Ravine wall. The walls, platform, and tower are carefully positioned in order to control access to the upper structures on La Raya.

Adobe construction is rare on the mountain. Some adobes were used in rooms on the East Spur (see below), but the only large adobe structure is an eroded and looted mound in Sub-Sector III of the East Spur. This may be the upper area which Bennett[3] excavated.

The northern point of the East Spur (Sub-Sector IV) consists of superimposed, stone-faced stepped platforms which rise from the north to the south. The lowest, southernmost platform was reached by a path skirting the side of the East Spur; from this small platform

overlooking Huaca Larga, a flight of steps leads to a larger, slightly trapezoidal terrace measuring about 25 m (82 ft) on one side. Kvietok's clearing operation here showed the foundations of numerous small subdivisions. An alternative route on to the stepped terraces led along the west side of the upper terraces to the base of the Trapezoidal Terrace. From here, a broad flight of steps continued up to the penultimate level, with a ramp, 3 m (10 ft) wide, leading up to the highest level. This is a 30-m (98-ft) long terrace which narrows from over 10 m (33 ft) at the north end to about 5 m (16½ ft) at the south end. The uppermost terrace can be circumvented by following a path along the east side at the level of the penultimate terrace.

All the Sub-Sector IV terraces have stone-faced sides and artificially flattened surfaces, but on the uppermost terrace, an unmodified piece of bedrock was left projecting (*ill. 163*). In front (north) of this rock, Kvietok cleared the foundations of a row of niche-like structures, each about 1 m (3 ft) square. Considering the centerpiece of the Stone Temple next to Huaca Larga (see Chapter 4) and recalling the Andean tradition of venerating natural stones, I believe that this outcrop was a sacred place. Such a status would explain the tremendous investment of labor in building the stepped platforms of Sub-Sector IV of the East Spur, which all culminate in the Terrace of the Stone.

In Sub-Sector I of the East Spur (see *ill. 161*), we found two areas of agglutinated stone structures, above and below a terraced hillslope with rows of small storage structures. From Sub-Sector I of the East Spur a series of terraces climbs the east face of the mountain to the summit. The top of the mountain is ringed by the remains of stone facing-walls, in places still measuring over 6 m (20 ft) in height. Above these walls is a small and jagged area where only a few people could have gathered. Just below the summit on the northeast side is a sub-rectangular platform overlooking the East Spur, the North Ravine, and Huaca Larga. Anyone approaching the peak of La Raya from the East Spur would have been clearly visible from this platform. A similar platform may have been located on the southeast side of the summit overlooking the South Ravine. Taking into account these platforms, those in the North and South Ravines, and several other small platforms around the mountain, it seems likely that La Raya was ringed with a series of lookout points, each in sight of at least one other and in total overlooking all possible routes up the mountain.

During the mapping project, Ojeda noted the remains of a pathway circling the mountain at the level of the uppermost stone-faced terraced platforms. This 'circum-Raya pathway' is often defined by stone walls and leveling fill. On the east side of the mountain the path leads to a large stone-faced platform built at the mouth of the White Cave, just below Sub-Sector I of the East Spur. Although well known to locals, previous investigators had not remarked on this cave. Indeed, we were unaware of it for quite some time. The results of test excavations in 1991 are detailed in a later section.

Field work in Sub-Sector I of the East Spur

Field work in Sub-Sector I included clearing, surface collection, mapping, and excavation. These operations gave insight into the function and chronology of this sector of La Raya. For the purposes of collection and mapping, I divided Sub-Sector I into four Units (see *ill. 161*). To the north, *Unit I* is a flat area between the North Ravine and the steep eastern face of La Raya. It is the lowest part of Sub-Sector I and consists of agglutinated, rectangular rooms. *Unit II* is a terraced hillslope rising to the south of Unit I. A natural outcrop with a stone facing-wall delimits the eastern side of Unit II, while an unmodified outcrop on the west separates it from Unit III. A series of stone steps winds up through Unit II, providing access to the terraces and eventually reaching Unit IV. The terraces of Unit II average about 4 m (13 ft) in width (north–south) and 15 m (50 ft) in length (east–west). The downslope (north) faces of the terraces are stone retaining walls, with lines of small storage units backed against the wall of the terrace above. *Unit III* lies to the west of Unit II, at the head of the North Ravine. Like Unit II, it is a terraced hillslope. *Unit IV* is a flat area above and south of Units II and III; Unit IV consists of agglutinated rectangular rooms. From here, a series of steep terraces rises toward the summit of La Raya.

Excavations

Excavations in Sub-Sector I sampled several rooms in Unit I and a row of storage structures in Unit II; Kvietok later excavated a similar row of storage structures. The material remains recovered from the excavations are similar to those found in the surface collections. This makes sense: artifacts from other parts of the site cannot roll uphill to be deposited on the mountain, and it seems unlikely that anyone would go to the trouble of hauling heavy material up La Raya from elsewhere.

We have only one radiocarbon date from La Raya, from a pit in Room I-B in Unit I: 600 ± 70 BP (BGS-1618), calibrated to AD 1310 to 1433 with a mean calibrated date of AD 1405. The sample came from a fill level near the base of the deposit and should date to, or just prior to, the beginning of construction in Sub-Sector I.

Surface collections

We made a complete surface collection from Units I, II, and IV; time did not permit collection from Unit III. We also made spot collections and inspections of surface material on the rest of the mountain. The most abundant class of surface material was pottery, especially fragments of the hook-rim plates which Donnan[4] has identified as diagnostic of the Late Horizon (or Inca Period) in Lambayeque. Other common pottery forms include open bowls, carinated-rim *ollas* (cooking jars), jars with highly everted rims (probably Inca-influenced), and *porrones* (large cooking jars) (see Chapter 6).

The most common decoration on the pottery is paddle-stamping or *paleteada*, as it is throughout the site. However, the collections from La Raya show a much higher percentage of single-image, often representational designs (see *ill. 136*), as compared to the repetitive, geometric designs found elsewhere (see *ill. 135*).[5] Shimada[6] refers to the representational images as 'logographic' or 'semasiographic' and suggests that they are short-lived. The most common logographic motif on La Raya *paleteada* pottery is a double-spout-and-bridge bottle, often showing appendages on the bridge and under each spout (*ill. 136 j, k*); this vessel form is diagnostic of the Lambayeque or Sicán pottery tradition. The single-image geometric designs tend to be concentric circles or polygons and usually include pendant triangles.[7]

ACTUAL CONDITION

- Natural
- White
- Grey
- Red

RECONSTRUCTION

164 An imported Cajamarca rim sherd found on La Raya Mountain, Sub-Sector I of the East Spur. The pendant triangles show possible Inca influence.

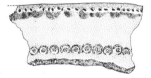

165 An imported Casma Incised rim sherd, La Raya Mountain, Sub-Sector I of the East Spur.

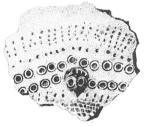

166 An imported Casma Incised potsherd, La Raya Mountain, Sub-Sector I of the East Spur. The nubbin shows possible Inca influence.

In the surface collection from Sub-Sector I, three pieces of exotic pottery stand out. One is a rim sherd from a flat Cajamarca plate with red and gray paint on a white background (*ill. 164*). Cajamarca is the highland area immediately inland from Lambayeque. The painted decoration includes pendant triangles on the rim, which may be influenced by Inca design canons. The other two sherds are Casma Incised pottery,[8] the predominant late prehispanic pottery style from the coastal Casma Valley some 380 km (236 miles) south-southeast of Túcume. One of these sherds is a rim from an *olla* (*ill. 165*), while the other is a body sherd with an animal-head nubbin in the Casma style but very similar to ones on Inca pottery (*ill. 166*). I believe that these sherds, like the rest of the diagnostic pottery on La Raya, date to the Late Horizon or Inca Period.

In addition to pottery, surface collections included stone polishing tools, shell beads, quartz crystals, gourd fragments, copper objects, spindle whorls, wooden artifacts, animal coprolites, fish and terrestrial animal bones, and shells including the warm-water, sacred mollusk *Spondylus*. In fact, *Spondylus* occurred more frequently on La Raya than anywhere else at the site except in the burials.

Architecture

As elsewhere on La Raya, the terraces and agglutinated rooms in Sub-Sector I are made of rough-quarried, local stone. Subdivisions within rooms are of stone or adobe. As in Sector V and most other parts of the site (see Chapter 6), the adobes used in Sub-Sector I of the East Spur are bread-loaf shaped (or plano-convex) and vary widely in color. During clearing and excavation, we found postholes and several toppled posts, indicating that many of the structures once had roofs. Some walls still conserved mud plaster, and most likely all were originally plastered.

The agglutinated rooms of Units I and IV have double-faced external walls of stone set in mortar, while internal walls consist of single lines of adobes or stones; in some cases, adobes rest on stone foundations. Excavations in Unit I uncovered adobe benches set against several walls. Floor plans in both units are rectangular to sub-rectangular and are oriented in accordance with the topography rather than strictly following the cardinal directions. This observation holds true for Units II and III as well; in these units, walls run perpendicular to the slope to form flights of terraces. The terraces form the base for small subdivisions of variable size and shape, which seem to be storage structures. The interiors of these units were plastered with gray mud, and access was from above. None of the original contents remained in any of the excavated units, and we found only loose fill above the floors. The terraced hillside of Units II and III is reminiscent of the Inca custom of building lines of storehouses on hillslopes overlooking their administrative centers.[9] However, the scale on La Raya is much reduced.

Excavations in Units I and II showed changes through time in the architecture, seen in sequences of floors, fills, midden, walls, and sealed doorways. These are changes in details only, not in form or function. The overall plan of Sub-Sector I originated with the first construction and remained unaltered throughout the entire occupation.

Excavations in the White Cave

The White Cave opens in the east side of La Raya, below Sub-Sector I of the East Spur (*ills 167–168*). It is set in a localized deposit of soft white rock, and is a natural feature. In front of it is the highest of the stone-faced, rubble-cored, terraced platforms. Access to this platform was via a road (the circum-Raya pathway) winding around from the south. The remains of several walls in front of the cave show that the platform once supported structures. The presence of the platform and road show that the White Cave was deliberately incorporated into the plan of construction that converted La Raya into a giant pyramid.

Before excavating, I was certain that the White Cave would at last yield evidence of the preceramic hunter-gatherers who must once have

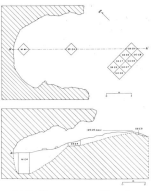

167 *Plan and profile of the White Cave on La Raya Mountain, showing the location of excavations and a reconstruction of the original cave profile. (From an original map by B. Ojeda.)*

168 *The White Cave on La Raya Mountain.*

lived in the resource-rich Lambayeque Valley. The cave faces east with a good view across large areas of the valley floor to the Andean foothills some 6 km (4 miles) away; it seems like a natural place for hunters to take shelter while watching for herds of wild camelids or other game. To test this hypothesis and to investigate the later functions of the cave, I placed three excavation units in a line from the rear of the cave to the mouth.

Despite careful sifting of all excavated material with fine-mesh screen, we found absolutely no evidence of human activity prior to the late prehispanic time (probably Inca Period) when the terraced platform was built. The deposits immediately above the bedrock base of the cave consisted of culturally sterile roof fall, capped by a smooth, floor-like level which was apparently built at the same time as the platform in front. Above this level, the deposits included roof fall and water-borne sediments that incorporated scarce cultural material (mostly pottery) from the platform fill.

By plotting the location of the bedrock floor of the cave in our excavation units, we could see that the original form resembled a bag; perhaps this shape was simply too inconvenient to use as a shelter before roof fall eventually raised the base to a more comfortable level. Another possible reason for the lack of early occupation is that the area around La Raya was probably desert before construction of the Taymi Canal; however, preceramic hunting sites are known from desert areas elsewhere on the Peruvian coast.

The diagnostic pottery above the floor is generically late, representing the Lambayeque Tradition of the Late Intermediate Period and Late Horizon. This fact and the data relating sedimentation to platform construction show that the White Cave was used at the same time as the platform. The construction of this flat surface in front of the cave mouth allowed water from El Niño rains to wash material into the cave, thus filling it after the area had been abandoned. Prior to the platform, water had no way to enter the cave, explaining why the lower levels contained only roof fall.

Whatever the function of the White Cave was, it did not result in the accumulation of *in situ* midden or any interior structures.[10] If it is correct that the platforms and other structures on La Raya were built under Inca direction, then the White Cave may well have been a sacred place for observing the sunrise to the east. The Inca revered caves, worshipped the sun, were adept at solar astronomy, and used an east-facing cave as a solar observatory at least at one other site, Machu Picchu.[11]

Final observations on La Raya

From the first days of Túcume, La Raya must have been extremely important symbolically – mountains were worshipped throughout the Andean region, not just among highland groups such as the Inca. Conklin[12] argues persuasively for a very long history of mountain worship on the north coast of Peru as evidenced in architecture as well as ethnohistory. Moche pottery of the Early Intermediate Period often shows deities perched atop peaks which sometimes resemble La Raya. The pyramids and other structures of Túcume cluster around the mountain, which clearly is the magnetic center of the site. Nevertheless, available data indicate that construction on the mountain began late and was probably an Inca project. Indeed, Bennett[13] found only Inca Period burials in his excavations on La Raya, and Schaedel[14] suggested 40 years ago that the mountain structures were Inca, like similar hilltop sites throughout the Lambayeque region.

The structures in Sub-Sector I of the East Spur show that there was a small resident population living on the mountain. The exotic pottery found here provides a clue to the origins of the mountain-dwellers: the Inca may have staffed La Raya with *mitmaq* from other areas such as Cajamarca and Casma. Both of these places lie within the same *suyu*, or quarter, of the Inca Empire as Túcume.

If we had found any original contents in the storage units, we would have a better idea of the mountain residents' function; however, the fact the dwelling area is linked by a major pathway to the presumed temple and sacred stone and lies directly above the White Cave argues that at least some of these people were religious specialists. Others may have been their retainers. The number of people who could have resided in Sub-Sector I is small, in the tens at most. Such a small group could have been well-supplied from the storage structures in Units II and III of Sub-Sector I.

For the Inca, La Raya served many functions. By domesticating the mountain and converting it into a massive pyramid, La Raya became an impressive and omnipresent reflection of its overlords' power. The labor invested in clothing the mountain in platforms and other structures was tremendous, and all the more impressive if carried out during the 60–70 years of Inca domination. The wall/tower complexes and integrated lookout points guarding access to the upper structures suggest that La Raya was a fortress and/or place of refuge in the midst of a potentially hostile conquered people. However, the most important function of the mountain seems to have been as a sacred place.

Daniel H. Sandweiss and Alfredo Narváez

Túcume Past

TÚCUME IS ONE of the largest and most complex sites in north-ern South America, and our five years of excavations have barely scratched the surface. Nevertheless, we now know much more than when we started; in this chapter, we outline current thought on Túcume and its role in late prehispanic Lambayeque.

Túcume through time

Túcume arose and grew through three periods, which we refer to as the Lambayeque Period (c. AD 1050 to 1350, equivalent to the early part of the Late Intermediate Period in the standard Peruvian sequence); the Chimú Period (c. AD 1350 to 1470, equivalent to the late part of the Late Intermediate Period); and the Inca Period (c. AD 1470 to 1532, equivalent to the Late Horizon). Earlier scholars believed that most construction at Túcume dated to the Lambayeque Period, before the Chimú conquest of the region.[1] We can now state that major building at Túcume continued through the Chimú and Inca Periods, and that the site reached its architectural and probably demographic and polit-ical apogees only at the end of the prehispanic sequence.

Lambayeque Period

Túcume was founded around the time that the nearby religious center of Batán Grande was burned and largely abandoned.[2] Kosok believed that the entire Lambayeque Valley Complex was hydrologically united through intervalley canals at this time.[3] Of particular importance for

Túcume is the extension of the Taymi Canal, which allowed irrigation of the coastal plain around the site; without this Túcume probably could not have been built or inhabited.

Our evidence for the Lambayeque Period at Túcume is rather sketchy, as most remains are covered by massive later construction. The first version of Huaca 1 was built at this time, and it is likely that most of the other pyramids in the Monumental Sector began then. In the Lambayeque Period, Huaca Larga was not a long platform at all, but rather a free-standing pyramid like the rest of the Monumental Sector mounds.

Outside the Monumental Sector, occupation in the Lambayeque Period seems less dense than later. There is no evidence for any Lambayeque Period construction on La Raya Mountain or in Sector V; probably most of the small mounds and workshops in the non-monumental sectors of the site were built in the Chimú or Inca Periods. The one possible exception is Huaca Las Balsas, which on iconographic grounds appears to be entirely Lambayeque in date despite the single Chimú-to-Inca Period radiocarbon date. The two pyramids just north and east of Huaca Las Balsas remain unstudied, but comparison with the Monumental Sector suggests that they date initially to the Lambayeque Period; apparently, this area on the south-west edge of the site formed a secondary center within the overall site plan. The Huaca del Pueblo is the third focus of Lambayeque Period monumental construction.[4] Finally, the South Cemetery contains a number of burials dating to the Lambayeque Period.

Our overall impression of Lambayeque Period Túcume is that the site was a pyramid center without a large resident population, not an urban site by any standard definition. Nevertheless, it was the largest site of its time in the region. Shimada argues that Túcume was built to replace Batán Grande as the 'dominant political and religious center of the Lambayeque Valley Complex.'[5] Our data suggest that the religious function was probably dominant early in the site's history, with an increasingly visible political role emerging under foreign control by the Chimú and later Inca empires, at the same time as the site acquired a more urban aspect. The importance of Túcume as a religious center from the beginning is shown by the initial construction of the Temple of the Sacred Stone during the Lambayeque Period and by the probable dating of Huaca Las Balsas to the same period. The continued use and modification of the Stone Temple shows that the site remained an important place in the Lambayeque religious landscape through the Inca Period.

Chimú Period

In the Chimú Period, Túcume continued to grow. In the monumental sector, Huaca 1 (and presumably the other pyramids) continued in use, with a major remodeling some time during the Chimú occupation. At Huaca Larga, the free-standing pyramid of the Lambayeque Period was converted into the long, massive platform still visible today; the investment in labor must have been tremendous. Huaca Larga seems to have been the Chimú administrative center for the Túcume area, and given the lack of similarly monumental architecture around Batán Grande at this time, that region may also have fallen under the jurisdiction of the Túcume center. However, the ethnohistoric record refers to two major, pre-Inca polities in the northern Lambayeque area, Túcume and Jayanca, and Batán Grande may have been part of Jayanca. The immense site of Apurlec was probably the capital of the Jayanca polity.[6]

Schaedel postulated that Huaca Larga was a precursor to the huge walled compounds of Chan Chan, the Chimú capital in the Moche Valley.[7] However, the discovery that the innovative form of this mound dates to the Chimú Period at Túcume indicates that Huaca Larga is probably modeled on the Chan Chan palaces, not vice versa. At Chan Chan, the palace rooms were isolated and protected by surrounding massive walls, while at Túcume, the Huaca Larga rooms were placed on top of a raised platform. Schaedel saw this difference as chronological, a developmental transition from the earlier, free-standing pyramids to the walled compound; we now see the form of Huaca Larga as a synthesis of Chimú and Lambayeque forms. Chimú architects apparently combined imperial Chimú design concepts with the Lambayeque pattern of high platforms to display power in the local idiom.

Outside the Monumental Sector, the site began to fill in with small, elite structures such as the West Mound in Sector V, workshops such as the Rectangular Compound, and residential units such as that in the South Cemetery. With an increasingly dense population and a growing diversity of functions, Túcume began to assume an urban aspect. At Túcume urbanism thus developed during the Chimú domination, rather than being a precursor to it as Schaedel proposed.[8]

Given its size and the Chimú labor investment in the expansion of Huaca Larga, Túcume was probably the Chimú-sponsored center of power for the lands watered by the Leche River and the Taymi Canal, if not for the entire Lambayeque Valley Complex.[9] No other Chimú Period site in the region comes close to Túcume in sheer magnitude. Like the later Inca, the Chimú ruled largely through the local lords.

Certainly they made many concessions to local privilege and tradition: the Lambayeque lords of Túcume seem to have continued to live on and presumably exercise power from the tops of pyramids such as Huaca 1, overlooking the Chimú administrators on Huaca Larga; the Temple of the Sacred Stone continued to receive offerings; and local potters continued to produce ceramics in the traditional Lambayeque style. In this context, we believe that the many small mounds in the west and southwest sectors of Túcume were, like the West Mound, the residences and burial places of elite lineages from the Túcume hinterland, drawn to the site by the prospect of Chimú power-sharing and perhaps the economic gain to be had from overseeing craft workshops.

Inca Period

The Inca conquered the Chimú capital in the 1460s, but then turned their attention to what is now Ecuador. Only a year or so later, around 1470, did an Inca army come marching down the coast from Tumbes, conquering the coastal polities that until recently had formed the northern part of the Chimú empire – among them Túcume.[10]

The Chimú were the greatest rivals of the Inca, and Inca policy towards them centered on a strategy of conquer and divide. Like the Inca empire itself, the Chimú empire was composed of many subordinate polities taken by force or its threat. Both empires ruled largely through the local, hereditary elite; through time, the Inca made these local lords directly subordinate to Cuzco, rather than ruling them through the Chimú royalty. Within one or two generations, the former lords of Chimú ruled only the Moche Valley, and that in the name of the Inca.[11]

Cabello noted in 1586 that the inhabitants of Túcume had been great followers of the Chimú,[12] so it might be expected that they would not have had a privileged place in the Inca empire. Our archaeological research tells us otherwise. As in the Chimú and Lambayeque Periods, Inca Period Túcume remained the largest, most impressive site in the Lambayeque Valley Complex. In fact, labor investment in construction under the Inca was probably even greater than under the Chimú – it is at this time that the structures covering La Raya Mountain were built, the tomb in the Sector V West Mound was emptied and the late phase structure built over it, and, presumably, many other structures throughout the site were modified. During the Inca Period, the entire site was occupied: everywhere we dug (with the exception of Huaca Las Balsas), we found evidence from this date. We believe that, like the Chimú (and probably influenced by their use of the site), the Inca chose Túcume as their regional administrative center and the Huaca Larga as the house of their governor.

As under the Chimú, Inca domination saw the native lords of Túcume continuing to live on top of the pyramids overlooking the Inca administrators. Outside the monumental sector, work in the West Mound suggests some reorganization of the minor nobility; the body in the tomb was removed and a new but equally impressive structure built above it. Perhaps the ancestral mummy buried in the West Mound was taken to Cuzco as a hostage, or perhaps merely relocated to a new, possibly more prestigious location at the site – the Inca often elevated lower-ranking lords to local paramount status when they had cause to distrust the original highest-ranking lord. In any case, the inhabitants of the Inca Period West Mound building continued to use local pottery and live in a large and elaborate structure; presumably these occupants were still native lords.

There are many specific indicators of Túcume's importance under the Inca. First, the use of stone on La Raya and on top of Huaca Larga is an intrusive trait at the site, suggesting Inca involvement. Schaedel was the first to note that there are a number of other sites in the Lambayeque Valley Complex with stone architecture on upper slopes in association with Inca-influenced pottery, but none reach the size or complexity of the La Raya structures.[13]

Second, the conversion of La Raya Mountain into a monument must have impressed all viewers with the power of the site's Inca rulers, especially considering the ancient tradition of worshipping mountains. At the same time, La Raya was prepared to serve as a fortress in case of trouble. Given the effort made to provide access to the White Cave, it may well have been used for Inca solar worship.

Third, the evidence that Huaca Larga housed an Inca *Acllahuasi* (house of the chosen women) seems overwhelming. Such institutions were generally reserved for state centers. Fourth, the principal mummy bundle from Room 1 on Platform 2 of Huaca Larga appears to be the body of an Inca official, probably the last Inca governor of Túcume. Fifth, classic Inca figurines like those offered to the Temple of the Sacred Stone are known only from a handful of sacred sites throughout the Andean region.

Finally, the stone-lined, Inca shaft tombs in Huaca Facho are an intrusive grave type and contain Inca ceramics. The presence of these tombs and those on Huaca Larga provide our best evidence that Túcume housed Inca officials in addition to the local lords empowered to act on behalf of the Inca state. This is a particularly important point considering the lack of documentary evidence for Inca administrators living among the conquered ethnic groups within the empire.[14]

Unfortunately, excavations in other Lambayeque Valley sites dating to the Inca Period are relatively few, so it is difficult to assess fully the idea that Túcume was the Inca administrative center for the entire region. Indeed, in noting the absence of Inca architecture on the north coast, Hyslop suggests that this region was ruled from the highlands or at least the upper valleys to the east of the coastal plain; if this is correct, he further speculates, there may not have been any north coast administrative centers.[15] Although Inca-influenced pottery and other media support the clear ethnohistoric evidence that this area was part of the Cuzco empire, the few 'pure' Inca sites known seem clearly insufficient for imperial administration of such a large, populous, and prosperous area, even considering the policy of rule through local elites. Thus, our work begins to fill a major gap in north coast Inca studies – Hyslop and others have shown that the Inca co-opted local centers for state functions in other parts of the empire, but only our work at Túcume, and especially the discoveries on Huaca Larga, has provided strong archaeological support for this practice on the north coast.

In the Lambayeque Valley Complex, Tambo Real is the only 'pure' Inca facility yet known. This site lies on the Inca coastal road near Batán Grande, less than 10 km (6 miles) from Túcume; if it was truly a *tambo*, then it served as a way station for state-sponsored travelers along the road. In any case, excavations and analysis by Frances Hayashida have shown that this site was an Inca Period pottery workshop, producing mainly utilitarian wares. Preliminary results comparing the chemical composition of pottery made there with similar types found at Túcume and other Inca Period sites in the area suggest that Túcume did not obtain its ceramics from Tambo Real.[16] If confirmed, does this mean that the Inca used Túcume to govern only a very limited area of the Lambayeque Valley Complex? Or was Tambo Real a minor workshop supplying a very local clientele, while undiscovered workshop(s) provided pottery for Túcume? These are among the many mysteries of Túcume yet to be solved.

Túcume and the Lambayeque Tradition

The Lambayeque cultural tradition was long and vibrant, expressed in pottery, textiles, metalwork, friezes, architecture, and mythology. Shimada traces its roots to the late first millennium AD and identifies Batán Grande as its first center.[17] For the final five centuries before the

Spanish Conquest (c. 1050–1532 AD), Túcume was the principal Lambayeque site, recognized as such by Chimú and Inca alike.

Although Lambayeque as an independent culture dates between about AD 750 and 1350, the Lambayeque cultural tradition continued under Chimú, Inca, and even Spanish domination at least through the 16th century. Within this tradition, there are several phases. Both Donnan and Shimada have shown a major disjunction at about AD 1100, around the time Batán Grande was largely abandoned and Túcume founded. Both scholars also point to Lambayeque cultural continuities through the succeeding periods. For instance, Donnan has found that the utilitarian pottery at Chotuna and Chornancap was made without modification from about AD 1100 through the early years of the Colonial Period. With each successive wave of foreign conquest (Chimú, Inca, and Spanish), new elements were added to the corpus but the basic types remained the same.[18]

At Túcume, we see a number of continuities through the sequence. As at Chotuna and Chornancap, so at Túcume pottery changes only by the addition of new elements. Decoration like that found on Shimada's Late Sicán pottery (AD 1100–1350) was still used at Túcume in the Inca Period, as were Middle Sicán (AD 900–1100) Huaco Rey pots.[19] The latter show the persistence of the Lambayeque Tradition at the site, as do the Huaca Las Balsas murals and, on a larger scale, the construction of massive stepped pyramids with ramps. Adobe types and construction techniques are among other persistent Lambayeque traits at Túcume; 'temple entombment'[20] as seen at the Huaca 1 Annex and the West Mound in Sector V reflects a very ancient tradition of regional and even Andean scope.

More complex than the question of continuities or otherwise in material culture is that of political organization in the Lambayeque Valley Complex. Shimada argues that prior to the construction of Túcume, Batán Grande was the center of a Lambayeque religious polity whose authority was based on religious prestige rather than military force. With the burning and abandonment of the major pyramids of the Batán Grande Religious-Funerary Precinct around AD 1050–1100, the center of power shifted to Túcume.[21] Schaedel likewise saw Túcume as the center of a strong Lambayeque polity controlling not only the Leche River section of the Lambayeque Valley Complex, but also the larger, more productive Lambayeque River section to the south. Schaedel based much of his assessment on his inference that Túcume was already an urban site at this time.[22] As noted above, our work suggests otherwise: Lambayeque Period Túcume was probably a non-urban pyramid center with a low resident population. We suspect that, like Batán Grande before it, Túcume at this time had great prestige as a religious center, but lacked secular, political authority over a wide region. We cannot be sure, however, for data from Lambayeque Period sites are insufficient to recognize political hierarchy in any more sophisticated way than on the basis of size (which argues for Túcume's predominance).

At the time of the Spanish Conquest, the Lambayeque Valley Complex was divided into a number of polities, often in competition and occasionally at war. The ethnohistoric record implies that these polities already existed at the time of the Chimú conquest of the area.[23] Perhaps Lambayeque Period Túcume was the leader of a loose regional federation, rather than the capital of a hierarchical state. The manipulation of myth and kinship for political ends was part of the Andean repertoire of statecraft, at least among the Inca,[24] and the Naymlap myth recounting the installation of the dynastic founder's grandchildren at sites throughout the area would have provided a (probably fictitious) kinship basis for such a federation. Kosok came to a similar conclusion: 'The Naymlap legend refers at best only to a kind of kinship-dominated "federation" of local "states" . . . in which the local ruler of Lambayeque was looked on as a kind of senior partner or leading chief.' However, his use of the legend implies a greater belief in its exact historicity.[25]

In any case, both the Chimú and later Inca conquerors of Lambayeque chose Túcume as their regional administrative center, probably to co-opt the site's prestige as well as for strategic reasons. Only under these foreign invaders did the site take on an urban aspect and regional-scale political authority. Though both conquerors wrought major changes in the layout and composition of Túcume, many elements of the Lambayeque cultural tradition continued (as noted above), and there is no doubt that the vast majority of the site's inhabitants and its subjects were ethnically Lambayeque. Nevertheless, we might conclude that urbanism and political centralization were imperial innovations imposed – or inspired – by foreign conquerors for state needs.[26]

The Spanish Conquest and the end of Túcume

In 1532, the Spanish conquistadors under Pizarro landed at Tumbes, marched down the north coast, turned east into the highlands, and began their rapid conquest of the Inca empire. Although they passed close to Túcume, we have no description of the site until some 15 years later, when Pedro Cieza de León described the 'many buildings . . . [as] ruined and brought down.'[27] What happened? How did such an important site fall to ruin so quickly, after five centuries of continuous growth and successful adjustment to two previous foreign conquests? Perhaps Túcume was abandoned at the very beginning of the Spanish Conquest, an event which caused an ideological as well as demographic and economic disruption greater than any that had occurred before. Certainly, part of the answer must lie in this great upheaval. Or perhaps the decline of Túcume had already begun a few years earlier, during the civil war between Atahuallpa and Huáscar, and the Spanish Conquest merely hastened the process.

Still, the ethnohistoric record speaks of the lords of Túcume and their followers long after Cieza's visit in 1547, and the Toledan resettlements (see Chapter 3) did not take place for another three decades. Furthermore, people continued to be buried in the South Cemetery during the early Colonial Period, even though there is little evidence for post-Conquest occupation elsewhere on the site. Although Francisco Pizarro divided Túcume between two *encomenderos* as early as 1536,[28] other polities were similarly divided and yet their capital cities did not so quickly fall to ruin.

Trimborn suggests that the destruction of Túcume resulted from a war with Jayanca during the Inca Period, noted by Cabello.[29] This seems unlikely – our data show no destruction or abandonment during the Inca Period. Rather, the burials of the Inca governor and chosen women in Rooms 1 and 3 on Huaca Larga seem to have taken place at the close of the prehispanic era, and the fill which buried these rooms was laid down in the early Colonial Period. Similarly, the deliberate burial of the West Mound in Sector V must have occurred very late in the Inca Period or at the start of the Colonial Period.

It is easier to understand why intrusive Inca sites such as the vast administrative center of Huánuco Pampa were quickly abandoned after the Spanish Conquest – they were built to serve state needs, and without the Inca state, they had no *raison d'être*. Túcume is another matter. Its location is strategic in relation to irrigation water, the source of life on the desert coast. It had served for centuries as the major center of local people, upholding their cultural principles even under foreign domination by Chimú and Inca overlords. Why was the Spanish Conquest so devastatingly different? Perhaps we shall never know; perhaps this will remain the final mystery of the pyramids of Túcume.

Thor Heyerdahl

Túcume

and the Continuity of Peruvian Culture

L OOKING BACK on the results of the years of archaeological field
work in Túcume, it immediately becomes evident that the prehistory of the Lambayeque Valley cannot be understood except
through its relations with the surrounding Peruvian cultures. The
coming of age of the rather sophisticated culture in the area cannot be
seen as a strictly local phenomenon.

The question of whether or not there had been any sort of interaction between the many diversified pre-Inca cultures has been a major
issue ever since the scholars A. Stübel and M. Uhle laid the foundations of Peruvian archaeology at the end of the 19th century.[1] In the
early 20th century there was a growing tendency among professional
archaeologists to place the burden of proof on those who argued for
continuity of Peruvian culture. This was as a result of specialization.
As archaeology gained impetus as a disciplined science and the general
anthropological approach yielded ground to detailed research, it
became easier to detect traits separating cultures into distinct geographical areas and cultural periods. More widespread trends became
blurred under the scrutiny of specialists who often lost sight of the
pan-Peruvian characteristics which, when seen from the outside, separated Andean cultures from those of the world at large.

By the middle of the 20th century results from excavations in many
areas had vastly increased the previous store of knowledge, gleaned
mainly from studies of religious art objects brought to the surface by
huaqueros. More rigid classification required a new terminology which
divided the pre-Inca cultures on the coast and in the highlands into

ever smaller geographical and chronological units, defined by stratigraphic excavations with radiocarbon dating.

As archaeological information proliferated, most scholars began to see the various pre-Inca cultures as a series of separate phenomena. The Andean geography lent itself to this interpretation. Sky-piercing mountain ranges physically isolated the highland tribes from those along the coast. And along the Pacific littoral vast stretches of desert and impassable coastal cliffs divided the beach of one open valley from that of the next, all of them far apart and each with an identifiable art style. The aboriginal inhabitants were anonymous until classified and named, frequently after the pottery they produced. It became customary to ascribe to each valley its own Formative Period, when the previously primitive food gatherers began to establish settlements and the first evidence of pottery and agriculture appeared. From the Formative stage each separate region continued to develop its own particular culture independently, but along parallel lines until the Incas united them by force.

This 20th-century interpretation was very much in line with the written records of the 16th-century Spanish chroniclers, who came to a totally Inca-dominated Peru too late to know whether other dynasties had extended their influence throughout the land at the peak of their religious and political power. The chroniclers did, however, record the pan-Peruvian claim that the pre-Inca priest-king Con-Ticci-Viracocha had ruled the subsequent Inca territory from Tiahuanaco, in modern Bolivia, until he departed into the Pacific from the northern coast of what is now Ecuador. This strong tradition has been interpreted by some modern observers as memories of cultural diffusion from the Lake Titicaca region, since archaeologists found what they termed Coast Tiahuanaco (now considered to be Huari-influenced) pottery on the northern coast of the subsequent Inca territory.

Such a rigid isolationist view was no longer adhered to at the time extensive excavations began in the Lambayeque Valley. It was common to speak of such highland sites as both Tiahuanaco and Chavín de Huántar as cult and culture centers with wide influence in the Andean area. But, as could be documented in the case of the Inca expansion, a prevalent theory held that pre-Inca population movements must also have been from the interior mountains down toward the coast. It was assumed that no matter how high and wild the inland mountain ranges were, it was easier to cross them to reach the coastal valleys than to move by primitive raft from one valley to the next along the unsheltered Pacific coast.

The archaeology of Túcume clearly showed that the ancient inhabitants did not ignore the ocean. Although the pyramid site was 20 km (12 miles) from the seashore where Naymlap's balsa fleet had landed according to legend, our first surface survey found the entire temple area littered with sea shell fragments, in many places nearly covering the ground. Excavations uncovered fish bones, fragments of fish nets (*ill. 130*), tropical *Spondylus* shell, and various marine motifs, realistic and symbolic, in pottery, wood, adobe reliefs, and wall paintings, featuring a diversity of sea creatures, diving sea birds, and anthropomorphic waves. Clearly, the original culture in Túcume was based to a large extent on maritime activity. Fishing, as well as trade by sea and land, had been at least as important as agriculture to the pre-European population in Túcume.

The vast quantity of tiny beach shells, whole and broken, recalled the former custom, reflected in the Naymlap tradition, that a king could not put his sacred feet on the ground unless a royal servant had walked ahead of him strewing shell where he stepped. Our local workmen assured us, however, that these tiny shells had always been considered a delicacy in Túcume. People from Mórrope, halfway between Túcume and the sea, today dig them up with spoon-shaped sticks. Such minute shells, together with both fresh and sun-dried fish, were still brought almost daily to Túcume by truck and to all the isolated settlements in the surrounding forest by donkey. Traditions lived on in Túcume, and fish from the sea was still an important staple in the local diet.

The Túcume community today

As our archaeological excavations advanced, all who took part in the Túcume project gradually found themselves completely accepted as members of the living Túcume community. In time, we had as many as a hundred local men employed on the site, and we came to know all their families. We were invited into their homes and encountered friendship and hospitality in a village where we had at first not seen an open door or a window without the shutters closed. As the doors opened we were able to see that many of the houses had a desk at the entrance, where a few items like soap, matches, candles, candies, soft-drinks, and even an occasional roll of textiles were for sale. The tiny peep-holes and solid iron bars of the doors reflected what we had already learned from experience: the friendly inhabitants of Túcume housed in their midst a dreaded nest of highway robbers whose fortunes, earned by hijacking trucks at night, helped them out of jail as soon as some honest police caught them and put them in. Every night a horse or a cow disappeared, or a goat or a turkey, and they knew who the thief was. The worst was the charming young citizen nicknamed *El Zorro*, 'The Fox'. He was admired, respected, and feared by everyone because of his incredible agility in running, jumping, and climbing on to roofs and even speeding motor vehicles. Nobody dared to denounce him for fear of reprisals from his family and others who benefited from his very rewarding activities.

One of these agile outlaws assaulted my pickup one moonless night as we drove at full speed through the dark streets of Túcume on the way home from Chiclayo airport. My most important suitcase filled with scientific archives, irreplaceable photographs, and manuscripts was stolen. Pizarro, my faithful driver, himself from Túcume, immediately ventured back into the dark village and found a band of four masked men at the corner where we had turned. With a knife at his throat he retrieved my suitcase with the promise of a ransom of US $400, to be delivered by midnight the following day. I refused to pay any ransom to thieves who stole from me, and suggested Pizarro move inside my fence with his family. News about the threat spread fast, and the general of the police in north Peru came and offered me police protection. This I also refused, and made it clear that I would live just like other people in Túcume, and if they themselves did not drive the gangsters out of their village, then I would leave Peru.

The effect was spontaneous and beyond any expectations. The next day large and small delegations of young and old from the village and the suburbs came to me and asked for my pledge that I would not leave them. The first delegation numbering 80 men and women of all ages was let into my house before I realized how many they were, and with their big hats in their hands they stood for a moment not knowing what to say. Then they all straightened up and began singing the national anthem. It was extremely touching. The last delegation my guardians let in consisted of two little girls, 6 and 8 years old. They forgot everything they had come to say when I offered them a soft drink. But as they left, they suddenly turned around and said together: 'The people want you to stay!' I sent them back to the village with the message that I would stay. We never heard of the thieves again. 'The Fox' moved to another town.

From then on I was considered a Tucumano like them. And I began to feel like one. Even those of our team who were not Peruvians were accepted as *mitimaq*, a term used since Inca times for immigrants who became part of the local community. We went freely in and out of their houses, both those squeezed together in the village streets and those scattered about in the forest. The village houses were built of the same sun-dried adobe blocks as the next door pyramids. Outside the village area the homes of people and animals alike were often just made of cane daubed with mud that hardened to give the appearance of sheets of adobe. Such houses were commodious, clean, and very picturesque, as if they had grown in the sandy ground in harmony with the mango trees and large-leaved banana plants around them. Windows were few or entirely absent, but the intense tropical sun managed to filter in adequate measure through the door and openings in the roof. The village houses seemed tiny from the street, with one door and a little window closed by shutters. At first we wondered how there could possibly be room for the horse, together with cattle and goats, which we sometimes saw being herded in through the door before sunset. But when we were invited inside ourselves, the first room we came to was a spacious reception room intended for parties and sparsely furnished with a long wooden table, with benches and chairs along the walls. Apart from this the room was empty, with the earthen floor clean and swept, ready for dancing. Other rooms opened behind in a long, narrow row that stretched back through the whole block to the next street on the other side. Past two or more bedrooms and a kitchen with huge ceramic pots and a glowing wood fire, was a small open backyard where there was a shed with a deep and narrow hole in the ground, and where chickens and a couple of ducks or turkeys kept company with the larger animals we had seen entering the front door. This strange architecture was so uniform that it had to be old. It also gave the impression that theft was not a recent phenomenon in these parts. There was no way for burglars to enter except from the flat, mud-covered roof, and that was where the Tucumanos kept their snarling dogs, some of which were of the edible, hairless type of their ancestors, with gray skin like elephants. The archaeologists mapped the floor plan of the Túcume houses as a guide for the better interpretation of foundation walls and postholes they found during excavation around and on top of the pyramids.

We shared the genuine joys of life with the Tucumanos. We ate with them at their long tables in polite silence, so that everyone could concentrate on the pleasures of the palate, and we learned the art of eating elegantly with two fingers and a thumb, at best assisted by a spoon. The food they favored was solid chunks of goat or duck served with beans and rice, or raw fish prepared with lemon, onion, and hot red pepper, making a delicious dish called *ceviche*. All was washed down, when our turn came to drink from the huge gourd bowl, with *chicha*, a gray, fermented brew of maize passed from person to person with ceremonial courtesy.

In Túcume, where young and old missed no occasion to celebrate, the men, and sometimes also the women, were great orators. They enjoyed both giving and listening to speeches, had a keen sense of humor, and welcomed jokes at any opportunity. Birthdays started with firecrackers and ended with dancing and dinner parties at which loudspeakers played music at such a volume that even the most distant hut in Túcume realized where the party was. Those of us who participated inside worried about our eardrums and felt completely deaf when we finally emerged after hours of celebration into the silent village. Letting off firecrackers and shooting shotguns usually began before the cock crowed, and we had to inform our own guests about this custom since several of them were convinced that the Shining Path was attacking when they were woken by sudden bombardments in the black night. Firecrackers were used in celebrations for both living villagers and every popular saint. If a person's birthday coincided with that of a saint, he would start his firecrackers and shots as soon as possible after midnight to be sure to be heard before the shooting started in honor of the saint.

Every new possession, whether it was an object, a construction, or a child, needed a godfather. To have a godfather was essential, and to be one was a great honor. It became my privilege to perform the role of godfather for everything from newborn babies, from whom I had to cut a strand of hair, to the village police station, schools, and other buildings on which I had to smash a bottle of *chicha* suspended above the door. When President Alan García presented a bulldozer to Túcume after his weekend with us, this technical marvel was parked in front of the church entrance for Padre Pedro to sprinkle with holy water, while I had to break a bottle of champagne on the newly blessed carapace of the iron monster.

The fertile irrigated fields and the mild coastal climate meant that the Tucumanos suffered less hardship than the mountain Indians of Inca descent. Their cleanliness gave them normally good health. Very rarely did we see children with runny noses and hardly ever did we hear children cry, but it took nothing to make them burst into laughter and dance with joy. It was a mystery to us how the Tucumanos kept so clean. The men always came out of their houses with spotless shirts, as if fresh from the laundry, and the women with equally clean, colorful gowns. Water had been piped to Túcume before the last disastrous flood, but we rarely saw a house with an indoor water tap. The ancient Moche canal, dry most of the year, filled with bathing people when the chocolate-colored water was released from the big dam in the mountains.

But tragedy knocked on the doors of Túcume as inevitably as in the rest of the world. There was no doctor and it was a long way to the nearest hospital for the few who could afford the trip. We helped with our own transport whenever called upon, but one day our own driver Pizarro rushed from the car to vomit – he had cholera, which spread with the speed of the highway trucks that brought unclean fish from infested ports further south on the coast. About the same time my cook Chona and my housekeeper and secretary Carmen got typhoid. All three recovered. But the cholera took many lives and it was clear that it came with the fish along the road since it took a long time before it reached the more isolated fishing villages on the coast northward.

Terrible and gripping were the long, slow marches to the cemetery along donkey trails from isolated homes. Loudly weeping women surrounded the coffin and men with damp, unhappy eyes and lips pressed together trailed behind. Once, when one of our workmen died, the family insisted on a long detour to our archaeological camp where I delivered a little speech and the man in the coffin could make his last farewell to the place where he had so happily worked.

It was not long before we began to realize that what we excavated from the weathered ruins in their midst was not indifferent to the local people. However, when I first arrived with Walter Alva to inform the mayor and the leaders in the village that I had come with permission from the government to start excavations among the pyramids, the population, with a single teacher as an exception, made it very clear that they wanted no *huaqueros* (tomb robbers) in their territory, even if we were professionals and came with permission from Lima. Walter had already had a bad experience. At his pyramid site in Sipán he went to work with a loaded pistol for fear of reprisals from the family of the local *huaquero* who had been shot when Walter first arrived with the police. As Walter gradually continued to discover more tombs containing burials with gold and silver, his site had to be constantly guarded by armed police behind barricades of sandbags. But when the Tucumanos saw that our first act was to build adobe houses for storage and public display at the very entrance to the pyramid area, their attitude changed to one of full collaboration. A strange notion began to dawn upon all of us, locals and excavators: jointly we were digging up their direct ancestral past. It was not as in Egypt, Iraq, or the Indus valley, where invading foreigners had taken over the land that once belonged to long-lost civilizations. The people we lived among in Túcume were directly descended from the pyramid builders. Whether their names were Pizarro, as my driver, Castro, as my foreman, or Siesquén, Tuñoque, and Musayón as some of my other neighbors, their ancestors were the original Peruvians. To judge from their physical appearance, there was not much blood of the Spanish conquistadors in the Tucumanos. And perhaps more surprisingly, these people on the north coast had none of the typical Quechua features of the Inca invaders who had conquered the Lambayeque Valley three generations before the Spaniards. The inhabitants of the area were themselves very conscious of this.

Túcume Vivo

It was my close collaborator and friend Suy Suy who opened my eyes to what he termed the continuity of Peruvian culture. Suy Suy came from the larger town of Moche, just south of Trujillo and the ruins of Chan Chan, the prehistoric capital of the Chimú kingdom. With his proud and impressive features I believed him when he insisted that he was of pure Moche descent. He was a living personification of the pre-Inca portrait vases representing Moche chiefs, and he used only the Moche part of his name, his full name being Victor Antonio Rodríguez Suy Suy. The Peruvian archaeologists on our site had all studied anthropology under him when he was professor at the National University in Trujillo, and they considered him the father of Peruvian anthropology.

Suy Suy, well past the age of retirement, accepted my invitation to direct a project I had decided to call *Túcume Vivo*, 'Living Túcume', to distinguish it from the archaeological project. The two became entirely separate organizations – the excavations were sponsored and financed by the Kon-Tiki Museum, whereas Túcume Vivo was a social-aid program. It received annual funds from the private Strömme Foundation, a benevolent organization run on donations from Norwegian families with the aim of providing help wherever it was needed in developing countries.

We quickly became aware that the people of Túcume, protecting their meager property behind barred doors and surviving on their income from tiny fields, needed outside funds to restore the modest living standard they had lost in 1983. In that year a terrible deluge of El Niño rain swept their animals and farms away and sent coffins drifting from the cemetery down the streets together with their furniture. Most of their houses were still badly in need of repair, others were crumbled beyond hope. The town lacked a sewer system and all liquids were thrown out of the houses to evaporate and blow in again as clouds of dust.

When the Lima director of the Strömme Foundation came to visit us in Túcume, we went together to see the three schools in the village, since the well-being of children is the main concern of the donors. We found the smiling and clean children sitting on some empty boxes and planks, as all furniture worth carrying away had been stolen. In one classroom even the entrance door had been stolen, and the opening was closed by bricks to safeguard a table and some desks that were left. Thus no thief could get in, but neither could the pupils.

We asked to inspect the toilet facilities, and once received a great shock. In a school for the youngest children, where the Village Pyramid towered majestically over the schoolyard, a teacher opened the door to a one-room shack and we stepped in – and ran out again. I held my breath and ventured to peep in once more. All I saw was a large room with a central hole in the ground for the common use of 500 little boys and girls, who were so afraid of falling in that many had not dared to venture right up to the edge.

Considerable funds were immediately promised from donors in Norway, and with Suy Suy as field director, the operations of Túcume Vivo began with the construction of modern facilities for all the schools, and a sewer system and running water for the village. School books were for the first time distributed to the children, who received them with cheers as if they were toys. When new desks were carried into the classrooms, the family fathers volunteered to build high walls around the schoolyards with bricks and cement from Túcume Vivo, so thieves could not get in. And more effective than any hairless watchdog was our idea of providing a shelter with a comfortable bed to a homeless old woman inside the schoolyard, for if a burglar managed to climb the wall, she would shout louder than any dog could bark.

Suy Suy expanded the activities of Túcume Vivo to every satellite settlement in the algarrobo forest around the pyramid area. There were about a dozen schools that could be reached by car on roads little better than mule tracks. Most traffic was barefoot pedestrians though occasionally one would meet some trotting horseman who lifted his hat, and tiny donkeys invisible but for their legs under burdens of twigs and maize leaves, or carrying some smiling farmer if not two or three laughing children. Sometimes long trains of donkeys passed us heavily laden with huge jars or sacks of salt or lime from the coast. All seemed the same as in the days before the donkeys replaced the llamas which our excavations showed had been common even here in the lowlands in pre-European times. Loads of illegally-cut algarrobo wood also passed unseen along these forest trails to the market in Chiclayo, evading the police.

Deeper inside the forest an estimated 1000 squatters had settled as outlaws in an almost impenetrable wilderness known as Batán Grande. They made their living as charcoal burners by cutting the sometimes millennia-old jungle trees protected by the government as Peru's only remaining virgin forest west of the Andes. The President had personally come on a visit with a hundred policemen, but they had failed to penetrate the trailless thickets controlled by the armed squatters. Once I managed to drive along back trails with our pickup full of Tucumanos and we could hear the axes illegally at work near and far. We had ventured in to inspect a huge dry river bed which in Niño years flooded the old Moche canal and thus had caused the last catastrophe in Túcume. But as we tried to return out along the same lonely mule tracks, we found the passage blocked by a barricade of freshly cut trees. When we attempted to remove them we saw men with sticks and guns emerging from the trees on either side of the trail. They lowered their arms when they recognized some of my companions, but bluntly refused to move the barricade even when we explained that we had come in the interests of all local people to see how we could dam or clear the bed of the Río Leche. We even used their own nickname for the hated Leche (Milk) River, which was Río Loco (Mad River), but to no avail. We had to go back along the trail until we managed to bump across some of their clearings and come out on some other tracks, where we were stopped by another gang hostile to the first, who finally let us out.

The area around Túcume and the surrounding villages was literally a large oasis, and the Tucumanos were in reality desert people whose prerequisite for life was the water that flowed in the ancient Moche canal system. The amount of water in the old Taymi Canal determined their harvest, formed a topic of daily conversation, and was a thermometer of their moods. Nobody spoke about the weather – the sky was always blue and the rare clouds dry. Drought in the distant Andes caused famine in the plains but real catastrophe occurred in the worst Niño years when torrents of water tore loose boulders, sand, and trees, burst dams and canals, and swept away houses, animals, and fields.

Seven years had passed since the last, almost Biblical flood, when we began excavations in Túcume. Another catastrophe was expected at any time, indeed it seemed almost overdue when finally in 1992 the fishermen on the coast began to talk about an undertow in the coastal current which pulled their nets in the wrong direction and brought strange fishes up from the deep. They had to cease fishing due to the numbers of huge sea lions which destroyed their nets and gathered on the beaches. We feared the worst, and I flew to Norway in an effort to raise additional funds from the Strömme Foundation for emergency work to stem a new possible flood. Our North American archaeologist Dan Sandweiss was a specialist in the history of the Niño years throughout the centuries, and he could point to unmistakable archaeological evidence showing how the worst Niño floods had destroyed coastal cultures and caused population movements.

Suy Suy had been a pioneer in the study of the ancient Moche canal system in the Lambayeque Valley, and for years he had campaigned for the repair of sections destroyed by floods in modern times, and for the reopening of branches that had fallen into disuse. His early field investigations had revealed that far more land had been cultivated in pre-European times, when the complete Moche irrigation system was in operation, with its widespread network ending in a neat pattern of small comb-shaped trenches still traceable in the barren land.

Guided by Suy Suy's knowledge of the ancient Moche canal system that could still be traced in its entirety from the distant mountains, we mapped and repaired all damaged and vulnerable stretches in the last kilometres above Túcume. If an overflow occurred along the 55 km (c. 30 miles) higher up, this would hurt Túcume less as most of it would enter another branch of the main Taymi Canal which bypassed the village of Mochumí and entered the ocean.

An emergency project of canal repairs was set in motion by Túcume Vivo and administered in my absence by my efficient Peruvian secretary Carmen Barrantes. Back from Norway with more funds I was to experience activities that must have been part of life in Túcume from the time the canals were first built. A whole army of local farmers of all ages followed me as we climbed down into the bone-dry Taymi Canal and began shoveling sand washed in from the desert up on to the banks high above our heads. In the meantime Carmen, with the aid of a local engineer and the farmer in charge of water distribution, purchased cement, iron, and logs for the fast repair of the many sections of the canal where the torrents and drifting trees in 1983 had broken through dams and barricades. Modern equipment was used only where danger was most imminent and voluntary manpower too slow. In general it was sufficient to line the channel with clayey soil and hammer down a barricade of willow posts. To our surprise, the moisture under the canal immediately made the posts shoot new growth and, more important, produce a thick web of roots that helped consolidate the earthen walls.

Clearing the local stretch of canal was in fact an annual event of communal duty, toil, joy, and celebration. Older people recalled practices that probably went back to Inca times, if not before. The entire population took part in the cleaning in August each year, which was also an occasion for *fiesta*. The signal was given by a certain señor Don Rumichi, who came out of his house and began beating a drum. Then a man went around blowing a trumpet, announcing to all the farmers that the annual clearing should begin. Soon the workers swarmed like bees into and all along the canal. Each land-owner had to contribute a certain number of men for a certain number of days. There was an official in charge of water distribution at the head, and the land-owners often controlled their own men.

The day was long, so little children brought their fathers home-brewed *chicha* during work. But time for food and rest came when the sun began to sink towards the horizon. Workers, foremen, cooks, and land-owners all joined on the banks, where special tents had been set up for everybody to relax on sheepskin rugs and eat and drink. They had reason to celebrate, for they all knew that their day's work assured another year of decent livelihood for their families. There was music from guitars and song and dance and all sorts of merry-making until well into the night. And when the clearing of the Taymi Canal was finished for the year, everybody, young and old, marched in solemn processions behind a wooden Virgin carried through the villages, from one to another.

Suy Suy was sure that even this ceremony was a survival from ancient times. And although most Virgins we saw looked like giant dolls in wedding gowns, I happened to help carry one that was very different. The statue was totally hidden behind a veil and dressed in the usual elegant feminine attire, but I had rather a shock when an unexpected gust of wind lifted the veil. Although it was hurriedly replaced I got a glimpse of an old tree trunk with a queer face carved in high relief at the center of a somewhat crooked cross formed by two natural branches. This was neither Christ on the cross nor the Virgin Mary, but something truly old and pagan that must have served in similar processions since before the day it was wrapped decently and consecrated to Christianity.

From the time I saw that covered-up image, I began to note the importance of such tripod tree-trunks with two lateral branches rising slightly upwards to resemble a somewhat distorted cross. I saw them in various sizes – tiny ones set up respectfully in houses with flowers in front, and huge ones in backyards painted white. Once, when we were invited to a lonely old school in the forest to inaugurate new classrooms we had helped set up, we took part in a feast celebrated to mark the occasion. As if slightly embarrassed, the school master first took us to a dead and barkless tree with a trunk and two branches cut to resemble something between a huge trident and a cross, which still stood in the middle of the playground. He wanted us to participate in an age-old local ceremony. I noted that the bare wood of the tri-forked trunk was hard and smooth as bone from human touch. With children and parents crowding around us as solemn spectators, the school master, smiling shyly, poured a little *chicha* down the dead tree, followed by some *ceviche* and maize corn.

One day Alfredo, supervising archaeological work at a Chimú–Inca burial ground southeast of the main pyramid area, sent for me to look at a huge, living algarrobo tree next to the site where a dozen of our men were digging. Nature had given the tree the form of a cross with two large out-stretched branches which were covered with green leaves. In every nook and hollow of the bark and branches metal coins had been stuck in, some of them very old and real collectors' pieces. Someone must have noticed our curiosity, for next day when we returned to look again, the tree was stripped of every single coin and stood there just like one of the thousands of other algarrobo trees around it.

February 23 is an important day for the populations of both Túcume and the neighboring town of Mochumí, which receives its water from the other main branch of the Taymi Canal. The two towns jointly celebrate the ancient settlement of a long-lasting strife over water by carrying a sacred Virgin along the Panamerican highway from the one town to the other. The procession is escorted by masked devil dancers from the two towns, taking over from each other at the halfway mark. The tiny and pale-painted wooden Virgin looks remarkably unaffected by the horrible hoard of black devils dancing along as her escort to the rhythm of trumpets and drums.

El Purgatorio

Significantly, the devils seem to have arrived together with the first introduction of the Virgin. Oral history in Túcume maintains that when the Spaniards first came in the 16th century, they built a colossal cathedral just to the north of the Huaca Larga pyramid. We were certainly impressed when we were shown the ruins of this enormous early Spanish structure. It had collapsed during the last century together with all the adobe houses in the original Túcume settlement, when a terrible Niño flood caused the population to move the main village to its present position around its more modest village church. Many old people told us that their grandparents were forced to chain their Virgin with her Child inside the new church, for more than once she disappeared at night to return to the people she had deserted in Old Túcume. But living memories went even further back, to the days when the first Spanish settlers came with the Christian faith. Most Tucumanos were readily converted, but not all. Then the devils came at the heels of the Virgin and Child, arriving at night at a terrible speed in a large wagon pulled by four horses. Although the Tucumanos realized that it was the Spaniards themselves painted black and wearing masks with horns and big teeth, the noise from the wheels and the bells hanging on the horses and the devils' clothes scared them into their houses. Those who would not accept Christian baptism were dragged out and burnt on the pyramids. At night the Spaniards carried wood for great fires on the top of the highest *huacas*, and they called the entire sacred area *El Purgatorio*, Purgatory. The flames from the pyramids flickering in the night sky were visible for miles around, and the Spanish clergy told the people that to approach the area was deadly dangerous, for this was the entrance to Hell. The modern clergy in Peru were not afraid to admit the grave errors of their predecessors in the days of this inquisition.

We began to wonder whether the local stories were not based on some truth. At the start of our excavations on top of Huaca 1 we dug with our trowels and brushes down through superimposed layers of time. Shortly below the present-day surface we came across the dried remains of a lizard with needles pierced through its skin. Next to it was the faded photo of a man, also pierced through with needles. Modern medicine men had been here with their sorcery. A little deeper lay well-preserved Inca burials. And deeper still we found the remains of a pre-Inca temple with walls beautifully decorated with reliefs of seabirds swimming in a row.

On the very summit of Huaca Larga, the largest of all the man-made pyramids, Alfredo and his team had not dug very deep before they found remains of huge wood fires that must have been visible from surrounding villages. The fires had burnt amidst crumbled temple walls, some of adobe and some of crude stone, and the heat had been so intense that several of the surrounding walls had vitrified and formed glassy slag. Among masses of charcoal and carbonized wood

169 *Alfredo Narváez examining a burnt skeleton from the final fill of Huaca Larga, Platform 2 (Early Colonial Period).*

were burnt human bones – crania as well as long-bones. Some of these human remains had been thoroughly burned and others not (*ill. 169*). But had they been burned dead or alive? And, were they burned before or after the arrival of the Spanish?

The mystery did not diminish when we discovered that the entire area of the summit was covered with ruins, some of stone and built in Inca time, and some of adobe and of pre-Inca origin. All had been intentionally buried under immeasurable quantities of sand carried up from below. The ruins on the highest platform of Huaca Larga had been covered with sand that must have come from a still older and already abandoned cemetery at ground level, for in this fill were numerous unburnt human bones and an impressive variety of pot-sherds from funerary vessels.

Huaqueros had attempted to dig a hole at the very summit but aban-doned their effort, presumably disheartened by the charred remains. They had, however, broken down a small section of the Inca stone wall, thus helping us to detect an older adobe wall behind, which was beauti-fully decorated with pre-Inca frescoes, painted in red, white, and black, of symmetric bands of diving seabirds with eyes like the symbol of the sun.

A marked difference in the evidence of burning at the two pyramids examined was discernible. The remains of fire on Huaca Larga were found on the very top of the structure, and the burning had taken place locally, to judge from the signs of heat on the stone walls and the adobe that had turned red as brick. The thick layer of pure ashes in the tiny enclosures on Huaca 1 was instead at the foot of the pyramid, and the fires must have burned elsewhere because the adobe blocks next to the ashes had retained their unbaked tan color. From where had that vast quantity of ashes been brought? Had they been carried in the large undecorated earthen pots that lay broken into large sherds together with the fine ashes? The ashes at the foot of Huaca 1 were obviously evidence of some ceremony associated with fire. Would we ever discover where such a ceremonial fire was lit since it so obviously had neither been on the top or at the foot of Huaca 1?

El Horno, The Oven

One day I was showing the impressive adobe walls of the former Spanish cathedral to my companion Jacqueline, when we unexpectedly came upon a curiosity that I felt might have a bearing on the mystery of the ceremonial burning. I was examining the imposing thickness of the adobe walls of the ruined cathedral and wondering whether they were part of an earlier pre-Colonial structure or had been constructed by baptized Tucumanos used to building colossal adobe structures. Jacqueline was roaming about in the surrounding algarrobo groves, exploring terrain that bore every evidence of having been thoroughly looted by generations of *huaqueros*. She came back and reported that hidden behind all the trees she had found a huge eroded pyramid with a splendid view of Huaca Larga, which was just on the other side of the canal. I told her that we knew that pyramid well, it was outside our area of investigations, but part of the main Túcume archaeological complex. Suy Suy was always interested in this area, known as *Túcume Viejo*, Old Túcume. He was sure that it had been extremely important at the time the Spanish conquistadors came, otherwise they would not have built such a huge cathedral just at this site. They usually built their first churches on top of the most sacred places of the people they converted, to force them to worship at the same spot but to the new divinity.

The real mystery began when Jacqueline asked a man who lived at foot of this pyramid and said it was his, what its name was. The huaca had no name. Jacqueline insisted, such a big man-made hill had to have a name. But no, no name, except that the whole area was Old Túcume and formerly it was known as *El Horno*, 'The Oven'. We asked why The Oven, but the man did not know. We asked other people independently, and they all said that Old Túcume was formerly known as The Oven. We asked yet more people in farms far away where The Oven was, and old people immediately answered it was Old Túcume, with the ruins of the old church.

Another old man showed us the real oven – right next to the immense door of the cathedral, only five steps from the corner and in line with the front wall. It looked like a huge heap of eroded adobe, and we had climbed over it many times when going round the outside of the church walls. The man pulled away some dry branches hiding an opening and peeping in we could see it really had been an oven, and a very large one, with adobe blocks in the vaulted ceiling fired red from heat.

Nobody could tell us when this oven had been built, or what it had been used for. A man a couple of decades ago had tried to bake bread inside, but it had not been a success. Everybody agreed that the oven was probably as old as the church if not older, for no farmer would come and build an oven at the very corner of the cathedral. It must have been there before the church, otherwise why was the whole area of Old Túcume known as The Oven, and not The Cathedral?

Who had built this strange and obviously important oven, the first Christians or their local predecessors? It was not for baking bread and nobody used ovens of this kind for firing pottery in Túcume. The entire area around was a burial ground before the church had been built, and every time we went inside the former cathedral, we found new, tiny makeshift crosses with flowers on the earthen floor. The Catholics did not practice cremation. But perhaps those who had carried the vast amounts of fine ashes to the foot of Huaca 1 did? It would have been a long way to carry an urn with ashes from The Oven to Huaca 1. But an urn was lighter than a coffin, and we had marched with old and young Tucumanos behind a coffin from a lonely farm further away, past The Oven and Huaca 1 to the modern cemetery on the other side of the present Túcume village. And with the canal, people could travel easily to the pyramid site even from distant parts of the former kingdom.

Trade and travel in ancient Túcume

Ample evidence was found at Túcume to prove that the ancient Peruvians traveled widely by both land and sea. Llamas were used as pack animals until the Spaniards introduced donkeys and the llamas completely vanished from the lowland population. Alfredo found thick deposits of llama dung along the inner walls of the temple plaza of Huaca 1. The tracks of their tiny hoofs were also preserved, together with footprints of barefoot children, in the mud they had been transporting to serve as mortar to bind the adobe blocks. Small boys, then as now, obviously accompanied the pack animals. At his habitation site Dan found well-preserved remains of a stable, full of llama dung. Tropical bird feathers as well as the steering oar of a balsa found at the same site, were further evidence that the ancient residents traveled widely and had contacts with remote jungle countries on the other side of the Andes or far up the coast in the Ecuadorian jungle.

Striking evidence of Túcume having been a center of early Peruvian intercommunications came when Alfredo followed hints from people living in modern Túcume's suburb La Raya, 'The Ray', named like the central mountain cone after the mythical fish. These people had earlier pointed out a large depression north of Huaca Larga, where they insisted a real ray had been swimming around in an artificial lake until recent memory. Now they claimed that a very small elevation in the ground not far from the lost lake and right at the foot of Huaca Larga had also been something very important. Alfredo had been working for some time on the pyramid top above, where, below the clay floor of the Inca stone temple, he had found the first well-preserved mummy bundles on one side, and a large number of elite weavers with aristocratic ornaments and beautifully carved tools on the other.

He sent some of his men down to check what the bump on the ground below was hiding, and thus discovered a small, horseshoe-shaped temple with an inclined stone, or *huanca*, in the middle. At first all seemed rather insignificant, but it was found that a ceremonial road had passed right by this little temple, called the Stone Temple or Temple of the Sacred Stone, and everywhere around and inside offerings had been buried (pp. 101–115). They included no fewer than 31 complete, newborn llamas. In one deep, round hole lay a decapitated human head, in another a hand. Among the offerings were also more than 250 samples of miniature art cut out from thin sheets of silver, representing birds, fishes, crabs, pumas, leaves, trees, clubs, ceremonial axes, shields, paddles – both single- and double-bladed – trumpets, pan-pipes and other flutes, drums, rattles, parasols, litters, hammocks, stirrup-spout jars and other pottery forms, sandals, human masks, various forms of ceremonial headgear, royal regalia and nondescript forms. The last were probably pieces left over from the sheets cut up for all the other images.

Most beautiful of all these offerings were two skillfully executed silver images, about 8 and 17 cm (3 and 7 in) tall and thus much larger than the silver miniatures and, unlike them, modelled into form. The naked silver figurines were fully dressed, one in woven cotton cloth fastened with a copper alloy pin. But more beautiful was the other, wrapped in a brightly coloured wool poncho and wearing a

170–171 (opposite above and below) Details of the Huaca Las Balsas frieze showing birdmen holding round objects. The one above (Phase HB-4) is from a section of wall cut by looters to the right (north) of the main panel, and is very reminiscent of the crouching birdman holding an egg so dominant in the religious art of Easter Island. The line of birdmen (below) come from a crested wall, bordering a ramp (Phase HB-2).

meticulously manufactured headdress of brilliant red down from jungle birds, obtained from very distant hunters. Alfredo recovered this figurine from a deep offering hole, its red wool cloak held together with a traditional silver pin, only to discover that another archaeologist had also found a feather-crowned image, identical in every detail to his.[2] However, the other one had been excavated in northern Chile, around 3000 km (2000 miles) from Túcume. Both figurines dated to the Inca Period and were evidence of long-distance contact in pre-European times. Complete *Spondylus* shells from Ecuador, in the opposite direction, were also found as offerings in and around this seemingly insignificant but obviously important shrine.

The most peculiar testimony to the mobility of the original Peruvians was a vast hoard of small potsherds packed together as a single offering in a small, covered hole. Our laboratory staff at the site immediately set about trying to piece together the many fragments, only to find that no two of them belonged to the same pot. They could be identified by their fabric, shape, and decoration as deriving from completely distinct parts of Peru and belonging to different cultural periods. How could this be explained? They had all clearly been deposited in one lot and had hardly belonged to a prehistoric art collector who treasured potsherds like some collect stamps today. The only explanation could be that pilgrims came to the important pyramids in Túcume from all over Peru, and true to local custom each of them picked up a potsherd somewhere along his or her route, to deposit as a symbolic contribution to the temple. At one time the temple guardian had found it fit to offer the entire collection to the deity of the shrine.

We do not know the routes by which the silver figurines in feather headdresses traveled to end up respectively in Túcume and Chile. Both may have been manufactured by the same Inca craftsman in a Cuzco workshop. But the *Spondylus* shells must have come from tropical waters off the coast of Ecuador, if not still further north. In Túcume

172 A Moche line drawing of reed boats propelled by human legs running across the tops of the waves.

we found what archaeologists and *huaqueros* have discovered in tombs and sacred structures all over Peru: travelers to or from the waters north of the subsequent Inca empire brought *Spondylus* shells with them southward as personal property or trade items for thousands of years. It was only after *c.* AD 600 that they became common enough to require organized sea trade.[3]

Rafts of some navigable type must have been used for long-range off-shore navigation, as was amply documented in historical evidence. At the time of the Inca domination the coastal population preferred commodious sailing rafts of balsa logs, the boats made of bundles of reeds being more common on the highland lakes without easy access to balsa timber. Although reed boats of pre-Inca form, with elevated bow and stern, were still used on the coast until recent times, it was the one-man, tusk-shaped raft of totora reeds that survived in daily use among the modest, independent fishermen.

Thanks to pre-Inca art we know that both reed-boats and log-rafts had been used along the Pacific coast of Peru since early Moche times. To judge from the overwhelming number of reed vessels depicted (*ills 173–174*) as compared to more exceptional illustrations of log-rafts, it might be assumed that reed was a more popular building material for watercraft than balsa logs in Moche and Chimú times. However, this imbalance may partly be due to the fact that both in profile line drawings and in three-dimensional modeling a stout, moon-shaped boat is easier and more tempting to depict than a flat platform of a raft. Divine royalties travelling on log-rafts pulled by swimming men do occur in three-dimensional Moche effigy vessels, although not so common as free-standing pottery models of reed-boats propelled by paddlers fore and aft. Such moon-shaped reed-boats are also very common in textile decorations and as motifs on silver bowls and other artifacts of metal and wood.

Much more speculation has surrounded the complex Moche line

drawings on pottery which show ships of reed bundles with upturned
bow and stern – very often a curious double stern – with the elevated
parts terminating in heads of sea-monsters or mythical snakes. These
reed ships commonly have a two-story deck, such as seen by early eye-
witnesses on balsa log-rafts in Peru (ill. 172). On the lower decks rows
of water jugs are sometimes depicted, in other cases there are lines of
small men who occasionally seem to be roped prisoners. On the upper
deck stands the solar deity or divine personage with his company of
usually bird-headed men. Sometimes other bird-headed men pull the
reed-ship through the water with ropes, and these assistants have the
very long beaks of marine birds, whereas those on deck have short,
hooked beaks like birds of prey.

Most scholars who have studied these fascinating Moche navigation
scenes have noticed that the ships are often shown as if running over
the water with anthropomorphic legs, depicted with thighs so broad
that they seemed to represent *guaras*, or navigation boards. One day a
group of us studying a selection of such Moche boat illustrations

included the visiting Director of the Kon-Tiki Museum, Dr Öystein Koch Johansen. He happened to be an archaeologist and at the same time a specialist in ancient religions. Familiar with the Inca legend which described their ancestral priest-king departing from Peru 'walking on the water', he pointed to the legs carrying the vessel in the Moche line-drawing over the tops of the waves. Clearly the Incas had borrowed this poetic verbal expression from the graphic illustrations of their coastal predecessors.

Revival of reed-boats

A German film team once visited us in Túcume as they wanted the local fishermen to help them build a large reed-boat to sail to the Galapagos Islands, off the coast of Ecuador. Almost 200 one-man bundle-boats of totora reeds (known as 'caballitos') were in use in the nearest fishing village of Pimentel and there were more of them in Santa Rosa, a little further south. But the totora reeds formerly culti-

174 Balsa rafts of reed bundles are far more common than log balsas in the art of pre-Inca periods on the coast. This blackware effigy jar from the North Coast has a fixed support for a removable mast, locally known as a zapato, or shoe. Carved from a solid block of wood, the zapato is still used by fishermen in the same area on their small sailing rafts of balsa wood. (From the collection of the Cassinelli Museum, Trujillo, Peru.)

vated in vast quantities along the coast were becoming scarcer with the advance of modern civilization, and we were supporting the fishermen in their appeals to the authorities to reserve land for cultivation of the reeds. As we had by now tested out the single-stern reed-ship in three major oceans, I suggested to the Germans that they reconstruct one of the Moche variety with a double stern. Truckloads of totora reed were brought from an area still providing this material for reed-boat fishermen in Huanchaco, near the former Chimú capital of Chan Chan.

Paulino, an Aymara Indian from Lake Titicaca, was an experienced reed-boat builder who had helped us construct our reed vessels. First he had traveled to Morocco to build *Ra II* for the Atlantic crossing; then he came to Oslo to help preserve the same vessel as it lost its shape when reeds and ropes dried out after the voyage; next he went to Iraq to build *Tigris* for the Indian Ocean crossing. Later he built the *Uru* for Kitín Muñoz's Pacific voyage, and finally, in Denmark, he built a reed-ship for exhibit at the Viking museum in Roskilde. He now came at the Germans' request to northern Peru to show the local fishermen how their ancestors had built the large double-sterned vessels. This time Paulino arrived with his own visiting card, which gave his title as *constructor de balsas transoceánicas* ('builder of transoceanic rafts'), and his address as *Suriqui Island, Lake Titicaca*.

The Germans built their vessel, called the *Chimok*, and with its double stern it was so safe and steady in the ocean swells that the director of the film team suddenly leapt on board with the doctor at the very moment of departure. The ship looked magnificent, and with one Aymara hoisting the sail and a local fisherman at the rudder-oar, it took off into the open ocean. I was invited to jump on board from the pier and see them off, and found the doctor and the film director stretched out, one in each upturned stern, using them as deck chairs, seasick beyond cure. Fortunately for the two of them, the Ecuadorian authorities denied them access to the Galapagos unless they first sailed into port in Guayaquil to obtain a landing permit for this Ecuadorian territory. The film team decided to end their expedition in Peruvian waters and disembarked on the north Peruvian coast. The proud but abandoned *Chimok* sailed alone with the Humboldt Current. Nicolás, the Peruvian fisherman on board, used to one-man reed craft, was reluctant to part with the large reed ship which he had managed to sail in a large circle when passing the Lobos Islands.

From the moment the fishermen on the north coast noticed our interest in their humble but traditional types of watercraft, they began to organize paddling competitions with large numbers of their regular one-man bundle-boats of totora reeds, and also real sailing regattas for their somewhat larger fishing vessels of balsa logs. They even began building big reed-ships following their own design and sailed them in balsa festivals. First there was a Festival of the Ocean in Huanchaco, with men and women in costumes portraying King Takaynamo landing with his entourage to found Chan Chan. Next the fishermen of Pimentel and Santa Rosa reconstructed reed-ships to relive the story of King Naymlap and Queen Ceterni arriving on the Lambayeque coast.

Before the German film team built the majestic *Chimok*, the fishermen in Pimentel had helped me test a smaller and rather makeshift reed boat with a double stern. This was finished in a couple of days and with eleven fishermen on board, and the old father of Nicolás as captain, we sailed this forked reed vessel northward to the next town of San José, with an escort of almost 100 one-man reed balsas in our wake. The advantages of a double stern were clear even from this simple experiment. Apart from better stability and increased space for a larger bamboo deck, it also solved the awkward problem of getting back on board if one dived into the sea or fell overboard. A reed-ship is like a big barrel floating high on the water, making it exceedingly difficult to get on board again unless someone throws out a rope or a ladder. But with a split stern it is possible to swim into the fork and climb up with ease.

More important was its superb ability to ride with a steady course when landing through wild surf on an open coast. Any type of canoe, catamaran, or boat-shaped vessel is in danger of turning sideways and capsizing in a high surf unless the crew can control the vessel in the waves. When the surf runs into a forked stern it pushes the two sides in opposite directions, and the reed-ship rides straight up on to the beach.

Given the modern fishing fleet of present-day Peru, it was remarkable to observe the survival of home-made balsas of traditional types on the open beaches and secluded coves of the northern coast. The balsas of the Lambayeque valley were all of totora reeds, but immediately to the north they were consistently made from balsa logs. Larger rafts of balsa logs from the jungle east of the Andes are still used by some of the fishermen in the port of Ilo in southern Peru, right below Lake Titicaca, while the finest reed balsas of modern times survive on that stormy mountain lake. We were to discover that both types were known in Túcume prior to the Inca conquest of the coast.

Archaeological evidence of seafaring in ancient Túcume
In his habitation site, Dan found a ceramic vessel dating to the Chimú period or later, in the form of a stout reed boat with upturned bow and

175 (right) A detail of the left-hand raft of the Balsas Frieze (Phase HB-4), showing the cabin probably made from woven bamboo.

176 (below) A miniature double-bladed oar from an excavation in the South Plaza next to Huaca 1.

a crew of two men (see *ill. 131*). Nearby he also excavated a hard-wood rudder-oar of the special type with a short grip on top of the blade (see *ill. 119*), such as is still used on the rafts of balsa logs on the coast immediately north of the Lambayeque valley. Among the silver miniatures uncovered by Alfredo in the Temple of the Sacred Stone were representations of single-bladed paddles, as well as ones with a blade at either end. One of our Peruvian archaeology students even uncovered a miniature double-bladed wooden oar in a special structure inside the South Plaza next to Huaca 1 (*ill. 176*).

The most impressive reed-boat illustrations ever discovered in America were discovered by Alfredo in a most unlikely mound (see Chapter 5). Following a tip from a former *huaquero*, he sank a test pit into a low and insignificant little hill still further away from the main cluster of pyramids than Dan's habitation site. Here, in the extreme southern outskirts of the archaeological area lay two tall pyramids eroded into steep cones. Between them was the hillock. Signs of looting were apparent in the neighborhood.

Digging where his informant had seen 'something', Alfredo found that the looter had dug a deep and narrow pit destroying a section of an adobe wall. Following the undamaged part of the wall, Alfredo and his workmen saw to their amazement that the wall was covered with reliefs of a type rarely seen before. As excavation continued with trowel, brush, and air bulb, a large relief representing a maritime motif appeared. Bird-headed men were sailing on board two reed-boats. The artist had illustrated each boat with a cabin amidships (*ill. 175*) and a large number of oars in the water. Two mythical personages, wearing royal or ceremonial headdresses familiar from pre-Inca art, dominate all the space on each deck. All four have the heads of birds, but human arms holding the paddle shafts. In each boat one birdman has a human body and limbs, the other has a bird's body and human arms. Around the boats are fish and diving seabirds (*ill. 111*) – one bird is diving under the stern of a balsa. A row of swimming marine birds forms a frieze along the stamped floor of what was clearly a temple.

Below the vessels is a line of decorative symbols which in pre-Inca art are known as 'anthropomorphic waves' because the crests of the breaking seas normally end in human heads. In this special case the waves are capped with the heads of birds (*ill. 170*). In their hands they hold a round object which is very conspicuous in the symbolic design. It was only when Alfredo expanded the excavations to the rear of this wall that the identity of this round object became obvious.

The narrow pit attempted by the unsuccessful *huaquero* had disclosed the existence of another independent wall immediately behind the one with the reed-boat frieze, and the limited section we could expose without damaging the wall with the balsas showed a Moche-style motif of a ceremonial offering of animals. In this scene a priest leads a llama by a rope for the sacrifice, while other mythical animals are waiting behind. Also depicted are people dancing, some with masks and one upside down. There was even a third, and presumably still older, wall behind the second, also with reliefs. And behind all, on the outer side of the temple, was a ramp with sophisticated geometric decoration along one side, together with a long row of crouching birdmen, each holding the same round object in their hands as in the friezes under the reed-rafts (*ill. 171*).

The round and sometimes egg-shaped object in the hands of the birdmen dominating the reliefs from Huaca Las Balsas puzzled the Americanist archaeologists in our team, but was instantly recognized by those who had experience of Oceanic archaeology. Arne Skjölsvold, senior archaeologist in our team, who had worked in

177 *Silver miniatures from the Temple of the Sacred Stone. The paddle, 8.1 cm (3 in) long, represents a conventionalized form of the* ao *paddle carried as a badge of rank by aboriginal chiefs both in the Lambayeque Valley and on Easter Island. The crouching birdman is also a typical element in Easter Island art.*

Polynesia since we had begun excavations on Easter Island in 1955–56, immediately identified the small, round object held by the crouching birdmen as an egg. Crouching, wingless birdmen holding an egg in one hand was the dominant motif in the religious art of Easter Island, carved in relief on rocks and stones and painted on slabs. Since the Routledge expedition in 1917 brought the world's attention to the paramount importance of the bird-man cult to the aboriginal population of Easter Island, ethnologists and archaeologists have been searching the entire Pacific in vain for the origin of this non-Polynesian culture trait. During their annual birdman ceremonies the Easter Islanders competed by swimming on tusk-shaped reed bundles to certain offshore bird islets in search of the first egg of the year of the sooty tern. Their peculiar watercraft were identical to those still in use along the coast of Lambayeque, even in the building material – totora (*Scirpus riparius*), a South American fresh-water plant cultivated in irrigated fields on the desert coast of Peru by the aboriginal fishermen.

That full-size bundle-boats of totora reeds, such as illustrated in pre-Peruvian art, could have reached Polynesia had then just been demonstrated by Kitín Muñoz, one of the first to visit the reed-boat reliefs in Túcume after personally having sailed such a totora vessel from Callao harbour to the Marquesas Islands, twice the distance to Easter Island. At the peak of their culture the ancient Peruvians sailed the ocean with regular fleets of balsa rafts in an organized search for new land, such as Tupac Yupanqui, the grandfather of the ruling Inca met by the Spaniards, or the more legendary founders of the Chimu and Lambayeque kingdoms.

The stongest evidence for contact with Easter Island was, however, brought to light by Alfredo in the Temple of the Sacred Stone. One of the miniature paddles of silver or silver alloy he excavated (*ill. 177*) represented what the Easter Islanders call an *ao* – a double-bladed paddle, with no practical function, carried by chiefs during ceremonies. This type of specialized emblem has a long history in the Lambayeque Valley, as the silver miniature of Late Chimú or Inca times is a true replica of the full-size wooden paddle illustrated since Lambayeque and Chimú times held by chiefs on both redware and blackware pottery vessels. The diagnostic characteristics of the *ao* common to Easter Island and Lambayeque with Túcume are the purely ceremonial function of a double-bladed paddle with an upper and a lower blade asymmetrically carved and decorated. The lower blade is oar-shaped or spade-shaped and undecorated, whereas the upper blade is carved and sometimes also painted with the contours and features of a human mask. Eyes and nose are clearly marked and ears are carved as pendant additions on either side. Rows of vertical lines on top of the head depict a feather-crown which mark the rank of a chief, as do the extended ear-lobes of a typical 'Long-ears'. The occurrence of the same combination of particular traits in a ceremonial paddle, symbolic of navigation, and common to the Lambayeque Valley and the nearest island in Polynesia, is more likely the result of contact than independent invention among people who used the same kind of watercraft.[4]

The tiny double-bladed but undecorated wooden paddle excavated in the plaza of Huaca 1 is far too short for practical purposes and is of unknown use in Peru. The same type of tiny, double-bladed paddle, far too small to be gripped in two hands, is known as *rapa* on Easter Island, where it is a common ceremonial artifact spun in one hand during certain traditional dances.

Although the navigators on the Túcume relief were mythical, possibly symbolizing the sea-faring members of the Naymlap dynasty, there were important lessons to be learned from the details of their vessels. It is not possible to tell whether their sterns were forked as so often the case in Moche line drawings, because in the relief they are in direct profile. The sterns are shown cut into reversed steps which would in fact serve the same purpose as a curved stern, for if a big ocean swell caught the vessel from behind, the steps would dissipate the force of the wave and stop it breaking aboard. Obviously the steps were achieved by cutting each layer of reed bundles straight off at the stern, and since we know reed-boat builders rarely make their bundles less than half a meter in diameter, it was easy to work out that the vessels on the Túcume relief were about 12 m (40 ft) long, the same size as our reed-ship *Ra II* which crossed the Atlantic.

The cabins of the reed-boats seemed to be built as experience had taught us would best resist the force of the elements at sea: woven from split bamboo like so many of the fishermen's huts on the same coast today. Planks splinter in breaking ocean waves, but plaited bamboo is as flexible as basketry and will resist any sea. We had also discovered that the cabin should be vaulted and as low as possible, so as not to catch the wind and thus interfere with the steering.

Perhaps the strange round oar blades shown on the frieze were the most interesting details to Kitín and me. We had both learned that rigid wooden steering oars were the only vulnerable parts of a reed-ship. We had seen an oar-shaft break like a match in high seas even when the thickness of a telephone pole. Some of the reed-ships depicted on Moche pottery as if running over the crests of the waves carried such huge, round oar-blades projecting both fore and aft. On these fine-line drawings the oar-blades are cross-hatched like the woven bamboo cabins on our Túcume reed-boats. We had conducted experiments with round steering oars, one in front and one aft, an arrangement usual for river navigation, and it was unexpectedly effective in keeping a steady course at sea as well. With Nicolás and our fishermen friends on the small double-stern raft, we tested a large steering-oar with a shaft of multiple bamboo canes tied together and a blade woven like basketry from split bamboo. The oar functioned perfectly and moved as flexibly as the tail of a fish in the water behind us when we sailed in the open Pacific below Túcume.

We sailed no farther from the coast than allowed us still to see the people following us like a swarm of ants along the beach, and when we steered towards the shore at the spot where legend said King Naymlap had landed, the whole town of San José assembled to receive the strange flotilla. The fishermen on board rejoiced with pride in their ancestral craft and the old man at the steering oar wept from emotion when the vessel rode like an arrow straight up on the beach. The whole flotilla of one-man reed balsas escorting us landed in our wake.

Our excavations, here reported by Dan Sandweiss and Alfredo Narváez, the two archaeologists responsible for field operations, could indeed only uncover a very modest sample of what lies buried under layers of windblown sand and eroded adobe. Much is yet to be learned from future excavations within the massive area of eroded pyramids, mounds, ceremonial plazas, and cemeteries, as well as in the surrounding terrain, such as the area around El Horno and the ruins of the old cathedral. No attempt has so far been made to penetrate any of the major pyramids in search of the tombs of the supreme elite. As Walter Alva said when he first brought me to the impressive site, it is certainly possible that the lords of Túcume were buried with the same splendour and wealth as the lords in the more modest pyramid site of Sipán. At Túcume, it was agreed by all, our work would be to study the daily life of the community in general, not, like the *huaqueros*, to empty tombs of the elite to the benefit of collectors and museum exhibits but depriving the Peruvians and the rest of the world of the complete knowledge of their glorious past.

It seems an obvious step to investigate the pyramids and associated mounds in future, both to avoid uncontrolled looting and to gain information on the origins and contacts of the rulers associated with the Naymlap tradition. Our investigations of Huaca 1 revealed that a smaller and older adobe pyramid was concealed inside another from which samples for radiocarbon dating were obtained. Near the southwest corner of the present, outer pyramid, the location of the inner pyramid could be ascertained from a section of the oldest plaza wall that ran through the wall of the outer pyramid, now heavily eroded but originally 7 m (22 ft) tall. Alfredo's excavations at the opposite (southeast) corner of the outer pyramid disclosed where the inner wall existed at the east side.

The burials discovered on top of the two pyramids examined, and those in the looted cemeteries, may not represent the earliest history of Túcume, although no evidence was found to indicate temple construction earlier than around AD 1100. About that time a dramatic event influenced cultures both along the coast and in the Andean highlands. An exceptionally disastrous El Niño flood caused devastating damage to buildings and agriculture all along the northern coast and the drought that followed in the highlands put an end to the Tiahuanaco empire. This is of particular interest to students of Polynesian archaeology, as the timing coincides with the beginning of a sudden and widespread migration event that affected all the principal islands, with new royal families replacing old ones. On Easter Island, AD 1100 is also the approximate date established by archaeologists for the end of the Early Period, and the beginning of a new, with the introduction of the birdman cult and the carving of long-eared images.

As a guide in the interpretation of the Naymlap tradition, so strong and widely held in the Lambayeque region, I believe that the chronology of Túcume would place the beginning of his dynasty at about AD 1100, as he is said to have built the Chotuna pyramid where he landed from the sea, and his grandson the second pyramid, at Túcume, a short walk inland. Given the long tradition of complex societies in the Lambayeque Valley, Naymlap and his descendants came to be such dominant figures in local oral tradition simply because their descendants played a leading role in the area at the time the Chimú and Inca conquerors arrived.

Future archaeology will certainly throw more light on the unwritten history of Túcume and the extremely important civilizations of pre-Inca times along the entire coast of what was later the Inca empire, a couple of generations before written history began. We owe gratitude to the government of Peru for permission to excavate, and to the skilled team of field archaeologists, graduate students and Túcume labour who made it possible to obtain a first glimpse of the life of the builders and residents of the largest pyramid complex in South America.

Notes

Chapter 1 (*pp. 9–37*)

1 Guaman Poma (1936 [1613]).
2 Las Casas (1994 [1559]: Chapter XLI).
3 Samanos (1844 [1526]: 196).
4 Xeréz (1872 [1534]).
5 Estete (1992 [1534]: 56–57).
6 Prescott (1847, Vol. I: 272).
7 Pizarro (1844 [1571]: 154, 157).
8 *Ibid.*
9 Cieza de León (1984 [1553]: 172, Chapter 54).
10 Garcilaso de la Vega (1869–71 [1609]: 432).
11 Xeréz (1872 [1534]: 13, 16).
12 Fernández de Oviedo y Valdés (1851–1855 [1535–48], Vol. IV, Bk. 46).
13 Andagoya (1865 [1541–46]: 36, 45, 58).
14 *Ibid.*
15 Zárate (1700 [1555], Bk. I, Chapter VI).
16 Benzoni (1857 [1565]: 242).
17 *Ibid.*
18 Juan and Ulloa (1748).
19 Espinoza Soriano (1987: 30).
20 Beechey (1831).
21 Spilbergen (1906 [1619]: 83).
22 Dampier (1729).
23 *Ibid.*
24 Juan and Ulloa (1748: 189, 193).
25 *Ibid.*
26 Stevenson (1825).
27 Paris (1841–45: 148).
28 For information about and photographs by Brüning, see Schaedel (1988) and Raddatz (1990).
29 Rostworowski (1977).
30 Rostworowski (1977: 218).
31 Garcilaso de la Vega (1869–71 [1609]: Vol. I, Bk. III, Chapter 16).
32 Valverde (1879 [1539]).
33 Sarmiento de Gamboa (1907 [1572]: 135).
34 Cabello (1951 [1586]: 322–323, Part III, Chapter 17).
35 Cabello (1951 [1586]: 323, Part III, Chapter 17).
36 Heyerdahl and Skjölsvold (1956).
37 Ringrose (1704: 58, 64).
38 Skogman (1854: 164).
39 Heyerdahl (1952: 572–574; 1978: Chapter 7).
40 Buck (1938: 22–23, 453).
41 Oliva (1857 [1631]).
42 Acosta (1664 [1590], Vol. I: 56).
43 Amherst and Thompson (1901, Vol. II: 463–468).
44 Translation by Rowe (1948: 28) of the *Anonymous History of Trujillo*, written in 1604 and first published by Vargas Ugarte in 1936.
45 Cabello (1951 [1586]: 321–330, Part III, Chapter 17).
46 *Ibid.*
47 *Ibid.*
48 *Ibid.*
49 *Ibid.*

Chapter 2 (*pp. 38–55*)

1 Cieza de León (1984 [1553]: 205, Chapter 67).

2 Alva (1988).
3 Alva (1990).

Chapter 3 (*pp. 56–78*)

1 Kosok (1965: 147).
2 Alcocer (1987 [1580]: 71–83).
3 Quilter (1991).
4 Richardson (1978).
5 e.g., Moseley (1975, 1992a, b).
6 Chauchat (1988); Richardson (1978, 1981); Sandweiss et al. (1989).
7 Quilter (1985); Moseley (1992a: 119).
8 Quilter et al. (1991).
9 See Burger (1992: Chapter 2); Moseley (1992b).
10 Alva (1985).
11 e.g., Burger (1992: Chapter 3); Burger and Salazar-Burger (1991); Pozorski and Pozorski (1986).
12 See Burger (1992); Bischof (1994).
13 Burger (1992: 91).
14 Alva (1987).
15 Shimada (1981, 1990). Shimada places Huaca Lucía in the Early Horizon, but his C-14 date of 3273 ± 163 (1323 bc, uncorrected) better fits Burger's (1992) assignment to the Initial Period.
16 Elera (1986).
17 Moseley and Richardson (1992).
18 Donnan (1978 *inter alia*).
19 Alva and Donnan (1993); Donnan and Castillo (1992).
20 Alva (1988, 1990); Alva and Donnan (1993); Donnan and Castillo (1992).
21 Moseley (1992a).
22 Moseley and Richardson (1992); Shimada (1978); Shimada et al. (1991).
23 Shimada (1990).
24 Shimada and Griffin (1994).
25 Shimada et al. (1982).
26 Shimada (1990).
27 Schaedel (1978); Donnan (1990a, b).
28 Shimada (1990).
29 Donnan (1990b); Netherly (1988a); Schaedel (1951b); Trimborn (1979).
30 Shimada (1990); Donnan (1990b).
31 Shimada (1990).
32 This volume and Donnan (1990b).
33 Much has been written about the Inca, drawing on historical sources and archaeological data. As a start, the reader is referred to the following sources: Hyslop (1984, 1990); Morris and Thompson (1985); Rowe (1946).
34 Hayashida (1992).
35 Cabello (1951 [1586]: 327–330. Part III, Chapter 17); Rubiños y Andrade 1936 [1781].
36 Trimborn (1979: 24) reads Cabello to mean that the Inca conquered Lambayeque when Oxa's son Llempisan was lord.
37 e.g., Donnan (1990b); Rowe (1948); Shimada (1990); Zuidema (1990).
38 Kosok (1965: 148).
39 e.g., Donnan (1990a, 1990b).
40 Shimada (1990: 303, 366).
41 Kosok (1965: 73, chart II); Means (1931). Means placed the arrival much earlier than

Kosok, during Moche times, by giving a much greater length to the interregnum.
42 Shimada (1990: 370).
43 Donnan (1990b: 268–271).
44 Cabello (1951 [1586]: 468, Part III, Chapter 32).
45 e.g., Trimborn (1979: 24, 28).
46 It is also possible that this detail is a *post facto* justification for the tension between Jayanca and Túcume, couched in the local idiom of kin relations.
47 Ramirez (1982: 125, Table 1).
48 See Netherly (1977); Rostworowski (1981); Sandweiss (1992) for the social, political, and economic organization of late prehispanic coastal polities.
49 Ramirez (1982: 128–129).
50 Espinoza Soriano (1975: 268–270); Ramirez (1985: 426).
51 Ramirez (1982: 127, Table 2).
52 Netherly (1988b: 270–271); Rostworowksi (1977: 191).
53 Netherly (1988b: 274).
54 Cieza (1984 [1553]: 205, Chapter 67).
55 Spanish official Gregorio González de Cuenca formally founded the Spanish settlement of Túcume in 1567 (Zevallos 1991), presumably at Túcume Viejo, but this place may well have been occupied earlier.
56 Lockhart (1994: 11).
57 Ramirez (1985: 425).
58 Zevallos (1991).
59 Alcocer (1987 [1580]: 71–83).
60 Haberland (1990); Schaedel (1988).
61 Brüning (1917: 198), cited in Trimborn (1979:51).
62 Schaedel (1988: Appendix VI) lists 39 shots of the ruins at Túcume among the more than 2000 photographs Brüning took in Peru.
63 Brüning (1923).
64 Kroeber (1930: 66).
65 See Chapter 10 for a consideration of how this name arose.
66 Kroeber (1930: 66).
67 Schaedel (1951b: 239). Nevertheless, Platform 2 was reused for burials immediately before being abandoned (see Chapter 4).
68 Bennett (1939: 114–117).
69 Kosok (1965: 163, 171).
70 Schaedel (1951a).
71 Schaedel (1951b: 232).
72 *Ibid.*
73 Schaedel (1951a: 23).
74 Schaedel (1951a: 23; 1951b: 239).
75 Bonavia (1985: 112–116, Plate 21, Figures 78–80); see Bonavia's Appendix (pp. 199–201) for a chemical analysis of the mural paints.
76 Trimborn (1979).
77 Trimborn (1979: 52).
78 Alva and Alva (1989).

Chapter 4 (*pp. 79–130*)

1 Huaca 1 is known locally as 'Huaca el Mirador' or 'Lookout Mound' (Trimborn 1979), but we decided to give it the neutral term Huaca 1 to avoid confusion with the

'Mirador' (lookout) which Walter Alva built on La Raya Mountain in 1986 for tourists. Kroeber (1930) had labeled the pyramid as Huaca F, but his terminology has fallen out of use.

2 The possible significance of flat adobes is considered further in the section on Huaca 1.

3 Bonavia (1985: 113–116).

4 Tschudi, Bandelier, and Laberinto Palaces.

5 Schaedel (1951a).

6 Topic (1982).

7 Moseley (1992a: 256–261).

8 Schaedel (1951b).

9 Moseley (1992a: 258).

10 However, Dan Sandweiss (Chapter 7) found evidence for a rainfall event earlier in the Inca occupation of Túcume, so there is a slight chance that the Stone Platform rainfall was not the same as that registered in the fill of the Stone Structure and the Benched Corridors.

11 Quinn *et al.* (1987); however, Hocquenghem and Ortlieb (1990) have argued that there was no El Niño event in 1532. I find it hard to believe that 16th-century Spanish writers would invent a rainfall. Also, the conquistadors traveled from Panama to Peru in record time, which should only be possible during El Niño years when the coastal currents are reversed.

12 The metal objects found in both bundles were carefully wrapped in cotton textiles, as though they were also being buried. The tweezers and earpicks were packaged together, while the other objects were individually wrapped. The *Spondylus* shells were also covered in cotton cloth.

13 Valcárcel (1987a: 167) cites Acosta: 'The imperial insignia was a red tassel of the finest wool which hung in the middle of the forehead and only the Inca [ruler] could wear it. Other lords had these tassels but they wore them to the side, over the ear.' Valcárcel (*ibid.*: 214) also cites Montesinos concerning the accomplishments of Inca Roca: 'recognition of the sun as the supreme god, foundation of the Acllahuasi [imperial house of the chosen women], establishment of the signs of rank of the nobles with the enlarging of the earlobes, authorization to the generals for them to wear headgear with a lateral tassel on the left and only on the right when they brought victory, and if they were defeated, [they had to go] without it.'

14 Valcárcel (1987b: 176) cites Polo de Ondegardo: 'In the time in which the captains of Atahuallpa captured Huáscar, the subjects of the latter made a great sacrifice to Viracocha so that he might be freed from his oppressors, sacrificing a considerable number of children, of llamas, of cloths . . .' According to Valcárcel, Polo's assertion is later refuted by an anonymous Jesuit. Valcárcel (1987c: 70) also cites Santa Cruz Pachacuti, referring to Topa Inca Yupanqui: 'The same Inca received from the Andes of Opatari 300 Indians carrying gold dust and small nuggets; but in the night there fell a most strong frost that finished off all of the crops, the Inca on advice of his wizards who considered that the frost was a curse of the gods, ordered that the 300 Indians with their cargo of gold be carried to the mountain of Pachatusán and there all buried with their treasure.'

15 See the discussion of *crisoles* in Chapter 8.

16 For instance, see Morris and Thompson (1985) for the Inca administrative center of Huánuco Pampa.

17 Rowe (1944).

18 Hosler *et al.* (1990); if it was a money ax, it is the only one known from Túcume.

19 Koepcke (1970).

20 Menzel (1976).

21 Moseley (1992a: 256–261).

22 The front, or north, face may have been deliberately flattened, but the stone is otherwise unmodified.

23 *Huanca* is a well-known Quechua term for a sacred stone. The local, muchik word is *alaec pong*, and the stone was probably known by this name when the Temple was built, prior to the Inca conquest.

24 Shimada (1990).

25 *Ibid.*

26 Arriaga (1920 [1621]: 47, Capítulo IV) discusses the use of such powders by prehispanic Peruvians.

27 Both this figurine and the courtyard figurine are made of soldered silver sheet.

28 See McEwan and van der Guchte (1992) for a review of all known finds of these figurines. See also Reinhard (1992).

29 Calancha (1974 [1638]).

30 Silva Santisteban (1982: 92) writes: 'In Huacho there was a huaca called the Basin of Gold, we don't know why, but the principal cult object was a carved stone nine feet in width. Another huaca called Carquín was also important, among whose sacred objects was a large stone "of poor aspect", to which sacrifices were offered.'

31 Donnan (1990a).

32 Also, the date reflects the cutting of the log, which may have lived many years and/or been used for a long time before burial.

33 Donnan (1990b).

34 *Ibid.*

35 Daggett (1983).

36 e.g., Conklin (1982).

37 Trimborn (1979: 66) dated a log sample and a charcoal sample from the face of Huaca 1, getting uncalibrated dates of 660 ± 60 BP and 680 ± 50 BP, respectively.

38 See Morris and Thompson (1985: 92–96) for further information on the mit'a and other forms of labor tax in the late prehispanic Andes.

39 Hastings and Moseley (1975).

40 Cavallaro and Shimada (1988).

41 Shimada (1990).

Chapter 5 (pp. 131–141)

1 Shimada (1985: 108; 1990).

2 McClelland (1990).

3 Millones (1975: 40).

4 Shimada (1990).

5 Donnan (1990a).

6 *Ibid.*

7 Alva and Alva (1983).

8 Schaedel (1978).

9 Also see Bonavia (1985: 113–116) for a discussion and photographs from 1953 of a section of these murals exposed by looters at that time.

Chapter 6 (pp. 142–168)

1 Shimada (1978).

2 Topic (1982, 1990).

3 Schaedel (1951a) had noticed this fact in the late 1940s, and his map shows the six-part division of the Rectangular Compound, although his placement of the rooms is slightly off.

4 Topic (1982, 1990).

5 For instance, see the 1887 photograph by H. Brüning in Schaedel (1988: 86).

6 Alva (1988, 1990).

7 See illustrations of Chavín iconography in Burger (1992). In fact, the fanged mouth band begins in the Initial Period and continues at least through the Early Intermediate Period in Moche art. There is no way of knowing whether the West Mound graffiti is a copy of ancient art or mere coincidence.

8 I first noticed the resemblance between the architectural model in the West Mound and the Inca structure at Chincha on an unpublished map of the Inca portion of La Centinela provided by D. Wallace.

9 S. Haoa, personal communication.

10 An alternative explanation is that the standard chronology for the Inca expansion out of Cuzco is too short (B. Bauer, personal communication).

11 Donnan (1990b).

12 Hyslop (1990: 236–237); see Hyslop for a list of other trapezoidal plazas.

13 Shimada (1990: 312–313 and Table 1).

14 Isbell (1992).

15 Alva (1988, 1990); Alva and Donnan (1993).

16 Shimada and Griffin (1994).

17 Donnan and Castillo (1992).

18 Isbell (1992).

19 Shimada (1990: Table 1).

20 Shimada (1990).

21 Conrad (1982). The enclosure at Galindo may be an earlier Moche Valley antecedent to these elite burial platforms (Bawden 1982; Moseley 1992a: 213).

22 Conrad (1982: 88).

23 Conrad (1982: 92).

24 e.g., Netherly (1990); Zuidema (1990); Conrad (1982).

25 See Conrad (1982).

26 e.g., Donnan and Mackey (1978).

27 Rowe (1946: 286–287); Brian Bauer (personal communication 1993).

28 See Silverblatt (1988) for a discussion of Inca manipulation of local mythology and ideology to legitimize imperial rule.

29 Donnan (1990b: Figure 16a, b and p. 268).

30 deFrance (1993).

31 M. Sandweiss (1991).

32 Cano and La Torre (1992).

33 deFrance (1993).

34 Shimada and Shimada (1985) have argued that camelids were bred and herded in this region at least since the Middle Horizon, and they point among other data to a thick deposit of camelid excrement in the side of the Huaca del Pueblo de Túcume.

35 e.g., Pozorski (1979); Sandweiss (1992).

36 Alva (1988: 514, 543).

37 Sandweiss (1992).

38 Fried (1967); Haas (1982).

39 Donnan (1990b).

40 Hayashida, personal communication; Donnan (1990b: Figure 16a, b and p. 268).

41 Rice (1987: 237–240).

42 Shimada (1990: 319).

43 Lanning (1963).

44 Rice (1987: 241).

45 Bankes (1985: Plate 4).

46 Bankes (1985).

47 Shimada (1990).

48 Hastings and Moseley (1975).
49 Cavallaro and Shimada (1988).
50 Cavallaro and Shimada (1988) indicate that the different structural requirements of the Middle Sicán chamber-and-fill technique require a joined (non-segmented) construction; while segmentary construction is viable for the solid adobe Moche huacas.
51 McClelland (1990).
52 Shimada et al. (1982); Shimada and Merkel (1991).
53 Shimada and Shimada (1981).

Chapter 7 (pp. 169–178)

1 Narváez (1989).
2 But see Donnan (1990b).
3 By Classic Lambayeque, I refer to the pottery made in the region during the centuries preceding the Chimú conquest of Lambayeque.
4 Shimada (1990).
5 Donnan and Mackey (1978).
6 Kroeber (1926).
7 Shimada (1990); Cleland and Shimada (1992).
8 Moseley (1992a: 216) illustrates a similar pot in a grave assigned to the Chimú period. I suspect that this is a case of mistaken identification and that both the vessel shown at the bottom of Moseley's illustration and the one found in the South Cemetery show incontrovertible Inca influence.
9 Shimada (1990).
10 Shimada (1990); Cleland and Shimada (1992).
11 Bonavia and Ravines (1971).

Chapter 8 (pp. 179–189)

1 Because the upper part of the mountain is steeper than the lower part, the platforms girdling the lower half cover far over 50% of the surface of the mountain.
2 Bennett (1939: 114–116).
3 Ibid.
4 Donnan (1990b).
5 Repetitive, geometric designs still predominate in the La Raya collections, but the representational designs are unusually common here.

6 Shimada (1990: 324).
7 Although apparently more common on La Raya, single-image logographic and geometric designs do appear occasionally on *paleteada* pottery elsewhere at Túcume, e.g., Sector V.
8 Daggett (1983).
9 For example, Huánuco Pampa (Morris and Thompson 1985).
10 Recent interviews of local residents by Alfredo elicited information that the White Cave had been mined for oxides to use in paint. Although this activity no doubt enlarged the cave, the archaeological data and context clearly show that it was a feature of the prehistoric landscape. The construction of the pathway to, and the platform in front of, the cave (part of the planned modification of the entire mountain) make no sense otherwise. Furthermore, the sedimentary sequence demonstrates that the cave is at least older than the platform and is not recent: the upper levels record multiple rainfall events (the rare El Niños) mixed with roof fall, while the lower levels have only roof fall and record a time before the platform existed to channel rainwater into the cave.
11 Dearborn et al. (1987). Schaedel (1951b) suggested that the structures on La Raya were observatories, but he did not mention the cave.
12 Conklin (1990).
13 Bennett (1939).
14 Schaedel (1951b).

Chapter 9 (pp. 190–198)

1 Schaedel (1951a, 1951b); Shimada (1981: 443, 1990: 346–347).
2 Shimada (1990).
3 Kosok (1965); Schaedel (1951b: 240).
4 Dated on the basis of Trimborn's (1979) radiocarbon dates; see Table 1.
5 Shimada (1990: 312).
6 Shimada (1990: 353); though very extensive, Apurlec has a notably smaller volume of pyramids than Túcume.
7 Schaedel (1951b).
8 Ibid.
9 Kosok (1965: 163) also believed that Túcume was the principal Chimú center in Lambayeque.

10 Rowe (1948: 44, based primarily on Cabello 1951 [1586]: 312–341, Part III, Chapters 16–18).
11 Rowe (1948: 45); Netherly (1988a: 115–116).
12 Cabello (1951 [1586]: 468, Part III, Chapter 32).
13 Schaedel (1951b); see also Netherly (1988a); Shimada (1990).
14 Rostworowski (1988: 118); see Hyslop (1990: 294).
15 Hyslop (1990: 249–251); he recognizes that Inca and Inca-influenced pottery indicate an Inca presence on the north coast and concludes that the Inca made use of local sites and structures, as we have seen at Túcume.
16 Hayashida (1992).
17 Shimada (1990); see also Cordy Collins (1992).
18 Donnan (1990b); Shimada (1990).
19 Shimada (1990).
20 Shimada (1986).
21 Shimada (1982, 1990).
22 Schaedel (1951b).
23 Cabello (1951 [1586]: 468, Part III, Chapter 32) noted that the Túcumes were closely allied with the Chimú at the same time as they were enemies of the neighboring Jayancas.
24 Silverblatt (1988).
25 Kosok (1965: 178; see also p. 148 and Chart II on p. 73).
26 See also Kosok (1965: 178–180). The process of centralization, hypothesized here as starting under Chimú domination, is the same seen elsewhere in the Andes under the Inca, for whom both ethnohistoric and archaeological evidence can be brought to bear. D'Altroy's (1992) study of the central highlands Wanka provides a clear example.
27 Cieza (1984 [1553]: 205, Chapter lxvii).
28 Ramirez (1985: 425).
29 Trimborn (1979: 51); Cabello (1951 [1586]: 468, Part III, Chapter 32).

Chapter 10 (pp. 199–229)

1 Willey and Sabloff (1980: Chapter 3).
2 McEwan and van der Guchte (1992) discuss all the known finds of this Inca figurine type.
3 Cordy-Collins (1990).
4 For comparison, see Heyerdahl (1975: Pls XIV, 55, 56 and 350).

Bibliography

Acosta, J. 1604 [1590] *The naturall and morall historie of the East and West Indies*. Trans. of *Historia natural y moral de las Indias*. Printed by Val: Sims for Edward Blount and William Aspley, London.

Alcocer, F. 1987 [1580] 'Probanzas de indios y españoles referentes a las catastróficas lluvias de 1578, en los Corregimientos de Trujillo y Saña'. In *Ecología e Historia*, ed. L. Huertas, pp. 38–190. CES Solidaridad, Chiclayo, Peru.

Alva, W. 1985 'Pampa de Eten'. In *Presencia histórica de Lambayeque*, ed. E. Mendoza S., p. 52. Ediciones y Representaciones H. Falconí e.i.r.l., Chiclayo, Peru.

—1987 'Resultados de las excavaciones en el Valle de Zaña, Norte del Perú'. In *Archäologie in Peru – Archäometrie: 1985*, ed. W. Bauer, pp. 61–77. Konrad Theiss Verlag, Stuttgart.

—1988 'Richest Unlooted Tomb of a Moche Lord'. *National Geographic* 174 (4, October): 510–550.

—1990 *New Tomb of Royal Splendor*. *National Geographic* 177 (6, June): 2–15.

Alva, W. and S. Alva. 1983 'Los murales de Ucupe en el Valle de Zaña, Norte del Perú'. *Beitrage zur Allgemeinen und Vergleichenden Archäologie* 5:335–360.

—1989 'Túcume Capital del Reino Lambayeque'. In *Antología de Lambayeque*, ed. C. Toro M., pp. 374–376. CONCYTEC, Lima, Perú.

Alva, W. and C.B. Donnan. 1993 *Royal Tombs of Sipán*. Fowler Museum of Culture History, University of California, Los Angeles, California.

Amherst, W. and B.H. Thomson. 1901 'Introduction'. In *The Discovery of the Solomon Islands*, ed. W. Amherst and B.H. Thomson, Hakluyt Society Ser. II Vols. 7–8, London.

Andagoya, P. 1865 [1541–46] *Narrative of the Proceedings of Pedrarias Davila in the Provinces of Tierra Firme or Catilla del Oro : and of the Discovery of the South Sea and the Coasts of Peru and Nicaragua*. Hakluyt Society Vol. 34, London.

Arriaga, P.J. 1920 [1621] *La extirpación de la idolatría en el Perú*. Sanmartí, Colección de libros y documentos referentes a la historia del Perú, tomo 1, 2a serie, Lima.

Bankes, G. 1985 'The Manufacture and Circulation of Paddle and Anvil Pottery on the North Coast of Peru'. *World Archaeology* 17:269–277.

Bawden, G. 1982 'Galindo: a Study in Cultural Transition in the Middle Horizon'. In *Chan Chan: Andean Desert City*, ed. M.E. Moseley and K.C. Day, pp. 255–284. University of New Mexico Press, Albuquerque, New Mexico.

Beechey, F.W. 1831 *Narrative of a voyage to the Pacific and Beering's Strait . . . in the years 1825, 26, 27, 28*. H. Colburn and R. Bentley, London.

Bennett, W.C. 1939 *Archaeology of the North Coast of Peru. An Account of Exploration and Excavation in Viru and Lambayeque Valleys*. Anthropological Papers of the American Museum of Natural History 37, Part I, New York.

Benzoni, G. 1857 [1565] *Historie of the New World*, translation of *Historia del Nuevo Mundo*. Hakluyt Society Vol. 21, London.

Bischof, H. 1994 'Toward the Definition of Pre- and Early Chavín Art Styles in Peru'. *Andean Past* 4:169–228.

Bonavia, D. 1985 *Mural Painting in Ancient Peru*. Trans. P.J. Lyon. Indiana University Press, Bloomington, Indiana.

Bonavia, D. and R. Ravines. 1971 'Influence inca sur la côte nord du Pérou'. *Bulletin de la Société Suisse des Américanistes* 35:3–18.

Brüning, H.H. 1917 'Provincia de Lambayeque – contribución arqueológica'. *Boletín de la Sociedad Geográfica de Lima* 32.

—1923 *Estudios monográficos del Departamento de Lambayeque Fasículo IV Reglamentación de las aguas del Taimi*. Dionisio Mendoza. Chiclayo, Peru.

Buck, P.H. 1938 *Ethnology of Mangareva*. Bernice P. Bishop Museum Bulletin 157, Honolulu, Hawaii.

Burger, R.L. 1992 *Chavín and the Origins of Andean Civilization*. Thames and Hudson, London and New York.

Burger, R.L. and L. Salazar-Burger. 1991 'Recent Investigations at the Initial Period Center of Cardal, Lurín Valley'. *Journal of Field Archaeology* 18:275–296.

Cabello Valboa, M. 1951 [1586] *Miscelánea Antártica*. Universidad Nacional Mayor de San Marcos, Lima, Peru.

Calancha, A. 1974 [1638] *Crónica moralizada de Antonio de la Calancha*. Cronicas del Peru 4–9, Universidad Nacional Mayor de San Marcos, Lima, Peru.

Cano, A. and M.I. La Torre. 1992 'Estudio botánico de los restos vegetales y evaluación preliminar de la flora actual'. Unpublished Túcume Archaeological Project Report.

Cavallaro, R. and I. Shimada. 1988 'Some Thoughts on Sicán Marked Adobes and Labor Organization'. *American Antiquity* 53:75–101.

Chauchat, C. 1988 'Early Hunter-Gatherers on the Peruvian Coast'. In *Peruvian Prehistory*, ed. R.W. Keatinge, pp. 41–66. University of Cambridge Press, Cambridge.

Cieza de León, P. 1984 [1553] *Crónica del Perú Primera Parte*. Pontificia Universidad Católica del Perú, Lima, Peru.

Cleland, K.M. and I. Shimada. 1992 'Sicán Bottles: Marking Time in the Peruvian Bronze Age – a Five-part Typology and Seriation'. *Andean Past* 3:193–235.

Conklin, W.J. 1982 'The Information System of Middle Horizon Quipus'. In *Ethnoastronomy and Archaeoastronomy in the American Tropics*, ed. A.F. Aveni and G. Urton, pp. 261–281. Annals of the New York Academy of Sciences 385, New York.

—1990 'Architecture of the Chimú: Memory, Function, and Image'. In *The Northern Dynasties: Kingship and Statecraft in Chimor*, ed. M.E. Moseley and A. Cordy-Collins, pp. 43–74. Dumbarton Oaks, Washington DC.

Conrad, G.W. 1982 'The Burial Platforms of Chan Chan: Some Social and Political Implications'. In *Chan Chan: Andean Desert City*, ed. M.E. Moseley and K.C. Day, pp. 87–117. University of New Mexico Press, Albuquerque, New Mexico.

Cordy-Collins, A. 1990 'Fonga Sigde, Shell Purveyor to the Chimú Kings'. In *The Northern Dynasties: Kingship and Statecraft in Chimor*, ed. M.E. Moseley and A. Cordy-Collins, pp. 393–417. Dumbarton Oaks, Washington DC.

—1992 'Lambayeque'. In press in *Andean Art at Dumbarton Oaks*. Dumbarton Oaks, Washington DC.

Daggett, C. 1983 'Casma Incised Pottery: an Analysis of Collections from the Casma Valley'. In *Investigations of the Andean Past*, ed. D.H. Sandweiss, pp. 209–225. Cornell University Latin American Studies Program, Ithaca, New York.

D'Altroy, T.N. 1992 *Provincial Power in the Inka Empire*. Smithsonian Institution Press, Washington DC.

Dampier, W. 1729 *A Collection of Voyages*. In four volumes. J. and J. Knapton, London.

Dearborn, D.S.P., K.J. Schreiber, and R.E. White. 1987 'Intimachay: a December Solstice Observatory at Machu Picchu, Peru'. *American Antiquity* 52:346–352.

deFrance, S.D. 1993 'Analysis of Vertebrate Faunal Material from the Túcume Site, Peru'. Unpublished Túcume Archaeological Project Report.

Donnan, C.B. 1978 *Moche Art of Peru*. Museum of Culture History, University of California, Los Angeles, California.

—1990a 'The Chotuna Friezes and the Chotuna-Dragon Connection'. In *The Northern Dynasties: Kingship and Statecraft in Chimor*, ed. M.E. Moseley and A. Cordy-Collins, pp. 275–296. Dumbarton Oaks, Washington DC.

—1990b 'An Assessment of the Validity of the Naymlap Dynasty'. In *The Northern Dynasties: Kingship and Statecraft in Chimor*, ed. M.E. Moseley and A. Cordy-Collins, pp. 243–274. Dumbarton Oaks, Washington DC.

Donnan, C.B. and L.J. Castillo. 1992 'Finding the Tomb of a Moche Priestess'. *Archaeology* 45(6):38–42.

Donnan, C.B. and C.J. Mackey. 1978 *Ancient Burial Patterns of the Moche Valley, Peru*. University of Texas Press, Austin, Texas.

Elera A., C.G. 1986 'Investigaciones sobre patrones funerarios en el sitio formativo del Morro de Eten, Valle de Lambayeque, costa norte del Perú'. Bachelor's thesis, Pontificia Universidad Católica del Perú.

Espinoza Soriano, W. 1975 'El valle de Jayanca

y el reino de los Mochicas, siglos XV y XVI'. *Bulletin de l'Institut Français d'Etudes Andines* 4:243–274.

—1987 *Artesanos, transacciones, monedas y formas de pago en el mundo andino, Siglos XV y XVI Tomo II.* Banco Central de Reserva del Perú, Lima, Peru.

Estete, M. 1992 [1534] 'El descubrimiento y la conquista del Perú'. In *Nouvelles certaines des Isles du Pérou: texte rapproche du français moderne*, ed. H. Cazes and I. de Soto, Amiot Lenganey, Cairon.

Fernández de Oviedo y Valdés, G. 1855 [1535–48] *Historia general y natural de las Indias, islas y tierra firme del mar océano Vols. I–IV.* Imprenta de la Real Academia de la Historia, Madrid.

Fried, M.H. 1967 *The Evolution of Political Society: an Esssay in Political Anthropology.* Random House, New York.

Garcilaso de la Vega, I. 1869–71 [1609] *First Part of the Royal Commentaries of the Yncas.* Hakluyt Society Vols. 51–55, London.

Guaman Poma de Ayala, F. 1936 [1613] *Nueva coronica y buen gobierno.* Institut d'Ethnologie, Paris.

Haas, J. 1982 *The Evolution of the Prehistoric State.* Columbia University Press, New York.

Haberland, W. 1990 'Enrique Brüning – un investigador alemán en el Perú'. In *Documentos fotográficos del norte del Perú Juan Enrique Brüning (1848–1928)*, ed. C. Raddatz, pp. 29–35. Hamburgisches Museum für Völkerkunde, Hamburg.

Hastings, C.M. and M.E. Moseley. 1975 'The Adobes de Huaca del Sol and Huaca de la Luna'. *American Antiquity* 40:196–203.

Hayashida, F. 1992 'Neutron Activation Analysis of Pottery from Túcume'. Unpublished Túcume Archaeological Project Report.

Heyerdahl, T. 1952 *American Indians in the Pacific: The Theory behind the Kon-Tiki Expedition.* Allen & Unwin, London.

—1975 *Art of Easter Island.* Allen & Unwin, London, Doubleday, New York.

—1978 *Early Man and the Ocean.* Allen & Unwin, London.

Heyerdahl, T. and A. Skjölsvold. 1956 'Archaeological Evidence of Pre-Spanish Visits to the Galápagos Islands'. *American Antiquity* 22 (2, part 3):1–71.

Hocquenghem, A.M. 1987 *Iconografía mochica.* Pontificia Universidad Católica del Perú, Lima, Peru.

Hocquenghem, A.M. and L. Ortlieb. 1990 'Pizarre n'est pas arrivé au Pérou durant une année El Niño'. *Bulletin de l'Institut Français d'Etudes Andines* 19:327–334.

Hosler, D., H. Lechtman, and O. Holm. 1990 *Axe-monies and their Relatives.* Dumbarton Oaks Studies in Pre-Columbian Art & Archaeology 30, Washington DC.

Humboldt, A. 1810 *Vues des Cordillères, et monuments des peuples indigènes de l'Amérique.* F. Schoell, Paris.

Hyslop, J. 1984 *The Inka Road System.* Academic Press, New York.

—1990 *Inka Settlement Planning.* University of Texas Press, Austin, Texas.

Isbell, W.H. 1992 'Chullpa Burial Monuments: Prerequisite for Ayllu Organization?' Paper read at the 58th Annual Meeting of the Society for American Archaeology, St. Louis.

Juan, G. and A. Ulloa. 1748 *Relación histórica del viaje a la América meridional . . . Vols. I–IV.* A. Marin, Madrid.

Koepcke, M. 1970 *The Birds of the Department of Lima, Peru.* Revised and enlarged from 1964 Peruvian edition. Livingston, Wynnewood, Pennsylvania.

Kosok, P. 1965 *Life, Land and Water in Ancient Peru.* Long Island University Press, New York.

Kroeber, A.L. 1926 *Archaeological Explorations in Peru, Part I: Ancient Pottery from Trujillo.* Field Museum of Natural History Memoirs 2(1):1–43, Chicago.

—1930 *Archaeological Explorations in Peru, Part II: The Northern Coast.* Field Musuem of Natural History Anthropology Memoirs 2(2): 45–116, Chicago.

Lanning, E.P. 1963 *A Ceramic Sequence for the Piura and Chira Coast, North Peru.* University of California Publications in American Archaeology and Ethnology 46(2):135–284, Berkeley, California.

Las Casas, B. de 1994 [1559] *Historia de las Indias.* Alianza, Madrid.

Lockhart, J. 1994 *Spanish Peru 1532–1560 A Social History.* 2nd edition. University of Wisconsin Press, Madison, Wisconsin.

McClelland, D. 1990 'A Maritime Passage from Moche to Chimu'. In *The Northern Dynasties: Kingship and Statecraft in Chimor*, ed. M.E. Moseley and A. Cordy-Collins, pp. 75–106. Dumbarton Oaks, Washington DC.

McEwan, C. and M. Van de Guchte. 1992 'Ancestral Time and Sacred Space in Inca State Ritual'. In *The Ancient Americas: Art from Sacred Landscapes*, ed. R.F. Townsend, pp. 359–371. The Art Institute of Chicago and Prestel Verlag, Chicago and Munich.

Means, P.A. 1931 *Ancient Civilizations of the Andes.* Charles Scribner's & Sons, New York.

Menzel, D. 1976 *Pottery Style and Society in Ancient Peru.* University of California Press, Berkeley, California.

Millones, L. 1975 'El mito peruano. Los duendes de Casma. Religión popular cerrana en un valle de la Costa Norte'. *Textual* 10:39–49. Lima, Instituto Nacional de Cultura.

Morris, C. and D.E. Thompson. 1985 *Huánuco Pampa – An Inca City and its Hinterland.* Thames and Hudson, London and New York.

Moseley, M.E. 1975 *The Maritime Foundations of Andean Civilization.* Cummings Publishing Company, Menlo Park, California.

—1992a *The Incas and their Ancestors.* Thames and Hudson, London and New York.

—1992b 'Maritime Foundations and Multilinear Evolution: Retrospect and Prospect'. *Andean Past* 3:5–42.

Moseley, M.E. and J.B. Richardson III. 1992 'Doomed by Natural Disaster'. *Archaeology* 45(6):44–45.

Narváez, L.A. 1989 'Chan Chan: Chronology and Stratigraphic Contents'. *Andean Past* 2:131–174.

Netherly, P.J. 1977 'Local Level Lords on the North Coast of Peru'. Ph.D. dissertation, Cornell University. UMI, Ann Arbor.

—1988a 'Las fronteras inka con el reino de Chimor'. In *La frontera del estado Inka*, ed. T.D. Dillehay and P.J. Netherly, pp. 105–129.

BAR International 442, Oxford.

—1988b 'From Event to Process: the Recovery of Late Andean Organizational Structure by means of Spanish Colonial Written Records'. In *Peruvian Prehistory*, ed. R.W. Keatinge, pp. 257–275. University of Cambridge Press, Cambridge.

—1990 'Out of Many, One: the Organization of Rule in the North Coast Polities'. In *The Northern Dynasties: Kingship and Statecraft in Chimor*, ed. M.E. Moseley and A. Cordy-Collins, pp. 461–487. Dumbarton Oaks, Washington DC.

Oliva, A. 1857 [1631] *Histoire du Pérou.* Bibliothèque Elzevirienne Vol. 67, P. Jannet, Paris.

Paris, E. 1841–45 *Essai sur la construction navale des peuples extra-européens, ou, Collection des navires et pirogues construits par les habitants de l'Asie, de la Malaisie, du Grand Ocean et de l'Amerique, 2 vols.* A. Bertrand, Paris.

Pizarro, P. 1844 [1571] *Relación del descubrimiento y conquista de los reinos del Perú.* Colección de documentos inéditos para la historia de España Tomo 5, Madrid.

Pozorski, S. 1979 'Prehistoric Diet and Subsistence of the Moche Valley, Peru'. *World Archaeology* 2:163–184.

Pozorski, S. and T. Pozorski. 1986 'Recent Investigations at Pampa de las Llamas-Moxeke, a Complex Initial Period Site in Peru'. *Journal of Field Archaeology* 13:381–401.

Prescott, W.H. 1847 *History of the Conquest of Peru, Vols. I and II.* Harper and Brothers, New York.

Quilter, J. 1985 'Architecture and Chronology at El Paraíso, Peru'. *Journal of Field Archaeology* 12:279–297.

—1991 'Late Preceramic Peru'. *Journal of World Prehistory* 5:387–438.

Quilter, J., B. Ojeda, D. Pearsall, D.H. Sandweiss, J. Jones, and E.S. Wing. 1991 'The Subsistence Economy of El Paraíso, Peru'. *Science* 251:277–283.

Quinn, W.H., V.T. Neal, and S.E.A. Antunez de Mayolo. 1987 'El Niño Occurrences over the Past Four and a Half Centuries'. *Journal of Geophysical Research (Oceans)* 92C:14,449–14,461.

Raddatz, C., ed. 1990 *Documentos fotográficos del norte del Perú Juan Enrique Brüning (1848–1928).* Hamburgisches Museum für Völkerkunde, Hamburg.

Ramirez, S. 1982 'Retainers of the Lords or Merchants: a Case of Mistaken Identity?' In *El hombre y su ambiente en los Andes centrales*, ed. L. Millones and H. Tomoeda, pp. 123–136. Senri Ethnological Studies 10, National Museum of Ethnology, Osaka, Japan.

—1985 'Social Frontiers and the Territorial Base of Curacazgos'. In *Andean Ecology and Civilization*, ed. S. Masuda et al., pp. 423–442. University of Tokyo Press, Tokyo.

Reinhard, J. 1992 'Sacred Peaks of the Andes'. *National Geographic* 181 (3 March):84–112.

Rice, P.M. 1987 *Pottery Analysis.* University of Chicago Press, Chicago.

Richardson III, J.B. 1978 'Early Man on the Peruvian North Coast, Early Maritime Exploitation and the Pleistocene and Holocene Environment'. In *Early Man in America from a Circum-Pacific Perspective*, ed. A.L. Bryan, pp. 274–289.

Archaeological Researches International, Edmonton, Canada.

—1981 'Modeling the Development of Early Complex Economies on the Coast of Peru: A Preliminary Statement'. *Annals of Carnegie Museum* 50:139–150.

Ringrose, B. 1704 'The Dangerous Voyage, and Bold Attempts of Capt. Bartholomew Sharp'. In *The History of the Bucaniers of America Vol. 2*, ed. A.O. Exquemelin, Part IV. Printed for Tho. Newborough . . . John Nicholson. . .and Benj. Tooke, London.

Rostworowski de Diez Canseco, M. 1977 *Etnía y sociedad, costa peruana prehispánica*. Instituto de Estudios Peruanos, Lima, Peru.

—1981 *Recursos naturales renovables y pesca, siglos XVI y XVII*. Instituto de Estudios Peruanos, Lima, Peru.

—1988 *Historia del Tawantinsuyu*. Instituto de Estudios Peruanos, Lima, Peru.

Rowe, J.H. 1944 *An Introduction to the Archaeology of Cuzco*. Papers of the Peabody Museum of American Archaeology and Ethnology 27(2), Harvard University, Cambridge, Massachussetts.

—1946 'Inca Culture at the Time of the Spanish Conquest'. In *Handbook of South American Indians Vol. 2*, ed. J.H. Steward, pp. 183–330. Bureau of American Ethnology Bulletin 143, Washington DC.

—1948 'The Kingdom of Chimor'. *Acta Americana* 6:26–59.

Rubiños y Andrade, J.M. 1936 [1781] 'Succesión cronológica: ó serie historial de los curas de Mórrope y Pacora en la Provincia de Lambayeque del Obispado de Trujillo del Perú. . .' ed. C.A Romero as Un manuscrito interesante. *Revista Histórica* 10(3):289–363.

Samanos, J. 1844 [1526] 'Relación de los primeros descubrimientos de Francisco Pizarro y Diego de Almagro, sacada del códice número CXX de la Biblioteca imperial de Viena'. In *Colección de documentos inéditos para la historia de España, Tomo V*, pp. 193–201. Madrid.

Sandweiss, D.H. 1992 *The Archaeology of Chincha Fishermen: Specialization and Status in Inka Peru*. Carnegie Museum of Natural History, Bulletin 29, Pittsburgh, Pennsylvania.

Sandweiss, D.H., J.B. Richardson III, E.J. Reitz, J.T. Hsu, and R.A. Feldman. 1989 'Early Maritime Adaptations in the Andes: Preliminary Studies at the Ring Site, Peru'. In *Ecology, Settlement, and History in the Osmore Drainage, Peru*, ed. D.S. Rice et al., pp. 35–84. BAR International Series 545(i), Oxford.

Sandweiss, M.d.C. 1991 'Estudio de los restos malacológicos del Sector V, sitio de Túcume'. Unpublished Túcume Archaeological Project Report.

Sarmiento de Gamboa, P. 1907 [1572] *History of the Incas*, trans. and ed. C. Markham. Hakluyt Society 2nd ser. Vol. 22, Cambridge.

Schaedel, R.P. 1951a 'The Lost Cities of Peru'. *Scientific American* 85(2):18–23.

—1951b 'Major Ceremonial and Population Centers in Northern Peru'. In *Civilization of Ancient America, Selected Papers of the 29th International Congress of Americanists*, ed. S. Tax, pp. 232–243. University of Chicago Press, Chicago.

—1978 'The Huaca Pintada of Illimo'. *Archaeology* 31(1):27–37.

—1988 *La etnografía muchik en las fotografías de H. Brüning 1886–1925*. Ediciones COFIDE, Lima, Peru.

Shimada, I. 1978 'Economy of a Prehistoric Urban Context: Commodity and Labor Flow at Moche V Pampa Grande, Peru'. *American Antiquity* 43:569–592.

—1981 'The Batán Grande–La Leche Archaeological Project – the First Two Seasons'. *Journal of Field Archaeology* 8:405–446.

—1982 'Horizontal Archipelago and Coast–Highland Interaction in North Peru'. In *El hombre y su ambiente en los Andes centrales*, ed. L. Millones and H. Tomoeda, pp. 137–210. Senri Ethnological Studies 10, National Museum of Ethnology, Osaka, Japan.

—1985 'La cultura Sicán: una caracterización arqueológica'. In *Presencia histórica de Lambayeque*, ed. E. Mendoza S., pp. 76–133. Ediciones y Representaciones H. Falconí e.i.r.l., Chiclayo, Peru.

—1986 'Batán Grande and Cosmological Unity in the Andes'. In *Andean Archaeology Papers in Memory of Clifford Evans*, ed. R. Matos et al., pp. 163–188. Institute of Archaeology, University of California, Los Angeles Monograph 27, Los Angeles, California.

—1990 'Cultural Continuities and Discontinuities on the Northern Coast of Peru, Middle – Late Horizons'. In *The Northern Dynasties: Kingship and Statecraft in Chimor*, ed. M.E. Moseley and A. Cordy-Collins, pp. 297–392. Dumbarton Oaks, Washington, DC.

Shimada, I., S.M. Epstein, and A.K. Craig. 1982 'Batán Grande: a Prehistoric Metallurgical Center in Peru'. *Science* 216:952–959.

Shimada, I. and J.A. Griffin. 1994 'Precious Metal Objects of the Middle Sicán'. *Scientific American* 270 (4, April):82–89.

Shimada, I. and J.F. Merkel. 1991 'Copper-Alloy Metallurgy in Ancient Peru'. *Scientific American* 265 (1, July):80–86.

Shimada, I., C.B. Schaaf, L.G. Thompson, and E. Mosely-Thompson. 1991 'Cultural Impacts of Severe Droughts in the Prehistoric Andes: Application of a 1,500-year Ice Core Precipitation Record'. *World Archaeology* 22:247–270.

Shimada, M. and I. Shimada. 1981 'Explotación y manejo de los recursos naturales en Pampa Grande, sitio Moche V: significado del análisis orgánico'. *Revista del Museo Nacional (Lima)* 45:19–73.

—1985 'Prehistoric Llama Breeding and Herding on the North Coast of Peru'. *American Antiquity* 50:3–26.

Silva Santisteban, F. 1982 *Historia del Perú Tomo I: Perú Antiguo*. Ed. Buho, Lima, Peru.

Silverblatt, I. 1988 'Imperial Dilemmas, the Politics of Kinship, and Inka Reconstructions of History'. *Comparative Studies in Society and History* 30:83–102.

Skogman, C.J.A. 1854 *Fregatten Eugenies resa omkring jorden aren 1851–1853 Vol. I*. A. Bonnier, Stockholm.

Spilbergen, J. 1906 [1619] *The East and West Indian Mirror Being an Account of Joris van Speilbergen's Voyage Round the World (1614–1617), and the Australian Navigations of Jacob Le Maire*. Hakluyt Society 2nd ser. Vol. 18, London.

Stevenson, W.B. 1825 *A Historical and Descriptive Narrative of Twenty Years' Residence in South America Vols. I–III*. Hurst, Robinson & Co., London.

Stiver, M. and G.W. Pearson. 1993 'High-Precision Bidecadal Calibration of the Radiocarbon Time Scale, AD 1950–500 BC and 2500–6000 BC. *Radiocarbon* 35:1–23.

Topic, J.R. 1982 'Lower-Class Social and Economic Organization at Chan Chan'. In *Chan Chan: Andean Desert City*, ed. M.E. Moseley and K.C. Day, pp. 145–176. University of New Mexico Press, Albuquerque, New Mexico.

—1990 Craft Production in the Kingdom of Chimor. In *The Northern Dynasties: Kingship and Statecraft in Chimor*, ed. M.E. Moseley and A. Cordy-Collins, pp. 145–176. Dumbarton Oaks, Washington DC.

Trimborn, H. 1979 *El reino de Lambayeque en el antiguo Perú*. Colectanea Instituti Anthropos 19, Haus Völker und Kulturen-Anthropos Institut, St Agustin.

Valcárcel, L.E. 1987a *Historia del Perú Antiguo, Tomo 2*. 4th edition. Editorial Mejía Baca, Lima, Peru.

—1987b *Historia del Perú Antiguo, Tomo 3*. 4th edition. Editorial Mejía Baca, Lima, Peru

—1987c *Historia del Perú Antiguo, Tomo 5*. 4th edition. Editorial Mejía Baca, Lima, Peru.

Valverde, V. 1879 [1539] 'Relación del sitio del Cuzco y principio de las guerras civiles del Perú hasta la muerte de Diego de Almagro, 1535 a 1539'. In *Varias relaciones del Perú y Chile; y conquista de la isla de Santa Catalina, 1535 a 1658*, pp. 1–195. Colección de libros españoles raros o curiosos, t. 13, Impr. de M. Ginesta, Madrid.

Vargas Ugarte, R. 1936 'La fecha de la fundación de Trujillo'. *Revista Historia* 10(2):229–239.

Willey, G.R., and J.A. Sabloff. 1980 *A History of American Archaeology*. 2nd edition. W.H. Freeman and Co., San Francisco.

Xeréz, F. 1872 [1534] 'A True Account of the Province of Cuzco'. In *Reports on the Discovery of Peru*. Hakluyt Society Vol. 47, London.

Zárate, A. 1700 [1555] *Histoire de la découverte et de la conquête du Pérou*, translation of *Historia del descubrimiento y conquista del Péru*. Chez J. Louis de Lorme, Amsterdam.

Zevallos Quiñones, J. 1991 'Túcume: introducción a su estudio etnohistórico'. Unpublished Túcume Archaeological Project Report.

Zuidema, R.T. 1990 'Dynastic Structures in Andean Cultures'. In *The Northern Dynasties: Kingship and Statecraft in Chimor*, ed. M.E. Moseley and A. Cordy-Collins, pp. 489–505. Dumbarton Oaks, Washington DC.

Acknowledgments

The Túcume Archaeological Project was a joint Norwegian–Peruvian enterprise, organized and financed by the Kon-Tiki Museum in Oslo with project approval and excavation permits from the Peruvian government and Instituto Nacional de Cultura in Lima. Respectively as project leader and field directors, the authors of this report are indebted to many individuals and institutions for support and advice.

We are deeply grateful for the full support of the Peruvian Ministry of Education for the opportunity in 1988 to sign the original agreement of collaboration with the Instituto Nacional de Cultura directed by Dr Germán Peralta. This friendly collaboration continued with Dr Fernando Cabieses and subsequent directors, and extended to the regional branches of the Institute, notably represented by the Director of the Brüning Museum in Lambayeque, Dr Walter Alva.

Without the financial support of the Kon-Tiki Museum the Project would never have existed. Our thanks go to the Board of the Museum, through its successive directors, Knut M. Haugland, Thor Heyerdahl Jr, and Dr Öystein Koch Johansen, and the Head of the Research Department, Prof. Dr Arne Skjölsvold. Additional support has come in particular from TIMEX Corporation and from Mortimer Zukerman, Sigurd Aase, and David Webb. The Peruvian National Tourist Agency (FOPTUR), led by Juan Gil Ruíz and Juan Lira, funded the construction of the temporary and permanent site museums at Túcume. The EPSCoR III Grant to the Institute for Quaternary Studies at the University of Maine supported D. Sandweiss during the writing of this book, including the final preparation of many of the illustrations.

Guillermo Ganoza originally brought Thor Heyerdahl to Walter Alva in Sipán and took the initiative to make them sign a document pledging Peruvian–Norwegian collaboration in a Túcume archaeological project. Norwegian Consul General Hans Stimman in Lima provided invaluable advice and assistance. In Túcume, the village priest Padre Pedro Vásquez constantly helped maintain good relations with the population, as did local representatives of the Strömme Foundation by providing important funding for the Túcume Vivo social development project, under the leadership of the Peruvian ethnologist Prof. Victor Antonio Rodríguez Suy Suy, and his successor, Carlos López.

Thor Heyerdahl's private secretary and assistant Carmen Barrantes was instrumental in coordinating between the two Túcume projects and provided much other assistance. Project accountant César Rodríguez Muro kept our finances in excellent order.

In the field and lab, we are very grateful for the help of the following assistant archaeologists (in alphabetical order): Pablo Carlos de la Cruz, César Cornelio Lecca, Bernarda Delgado Elías, Diana Flores Donet, Alfredo Melly Cava, Hugo Navarro, María del Carmen Rodríguez de Sandweiss, Jorge Rosas Fernández, Lidio M. Valdés, and Cirilo Vivanco Pomacanchari. We were also greatly aided by student assistants from the National University of Trujillo: Florencia Bracamonte, Noemí Castillo, Jesús Cherres, Marco Fernández, Miguel Fiestas, Guillermo Gayoso, Pedro Iberico, Jaime Jímenez, Franklin Jímenez, Alex Meléndez, Antonio Murga, Alfonso Reyes, Sixto Tejada, Ricardo Tello, Denis Vargas, Carlos Wester, and Lucía Zarate; from San Marcos University, Lima: Régulo Franco, Martín García, and Hector Walde. In addition to students from Cornell University and Ithaca College, we are also grateful for valuable help in the field from a number of foreign archaeologists, notably Sonia Haoa from Chile who joined the project from its initiation, Marili Apa from Italy, Belinda Clarke from Canada, Klaus Koschmieder from Germany, Peter Kvietok from the USA, Helene Martinsson and Paul Wallin from Sweden, Lars Pilo from Denmark.

The human skeleton material was studied by George Gill assisted by Patrick Chapman at the University of Wyoming. The mummy bundles were unwrapped by Sonia Guillén assisted by the textile expert Maria Luisa Patrón. Ethnohistorical information was provided by Dr Jorge Zevallos. The architects Rosana Correa and Edith Meneses Luy did the axonometric studies of excavated structures in the Monumental Sector. Percy Fiestas did the isometric reconstructions and other drawings from Sector V and La Raya Mountain. Esteban Sosa carried out topographic work at the site; Bernardino Ojeda mapped the structures on La Raya Mountain; Cristina Kvietok, Héctor Suárez, and Ronald Salas worked on the conservation and restoration of objects from Huaca Larga and Huaca 1. Fidel Gutierrez of the Metal Restoration Lab at the Brüning Museum worked on the metal miniatures from the Temple of the Sacred Stone and the last Inca governor burial on Huaca Larga.

Non-human organic material was studied by Asunción Cano, Susan D. deFrance, Franco León, Elizabeth Reitz, Teresa Rosales, María del Carmen Rodríguez de Sandweiss, Victor Vásquez, and Jonathan Kent. Jan Cristiansen and Fan Nian Kong conducted Geo-radar investigations. Stephen Bicknell at the University of Maine prepared several figures and the black-and-white prints. Uwe Brand and Howard Melville of Brock University kindly ran our radiocarbon dates at cost.

Germán Carrasco, Bettina Heyerdahl, Kristine Edle Olsen, and Quirino Olivera assisted with photographic work.

Finally, our sincere gratitude to the people of Túcume and in particular the many who participated in the Project as workmen. The list is far too numerous to reproduce here, so we thank them in the persons of the foremen Gilberto Tepo, Don Victor Bravo Cajusol, Osvaldo Chozo Capuñay, Julio Cumpa López, Antero Pacheco Llontop, and Teodoro Sandoval Acosta.

Illustrations

Archivo Museo Nacional Brüning de Lambayeque, Peru 20; Anders Berg/SebraFilm 55; Stephen A. Bicknell 1, 2, 31, 116, 167; Brüning-Archiv, Hamburgisches Museum für Völkerkunde, Hamburg 12; The Field Museum, Chicago, Neg.#74286.1 32; Roxana Correa and Edith Meneses 40, 47, 72, 73, 76, 94, 98, 101, 103; Bernarda Delgado 70, 112; Percy Fiestas 33, 53, 67, 68, 78, 117, 121, 122, 123, 124, 127, 128, 131, 132, 133, 134, 135, 136, 137,138, 139, 140, 141, 142, 161, 164, 165, 166; Bettina Heyerdahl 6, 15, 16, 22, 27, 50, 51, 52, 54, 64, 65, 88, 92, 106, 107, 108, 129, 147, 148, 149, 151, 152, 153, 155, 158, 159, 173, 174, 176; Thor Heyerdahl 38, 61, 74, 110, 111, 130, 154, 169; Alfredo Narváez 34, 37, 39, 43, 45, 49, 56, 57, 58, 59, 62, 69, 71, 75, 77, 79, 80, 81, 82, 83, 84, 85, 86, 87, 90, 91, 95, 96, 99, 100, 102, 104, 109, 113, 114, 115, 143, 144, 150, 156, 157, 170, 171, 175; Kristine Edle Olsen Title-page, 4, 5, 18, 19, 25, 26, 41, 46, 48, 97; Daniel Sandweiss 3, 14, 17, 21, 23, 24, 29, 30, 35, 36, 42, 60, 66, 89, 93, 118, 119, 120, 125, 126, 145, 160, 162, 163, 168; SebraFilm 105; Shippee-Johnson Expedition, American Museum of Natural History 28

Index

Numerals in *italics* refer to page numbers for illustrations and tables